D1284352

Derrida and Theology

Derrida and Theology

Steven Shakespeare

t&t clark

Published by T&T Clark International
A Continuum Imprint

The Tower Building   80 Maiden Lane
11 York Road   Suite 704
London SE1 7NX   New York, NY 10038

www.continuumbooks.com

All rights reserved. No part of this publication may be reproduced or transmitted in any form or by any means, electronic or mechanical, including photocopying, recording or any information storage or retrieval system, without permission in writing from the publishers.

Copyright © Steven Shakespeare, 2009

Steven Shakespeare has asserted his right under the Copyright, Designs and Patents Act, 1988, to be identified as the Author of this work.

British Library Cataloguing-in-Publication Data
A catalogue record for this book is available from the British Library

ISBN: HB: 978-0-567-18664-5
        PB: 978-0-567-03240-9

Typeset by Newgen Imaging Systems Pvt Ltd, Chennai, India
Printed and bound in Great Britain by MPG Books Ltd, Bodmin, Cornwall

For Sally

You, my love, is it you I thereby name, is it to you
that I address myself? I don't know if the question is
well put, it frightens me. But I am sure that the answer,
if it gets to me one day, will have come to me from you.
You alone, my love, you alone will have known it.

Jacques Derrida, *The Post Card*

Contents

Acknowledgements

I am grateful to friends and colleagues who have discussed Derrida's ideas with me as I prepared this book, including Hugh Rayment-Pickard, Don Cupitt, Gerard Mannion, Sally Bower, Patrice Haynes, Charlie Blake, Rob Loring and the members of the Liverpool Hope University Theological Society who attended a series of seminars I offered on Derrida in May 2008.

Abbreviations

The following abbreviations of Derrida's works are used in the text:

A   *Aporias* (Stanford: Stanford University Press, 1993).

AEL   *Adieu to Emmanuel Levinas* (Stanford: Stanford University Press, 1999).

AF   *Archive Fever: A Freudian Impression* (Chicago: University of Chicago Press, 1997).

AL   *Acts of Literature* (London: Routledge, 1992).

AR   *Acts of Religion* (London: Routledge, 2002).

AT   *The Animal That Therefore I Am* (New York: Fordham, 2008).

BP   'The Becoming Possible of the Impossible: An Interview with Jacques Derrida', in Mark Dooley (ed.), *A Passion for the Impossible: John D. Caputo in Focus* (Albany: State University of New York Press, 2003), pp. 21–33.

C   *Cinders* (Lincoln: University of Nebraska Press, 1991).

Circ   'Circumfession', in Geoffrey Bennington and Jacques Derrida (eds), *Jacques Derrida* (Chicago: University of Chicago Press, 1993).

D   *Dissemination* (London: Athlone, 1981).

FL   'Force of Law: The "Mystical Foundation of Authority"', in Drucilla Cornell, Michel Rosenfeld and David Gray Carlson (eds), *Deconstruction and the Possibility of Justice* (London: Routledge, 1992), pp. 3–67.

GD   *The Gift of Death* (Chicago: University of Chicago Press, 1995).

Gl   *Glas* (Lincoln: University of Nebraska Press, 1986).

GT   *Given Time 1: Counterfeit Money* (Chicago: University of Chicago Press, 1992).

Abbreviations

Abbreviations

SP   *Speech and Phenomena* (Evanston: Northwestern University Press, 1973).

WD   *Writing and Difference* (London: Routledge, 1978).

Note: All emphases in quotations used in the book are part of the original text from which they are sourced.

Introduction: Slogans

In the film *Deconstructing Harry* (Woody Allen, 1997), the eponymous writer, played by Woody Allen, gets into a heated argument with his sister, Doris. She objects to his corrosive scepticism and contempt for her return to her religious roots in Judaism, which he labels superstition. The conversation continues:

> Doris: It's *tradition*.
>
> Block: Tradition is the illusion of permanence.
>
> Doris: You have no values. Your whole life, it's nihilism, it's cynicism, it's sarcasm and orgasm.
>
> Block: Y'know, in France I could run on that slogan and win.

Allen's film plays on the caricature of the dissolute writer. Block objects to religious fanaticism, indeed to all religion as arbitrary and exclusive, undermining our universal obligations to all people regardless of creed and race. However, his own life is fragmented, shallow and bitter. He cannot help confusing real life and fiction, with disastrous consequences for the former. He seems incapable of sustaining any lasting relationship. In the end, it is only his fiction that offers him any redemption, any way of gathering the shards of his life together.

Deconstructing Harry might not be an academic exploration of what deconstruction in Derrida's work is really about. Nevertheless, it skilfully and hilariously exposes some of the popular images and anxieties that have been provoked by a body of work that seems to take away the 'illusion of permanence' from beneath our feet. Deconstruction, so the fear goes, infects our most cherished realities, our ethics and, yes, our religion with nihilistic fantasy and excess. 'France' – that byword for fashionable philosophy, anti-clericalism and dangerous liaisons – has come to our backyard and embittered our coffee.

For many years, Derrida was well aware of the stereotypes that surrounded his work, whether they were propagated by fanatical supporters or by the disapproving guardians of academic rigour. Time and again, he was moved to rebut suggestions that his thought was designed to destroy all ideas of truth:

> Interviewer: What's the most widely held misconception about your work?
>
> Derrida: That I'm a sceptical nihilist who doesn't believe in anything, who thinks nothing has meaning, and text has no meaning. That's stupid and utterly wrong and only the people who haven't read me say this . . . Anyone who reads my work with attention understands that I insist on affirmation and faith and that I'm full of respect for the texts I read.[1]

It is ironic that a philosopher often associated with the idea that we can make texts mean whatever we like should so often have felt compelled to challenge misreadings of his work. For those who believe that Derrida stands for nothing more than corrosive relativism, this merely exposes his own self-contradictions. As we will see, there has been no shortage of accusations that Derrida's thinking undermines all objective truth-claims, dissolves all stable meanings and traps us within the play of language. His famous statement that 'there is nothing outside the text' has led some to assume that he believes there is nothing outside language, nothing to constrain our most arbitrary fantasies.

Reading that statement in context, rather than as a detached slogan, has enabled scholars familiar with Derrida's work to lay that particular misinterpretation to rest to some extent. However, the scale and complexity of Derrida's written output have meant that he is one of those philosophers most likely to be 'read', judged and dismissed at second hand as typical of the worst pretensions and frivolities of 'postmodernism'.

After all, it is especially tempting to interpret Derrida's 'decon-struction' of metaphysics as intrinsically hostile to Western theology. Doesn't theology attempt to make systematic sense of faith in one God, one source and end of all things? And isn't that unification and objectivity of knowledge exactly what deconstruction sets out to undermine? On this view, Derrida is easily dismissed as one more denizen of the secular, postmodern playpen, who has nothing to offer but scepticism and relativism when everything of substance has been thrown out. Add to this that, in his own words, he 'rightly passes for an atheist' (Circ, p. 155) and we might well wonder what possible relevance he might have for theology.

However, that is a superficial view. For one thing it ignores the difficult and contested history of theology itself, which, even confining ourselves to the Christian tradition, is one of dialogues, appropriations of other languages, debates and disputes. It is also a history of the impossibility of adequate talk about God, and a meditation upon issues of transcendence, Trinitarian relationships, sacraments, revelation, commentary, incarnation and grace that defy the enclosed boundaries drawn around our conceptions of life and the world.

On the other hand, painting Derrida as the bogeyman nihilist is a bad reading of his texts, which has more to do with the politics of the academy than what his writings actually say and do. Derrida has never simply accepted the designation 'postmodern' as applied to his work, and we might all benefit from taking a holiday from that most abused, elastic and empty of labels. Nor does Derrida suggest that one can simply smash up and leap out of the questions and themes that have driven philosophy and theology in their search for truth and meaning. Such a fantasy of escape, he might argue, is no more than a naïve repetition of that search, freed from all the labour, faith and respect for the other that deconstruction demands.

Derrida consistently engages with the major themes of the philosophical tradition of metaphysics. His earliest work takes its orientation from phenomenology, which was at once the most stripped down and 'scientific' of philosophies at the same time as being the most ambitious. As we will see, Derrida's fascination with phenomenology led him to reflect on the origin of the world, the foundation of truth, the nature of God, the experience of revelation. He approaches all of these themes with an eye for irreducible complexity, a sense for the time and difference lodged at the heart of our most cherished ideals of eternity and unity. If Derrida cannot be claimed as a theologian, there is no doubt that his work attends to topics that carry enormous theological freight.

At the same time, I will argue that Derrida's thinking cannot simply be assimilated or added on to a pre-existing theological position. If Derrida challenges the rules of the game that separate the secular from the religious, he also disturbs the unity and self-identity of any theological tradition. Derrida's faith and his heresy cannot easily be disentangled, each one speaking with a plurality of voices that echo and distort the other.

One of the most valuable resources for exploring Derrida's relationship to religion and theology has been the series of 'Religion and Postmodernism' conferences held at Villanova University in the United States since 1997. Derrida was present at these conferences before his death in 2004, as a speaker and conversation partner, and the proceedings of each event have been published in an important series of volumes.[2]

In their introduction to the second such collection, John Caputo, Mark Dooley and Michael J. Scanlon note Derrida's anxieties about attending such gatherings. His concerns are based partly on his own professions of incompetence in the areas of theology and religious studies, but also on a fear that others would attempt to recruit him to some theological position or other. The editors reply that they 'do not expect him to do theology', and that it is up to the other participants to see where Derrida's work might engage with theological questions. They go on:

> That is a delicate operation, to be sure, one that must resist
> co-opting Derrida's work for religion, distorting his
> insights, or above all confining the energy of deconstructive
> analysis within the limits of a determinate faith. But it is
> also one that cries out to be done. For what else can one
> do with a philosopher who writes about the gift and
> forgiveness, hospitality and friendship, justice and the
> messianic, with someone who has radicalized these notions
> in such a way that anyone with an ear for these matters,
> with half an ear, can hear the biblical resonance, even if that

is not something that Derrida himself is conscious of or consciously monitors?[3]

Such a methodological caution is well advised. However, it needs to be taken somewhat further than accommodating Derrida's writings in other contexts where he claims no competence. The reality is that Derrida's engagement with theological and biblical motifs does not leave them unscathed. To hear a resonance is also to hear something distorted, doubled, repeated, interpreted. Derrida's performance of the theological is no mere dressing up in religious metaphors to add a surface twist to his purely philosophical arguments.

The increasing visibility of such a performative gesture in Derrida's later writings has raised the difficult and disputed question of whether he underwent some kind of religious 'turn' in his later years. Such a conversion might draw parallels with Heidegger's so-called *Kehre*, his move away from the underlying humanism of *Being and Time* to the more mystical reflections on language and the 'fourfold' of his later years; or it could reflect Wittgenstein's move from a kind of logical positivism in his *Tractatus Logico-Philosophicus* to the more pragmatic and grammatical treatment of language of his *Philosophical Investigations* and other late texts. The ageing philosopher, it seems, gets a little tired of the arid and lonely wastes of immanence, and acquires a wistful longing for a poetic and religious sensibility.

It's a nice story, but it is told with the benefit of hindsight and the taint of nostalgia. It obscures the lines of continuity and complexity that make such stories overly simplistic. Such is the case with Derrida. His wariness and suspicion of the 'theological' might indeed have been muted or nuanced by a more intimate engagement with mystical texts and messianic themes. However, there is no way of understanding his 'faith' adequately unless his critique of the metaphysics of presence, and his development of a writing of deconstruction, *différance*, and the trace from his earliest texts is not taken into account. As we will see, these constantly evoke *and* trouble theological questions.

This book invites the reader to spend time and attention on Derrida's early works, when the key parameters of notions such as deconstruction and *différance* emerged. It will also attempt to keep in view, not just what Derrida wrote but *how* he wrote. There is always a question mark about the status of his authorial voice, one he exploits through employing a plurality of voices and personas in his texts. This is not to say that his writings have no intended meaning. It is rather that, like Kierkegaard before him, Derrida is both questioning our preconceived ideas about meaning and evoking a radical and paradoxical structuring and de-structuring of truth that can never be directly stated, grasped or defined.

One of the tasks of this introduction is to provide a little more information about Derrida's life, background and content. However, it will soon become clear that these very ideas are not the stable starting points we might wish they were.

The accidents of life

'Ah, you want me to say things like "I-was-born-in-El Biar-on-the-outskirts-of-Algiers-in-a-petit-bourgeois-family-of-assimilated-Jews-but . . ." Is that really necessary? I can't do it. You will have to help me . . .' (P, pp. 119–20). These words are Derrida's response to an interviewer's question, inviting him to comment on his early life in Algeria, on 'where it all began for you'. His reluctance to play the game of direct autobiographical confession is characteristic. He questions the idea that one can base the meaning of a text in any straightforward way upon an author's supposed intention, or with reference to the so-called facts of his life. That 'biographical fallacy' is widely acknowledged within literary studies.

However, matters are not quite as simple as this. Derrida elsewhere admits that elements of his life and history are woven through several of his important texts. He employs an indirect style, in which his authorial presence is teasing, elusive and provocative. Nevertheless, just as it proves impossible to establish some absolute timeless basis for meaning, which escapes all the chances and ambiguities of writing, difference and time, so it is also an illusion to suppose we can strictly separate the 'personal' from the 'professional' or the 'academic'. The dividing lines between these identities and institutions are blurred and shifting.

Two elements of Derrida's exchange with the interviewer draw our attention to this. First, the question posed is about 'where it all began'. There is an assumption that it is possible to put one's finger on a definite beginning, a pure point of departure that is lifted above the general flow of time. As we will see, the question of whether we can identify such a simple origin has been a persistent focus of Derrida's texts throughout his career. To anticipate our discussion, we will see that for Derrida, ideas of simplicity, purity and beginnings are always secondary. They always arrive on the scene when the action has already started. And this has huge implications for how his work relates to theological issues.

Second, Derrida's refusal to speak autobiographically is not absolute. He asks for the interviewer's help. He invites a difficult dialogue. I suggest that this is done, not with any expectation that this will resolve all the problems that surround telling the story of one's life, but because such stories always involve more than one point of view, more than one voice. Derrida has confessed to a desire to compose a perfectly autobiographical text, to nail down each moment before it passes. At the same time he has acknowledged the impossibility of such a fantasy, not only for practical reasons, but because there is never any way of gathering the temporality and otherness of life into a single unambiguous, absolute narrative (AL, p. 34).

A number of Derrida's texts are therefore cast in the form of dialogues, of messages given and received, of columns divided by space and lines. It is not clear in these cases that there is one master voice or narrative that carries the day at the end of the text. Rather, we are invited into the space of an open-ended conversation.

This second point underlines the way Derrida's work makes meaning, truth and identity complicated. His style, the way the texts are performed, is not indifferent to what those texts are about. As Kierkegaard might have put it, the 'how' and the 'what' are inseparable. This too has major implications for how theological questions are approached, for the standpoint and authority theology claims for translating God into words.

These two aspects – the questioning of simple origins and the refusal to speak in a monologue – are clearly related. One particularly important consequence of this is Derrida's refusal to accept an absolute dividing line between what we might loosely call the ideal and the real, the universal and the empirical. This line draws together many otherwise opposed styles of philosophical enquiry.

On the one hand, we have timeless essences, forms, ideals, conditions, categories, rational principles or innate intuitions. These act as foundations and criteria for the identification of true knowledge and justified belief. On the other hand, we have the merely empirical and historical events, statements, objects and experiences that are contingent, passing and inessential. Typically, philosophy values the latter only as examples of the former, or as raw material to be analyzed and broken down into its enduring, timeless laws. Empiricists might claim to begin with sense-data rather than abstractions, but the way in which sense impressions are understood tends to abstract from any historical or cultural context. The aim is still to arrive at conclusions that any rational person would accept. An ideal of reason is continually presupposed.

For Derrida, this division between the universal essence or rule and its particular instantiation or example breaks down. It is not possible to maintain a pure distinction between form and matter, between the eternal and the historical, between general structures and contingent events. Neither can be what it is without the other, not according to some harmonious dialectic that reconciles all opposites, but in a strange relationship of mutual contamination.

It is appropriate to refer to Derrida's biography then, not because it offers the key to his writings, to what he 'really' meant, but because his writing concerns this unsettling of the border between universal truth and individual life. Individuality or singularity cannot simply be incorporated into a grand narrative. Rather, it is a piece of grit in the eye of the all-seeing system. It is the secret without which there could be no truth, no responsibility, no decision. We can only evoke this strange secret, never capture it; but unless we address it (and unless we are addressed by it) we are left only with the comical picture, offered by Kierkegaard, of the professor who became so obsessed with his world historical system of philosophy that he forgot his own name, forgot that he was an individual, existing human being.[4]

A short sketch of Derrida's life will be given later in this chapter. However, we turn first to some more specific episodes, which can give us pause for thought about the nature of the event, and the interweaving of life and thinking that Derrida offers us. These are the strange case of the Cambridge doctorate, the publication of Derrida's *Circumfession* (both in the early 1990s) and the appearance by him at the American Academy of Religion's annual meeting in 2002.

The doctor, the supplicant, the sceptic and the penitent

In 1992, a rather comical affair took place at Cambridge University. The famous philosopher Jacques Derrida was put forward for an honorary doctorate. Normally, these things go through the senate on the nod, but in this case there were objections. A vote was scheduled in the spring. Prior to the vote, various groups of academics put forward statements in the university publication, the *Cambridge University Reporter*, for or against Derrida's award.[5]

I was a graduate student in Cambridge at the time. I remember following the case and eagerly scanning the pages of the *Reporter* to find out which side my lecturers were on. I have to say there were one or two surprises, and it opened my eyes a little to the intellectual politics of the time. There were clearly theologians who thought Derrida was little short of the anti-Christ.

Those who opposed the award of the degree argued that Derrida was basically a nihilist or a relativist. That is, his philosophy of deconstruction amounted to an abandonment of all ideas of meaning, truth and knowledge. It was nothing short of an outright attack on everything a university should stand for. It would be self-defeating for a university to honour the one who had betrayed it.

Similar charges have often been mounted against Derrida's work. In the wake of the Cambridge affair, a letter appeared in *The Times* newspaper, signed by the philosopher Barry Smith and about twenty others. Part of it read as follows:

M. Derrida's voluminous writings in our view stretch the normal forms of academic scholarship beyond recognition. Above all – as every reader can very easily establish for himself (and for this purpose any page will do) – his works employ a written style that defies comprehension.

Many have been willing to give M. Derrida the benefit of the doubt, insisting that language of such depth and difficulty of interpretation must hide deep and subtle thoughts indeed.

When the effort is made to penetrate it, however, it becomes clear, to us at least, that, where coherent statements are being made at all, these are either false or trivial. (P, p. 420)

To his own obvious annoyance and weariness, Derrida continually had to refute the idea that he had abandoned all truth claims. Following a dispute with the speech-act philosopher John Searle, Derrida took issue with the idea that 'the deconstructionist (which is to say, isn't it, the sceptic-relativist-nihilist!) is supposed not to believe in truth, stability, or the unity meaning'. His reply is blunt:

this definition of the deconstructionist is *false* (that's right: false not true) and feeble; it supposes a bad (that's right: bad, not good) and feeble reading of numerous texts, first of all mine, which therefore must be read or reread. Then perhaps it will be understood that the value of truth (and those values associated with it) is never contested or destroyed in my writings, but only reinscribed in more powerful, larger, more stratified contexts. (LI, p. 146)

Later, he adds 'I say that there is not stability that is absolute, eternal, intangible, natural, etc. But that is implied in the very concept of stability. A stability is not an immutability; it is by definition always destabilizable' (p. 151).

If Derrida is not simply abandoning truth, but seeking to trace the complexity, the paradoxes that attend all our attempts to express or define truth, perhaps this is something theologians will want to pay attention to. In the politics of academic discourse – and their polite violence – it is easy to dismiss what seems to speak with another accent, to occupy another story, another camp. The division between analytical and continental philosophies

underscores this temptation as does the careless use of fairly meaningless labels such as 'postmodernism', which, as we have already
mentioned, Derrida never accepted as a description of his own
work. There is a clash of idioms, of languages, a political dimension that Derrida analyzed at length.

Fast forward ten years, and another story unfolds. As part of the
American Academy of Religion's annual meeting, a conference
was organized to reflect upon Derrida's significance for the study
of religion and the Bible. In a large hall in the Toronto convention
centre, an audience of about two thousand gathered for a panel
interview of Derrida. One or two of Derrida's most notable theological adversaries were present.

It was an extraordinary event. Derrida confessed his anxiety
and lack of competence. He recalled that the invitation to Toronto
was given to him when he was attending another conference on
Judaism or Jewishness, at which he says 'I knew that some of these
people would try and denounce me for not being Jewish enough,
for not being authentically Jewish. Others would try to convert
me to Judaism'.[6] Derrida, the Algerian-born French Jew, has often
attracted denunciation, but also perhaps unwelcome attempts to
recruit him to this or that cause. At the AAR, the question was:
which way would this go? Would Derrida, finally, be recruited as
a religious man? As a theologian?

The first question in Toronto was put by John Caputo, who has
been instrumental in drawing attention to the religious dynamic
of Derrida's thought. He quoted a passage in which Derrida said
that if one knew his experience of prayers, one would know
everything. Caputo asked what this meant. To whom did Derrida
pray and what answer did he expect? I quote from Derrida's
answer at some length:

> On the one hand, a prayer has to be a mixture of some-
> thing that is absolutely singular and secret – idiomatic,
> untranslatable – and, on the other hand, a ritual that
> involves the body in coded gestures and that uses a
> common, intelligible language. That is the way I pray,
> if I pray. And I pray all the time, even now. But there
> is a problem. My way of praying, if I pray, has more than
> one edge at the same time. There is something very

childish here, and when one prays one is always a child.
If I gather images from my childhood, I find images of
God as a Father – a severe, just Father with a beard – and
also, at the same time, images of a Mother who thinks I am
innocent, who is ready to forgive me. This is the childish
layer of my prayers, those I perform once a day, for
instance, before I go to bed, or a prayer that I might pray
right now. There is another layer, of course, which involves
my culture, my philosophical experience, my experience
of a critique or religion that goes from Feuerbach to
Nietzsche. This is the experience of a nonbeliever, someone who is constantly suspicious of the child, someone
who asks 'To whom am I praying? Whom am I addressing?
Who is God?' In this layer – this layer of a more sophisticated experience, if I can put it that way – I find a way of
meditating about the who that is praying and the who that
is receiving the prayer. I know that this appears negative,
but it isn't; it is a way of thinking when praying that does
not simply negate prayer. It is a way of asking all the
questions that we are posing at this conference, all of them.
These questions are a part of my experience of prayer.[7]

Here is the double nature of Derrida's relationship to religion, as
well as to values such as truth, meaning. He keeps faith with these
notions, because they cannot simply be surrendered. Anyone who
thinks they can just escape all talk of metaphysics and foundations
is being naïve, and bound to end up caught in the same problems
from which they are trying to escape.

So Derrida doesn't simply reject or make great rhetorical claims
about leaping out of past forms of thinking. Nor does he accept
them as given. He inhabits them, probing their logic and their
limits, and always looking out for what any organization of thinking, any theory or creed is suppressing. No system of thought is
self-contained and self-evident. It always presupposes something.
It always opens out on to an otherness that it cannot contain.

As we will see in greater detail later, a good example of this is
Derrida's analysis of law and constitutions. By what right is
a system of law or a constitution proclaimed? How can law be
introduced into the world? Only, it seems, by an act of force, or at

least by an act that lies outside the law. A sovereign moment is assumed: like a king who upholds and embodies the law, but can also suspend it. The law is made possible by illegality. And this is no accident; there is no other way for law to come into being, for the line between the ideal and the real to be crossed.

This strange structure means that no law is ever based upon sure foundations within the law itself. Perhaps something similar might be said about religious systems, and even the practice of faith. Derrida may 'pass for' an atheist, yet he insistently returns to religious themes and even confesses to praying, at the same time as wanting to question the very nature and object of prayer. In his reply to Caputo, he says that his scepticism is *part of the prayer*, part of an openness to the approach of the other that no secular or religious system can stifle.

These events in Derrida's life show a transition in the way his work is received. This is not to suggest that his erstwhile detractors have become enthusiasts. However, there is now an intense and constructive focus on what Derrida gives theologians, scholars of scriptures and philosophers of religion to think.

The third 'accident of life' I want to touch upon is the publication of *Jacques Derrida,* a work that appeared in 1991 in French, and in 1993 in English translation. It is a strange, doubled book. One part of it is written by Geoffrey Bennington, who aims to give a scholarly, systematic introduction to Derrida's thought. But on the bottom half of each page, under a line, there is a text by Derrida called *Circumfession.*

The title plays upon the ideas of confession and circumcision. Derrida's text is designed to expose the limits of any attempt to understand him systematically. It is written in a stream of consciousness style, with frequent autobiographical details, not least about the death of his mother, and his Jewishness. It is also an archly literary text, recalling above all the genre of confessions inaugurated by St Augustine (a fellow North African).

Throughout the text, Derrida plays with the initials *SA,* which stand both for the saint, his hidden partner in confession, and also for the *savoir absolu* or Absolute Knowledge craved by systematic philosophical thinking. It is as if one is played off against the other. The very act of confessing exposes the singularity of a life, while also underlining the fact that I can only have access to another's innermost life through an act of faith. That faith will never equate to knowledge or certainty.

Derrida resists Bennington's attempt to know and explain him from an elevated vantage point. In a sense, Bennington stands for the God, or at least the godlike philosopher, who has absolute knowledge in his grasp and in his vision. Derrida's flowing text is intimately personal, but it always points out that the secret of Derrida's life is being withheld. Even God, it seems, is denied absolute access to this secret.

At the same time, Derrida invokes the God known by many different names in his life:

> that's what my readers won't have known about me, the
> commas of my breathing henceforward, without continuity
> but without a break, the changed time of my writing,
> graphic writing, through having lost its interrupted
> verticality, almost with every letter, to be bound better and
> better but be read less and less well over almost twenty
> years, like my religion about which nobody understands
> anything, any more than does my mother who asked other
> people a while ago, not daring to talk to me about it,
> if I still believed in God, *nutrierat filios totiens eos parturiens,*
> *quotiens abs te deuiare cernebat* ['She had brought up her
> children, being in labor with them each time she saw them
> wandering away from Thee'], but she must have known
> that the constancy of God in my life is called by other
> names, so that I quite rightly pass for an atheist, the
> omnipresence to me of what I call God in my absolved,
> absolutely private language being neither that of an
> eyewitness nor that of a voice doing anything other than
> talking to me without saying anything, nor a transcendent
> law or an immanent *schechina*, that feminine figure of
> Yahweh who remains so strange and familiar to me, but the
> secret I am excluded from . . . (Circ, pp. 154–55)

Though he rightly passes for an atheist, on one definition of God, Derrida still finds in the language of God and faith a resource for articulating his resistance to the pretensions of knowledge. It is as if God names what must remain hidden, secret, other than certainty, other than transcendent law or revealed glory. However, this is not an invitation to escape into an other, parallel world, or to offer faith as an alternative source of certitude. Derrida continually returns us to the elusive flow of time and language, and to the very real fears and desires aroused by the mortality of his mother. These feelings are doubled when his own vulnerability is exposed by an attack of facial paralysis. Whatever God names for Derrida, it is not an exit from the passing nature of mortal existence. The God of consoling security is refused in the name of an other God, who accentuates the finitude and temporality of being.

Given this double nature of *Circumfession*, it is not so much what the text is about that is important as what it does. It affirms the singularity of its author's life and thought, while acknowledging that any life is bound up with languages, traditions and practices that no individual controls. Especially important to Derrida is his circumcision, the cut that happened to him before he can remember, which marked his identity, opened his identity to an otherness before all memory and knowledge. And Derrida was also given a middle name that he only found out about later in life: Elie, after the prophet Elijah, who would come to prepare the world for the coming of the Messiah. A past beyond memory and a future that no one can anticipate: these mark Derrida's identity in ways that modern philosophies of the isolated and rational ego fail to grasp.

It is significant that this is where he chooses to talk about his prayer. It is as if he is saying, or showing us, that one way in which to disrupt systems of thought that have totalitarian pretensions is to pray. Prayer – like the secret about which Derrida also writes at length – is the most intensely personal and private experience, and yet it has a subversive public power. It contests the limits we draw around the world, and the modern desire to expose the innermost recesses of the self to a speculative gaze, surveillance and control.

A short biography

The biographical incidents we have looked at so far have not been chosen in order to lay bare the secret of Derrida's work and motivation. If anything, they draw us to the inescapable necessity for interpretation and confession, for rationality and a kind of faith. As we will see, this belonging together of reason and fidelity plays an important role in Derrida's writing.

With this in mind, it might still be helpful to provide an outline sketch of Derrida's life, to offer another kind of orientation of his thinking. A full critical biography remains to be written, but some of the more basic facts about Derrida's life history can be traced.[8]

He was born in 1930 in the family's holiday home in El Biar, near Algiers in modern day Algeria, although it was then still a French colony. His family was of French Jewish ancestry, though on his mother Georgette's side, they had been in Algeria for several generations. Derrida maintained a sense of belonging to Algeria, although he was himself a French citizen. He was named 'Jackie', an Americanism he would later choose to alter to the more conventional 'Jacques'.

The family moved permanently to El Biar when Derrida was four years old. He describes himself as a 'a little black and very Arab Jew' (Circ, p. 58), a fragile child prone to tears and depression. His brother Norbert died in 1940, aged two; another brother, Paul, had died the year before Derrida's birth. He had been just three months old.

Matters could not have been helped by the influence of the Vichy years upon the French colony, and a growing atmosphere of anti-Semitism. Derrida was excluded from school in 1942 after the imposition of quotas that determined the acceptable proportion of Jews allowed into education. When his schooling resumed in 1943, Derrida frequently played truant. Indeed, his educational career was hardly stellar. He was not a model student, preferring dreams of professional football to study. He failed the *baccalaureat* in 1947, though it was a time of intense reading and the discovery of philosophy through writers such as Rousseau and Nietzsche.

Derrida studied philosophy for a further year in Algiers, discovering Kierkegaard and Heidegger. In 1949, he moved to the Lycée Louis-le-Grand in Paris. He tried to enter the École Normale Supérieure (ENS), one of the Grandes Écoles that are a distinctive feature of French tertiary education. They are not universities as such, but have a reputation for educating the national élite. The ENS had been founded to provide excellent quality teachers, but it had also become a training ground for top politicians and bureaucrats.

Derrida failed the entrance exam on more than once occasion, abandoning it due to stress, but was eventually admitted in 1952. By 1953 he was writing a startling and complex dissertation on Husserl, which was to be published later in his life. He had befriended Louis Althusser, the prominent Marxist intellectual who was on the staff of the ENS, as well as meeting Michel Foucault. However, Derrida's problems with education were not over. He failed the *aggrégation*, the exam that qualifies those who pass for teaching in higher education. He took it again and passed in 1956.

The following year was spent partly at Harvard, where Derrida was given a grant to carry our research on Husserl's archived material. There, he met and married Marguerite Aucouturier, with whom he was to have two sons, Pierre (1963) and Jean (1967). After a period of military service in which he was used as a teacher in Algeria, Derrida returned to France. He made his first contribution to a conference and took a teaching position at the university of Sorbonne in 1960. He began publishing in journals, and his first book, an introduction to Husserl's *Origin of Geometry*, appeared in 1962 (the year of Algerian independence). He was invited back to teach at the ENS in 1964, where he remained for twenty years.

The mid-1960s were when Derrida really emerged as a major figure. His contribution to the famous 1966 colloquium on 'Critical Languages and the Sciences of Man' at Johns Hopkins University in Baltimore marked his arrival on the intellectual scene of the United States. There he met Paul de Man and Jacques Lacan and renewed contact with Roland Barthes. In 1967, he published three groundbreaking books: *Speech and Phenomena, Writing and Difference* and *Of Grammatology*.

Derrida's own distinctive thinking was being formed. He was heavily influenced by Husserl's phenomenology, but (as we will see in the next chapter) problems of origin, time and language were making him critical of it. He was also becoming a critic of the dominant structuralism in French intellectual life, including its Marxist variant promoted by Althusser. Heidegger and Levinas had become major conversation partners for him, aided by an ongoing friendship with the latter. Derrida began to be invited to take up visiting teaching posts abroad, and developed especially strong links with a number of U.S. universities.

During the student protests in Paris in 1968, Derrida maintained a critical distance. Having been intermittently involved in left politics, he never subscribed to the prevailing Marxism and Maoism at the ENS. He broke with the critical journal *Tel Quel* for political reasons in 1972. In the same year there was another burst of major publications, including *Dissemination* and *Margins of Philosophy*.

However, in many ways Derrida remained an activist. One increasingly important front was the promotion of philosophical education in schools and universities. Derrida was a founding member of the *Groupe de recherche sur l'enseignement philosophique* in 1974, and a co-organizer of the government supported Estates General of Philosophy (1979) and the *Collège Internationale de Philosophie* (1983).

Politically, he was active in the 1980s and 1990s in a number of causes. He co-founded the Jan Hus Association in support of dissident intellectuals in Czechoslovakia. On a visit to that country in 1982, he was arrested on trumped up charges of drug possession. The intervention of the French government on his behalf helped to secure his release and made him a minor celebrity for a time.

Derrida also campaigned for the extension of voting rights to immigrants, the protection of Algerian intellectuals, and the UNESCO programme to create 'cities of asylum' as sanctuaries for those fleeing persecution. He supported anti-apartheid art projects and visited Israel, where he met Palestinian thinkers.

Deconstruction gained greater momentum in the United States from the mid-1970s, and Derrida found himself in demand on a global level, with visits to Latin America and Japan standing out. From 1984, Derrida became director of studies at the École des Hautes Études en Sciences Sociales, finally attaining a more senior academic position.

His own writing evolved in various ways. The experimental form of *Glas* (1974) marked a high point in innovative graphics that left its mark on many subsequent books. There was a greater explicit engagement with religious themes, with law, politics and ethics.

A strong influence was exerted by a number of controversies. The reissue of Heidegger's 1936 Rectoral Address, in which he aligned his philosophy with Nazism, led to a huge debate about whether there was an intrinsically fascist element to his thinking. Deconstruction, so heavily influenced by Heidegger, was tarred with the same brush. Derrida's response, especially in *Of Spirit* (1987), was to appeal to the depth and complexity of Heidegger's thought, without condoning his Nazi associations in any way. A related furore broke over the discovery that Paul de Man, foremost in promoting deconstruction on the United States, wrote anti-Semitic pieces during his time as a young journalist in occupied Belgium. Again, Derrida was compelled to address issues of politics and responsibility for very personal as well as intellectual reasons.

Derrida appeared in a film documentary in 2002 (*Derrida*, directed by Kirby Dick and Amy Ziering Kofman), in which he was filmed in various domestic and academic settings, and interviewed at length. He shows a characteristic awareness of the artificiality of the situation and a reluctance to divulge much about his personal life. He reputedly had a long-standing relationship with the philosopher Sylviane Agacinski, with whom he had a son, but he remained married to Marguerite until his death from cancer in 2004.

Destructure

The guiding thread for this essay will be the way in which Derrida challenges the idea of the simplicity of God. That God is simple implies that God cannot be divided or subject to change and suffering, that there is no unrealized potential in God, for God is the sum of fully actualized perfection. Only as such, for a tradition that stretches back through Aquinas into Greek metaphysics, can God be the necessary stopping point for any attempt to account for this changing, temporal world of creation. Only as simple can God's absolute distinction from creatures be assured.

Calling this idea into question does not mean dismissing it. Simplicity, with its associated values of full self-presence, certainty, clarity and unity, will always haunt the philosophical and theological quests for truth. If these ideas are caught in contradictions, they do not (simply) die. Derrida never merely rejects the philosophical search for enlightenment and emancipation. The critical vigilance he invokes must always bear a relation to truth in its most classical definitions.

His work consists in sounding these ideas, 'revealing' that what makes them possible also makes them unstable, internally divided – in a word, impossible. Much of his early published output consisted of readings of philosophical and literary texts which traced the ways in which the surface meaning was always being re-traced, warped and contradicted by what their texts were saying despite the author's best intentions. Such a way of reading can easily be misunderstood, as if Derrida were decoding texts to lay bare their 'real', unintended, unconscious references, much like the caricature of a Freudian analyst telling us the import of our dreams. In fact, Derrida understands meaning differently, not as an underlying truth, but as the interweaving of forces. Meaning, on this account, cannot be gathered into a simple presence. It differs from itself and always arrives too late for that. But this is not the end of meaning: it is how it works.

Such cryptic statements can only be justified by a closer analysis of Derrida's work. As already mentioned, his output is vast, but there is a consistency to it, and a certain number of key focal points around which an investigation of its theological importance can be arranged.

The organization of the rest of this book will (following a loose scriptural conceit) underline the uncanny recurrence of theological and even biblical motifs in Derrida's work. We will explore his engagements with genesis, the nature and name of God, the word, mysticism and messianism, the gift and incarnation. Finally, there will be a survey of how Derrida has been received and critiqued by theologians, and some concluding reflections. I have kept references to secondary literature to a minimum in the chapters on Derrida's own work, in order that space for a fuller engagement with these difficult texts is possible. A select bibliography is provided at the end of the book.

Chapter 1

Savage Genesis: Complicating the Origin

Anyone who has worked with the writings of Jacques Derrida knows that it can be both incredibly stimulating and extremely frustrating. His style is complex, teasing, playful – convoluted, you could say. He enjoys testing the limits of language, particularly the French language in which he most often writes and speaks. New words are coined, old ones are put together in new ways.

Of course, one of the important things to recognize about Derrida is that his style is not accidental to the meaning of his work. As already suggested, he does not want to play by the rules of common sense and plain speaking. The style is deliberate, because the way something is said is as important as what is said.

More radically: there can be no clear-cut division between style and substance. Language is performance. It is intervention. If language is structure, system and the shared rules of the game, it is also event, promise, call, interruption. It is not merely an empty, neutral vessel containing a sacrosanct meaning that is unaffected by the means of its transmission. It is not a regrettable detour or lapse, which a supreme effort of will or insight could set aside in order to get at the pre-formed reality somewhere behind it. Language's metaphors and other tropes, its grammar and context, all contribute to the making of what we call truth.

At times, Derrida's style may risk making him needlessly obscure. As we have seen, the way he contests the ideal of truth as simple timeless presence raises the ghostly fear that he is really against any sort of truth. But it is central to his project to call into question the ideas of clarity, certainty, foundation, self-evidence and presence that he believes are at the heart of the Western philosophical tradition and of so much of its political, ethical and religious thought.

To talk of Derrida's 'project' is at once to assume that he has some overarching theory running through all his work from the beginning. Given that his work is enormous in scope and variation, and often proceeds by close readings of other texts, this might seem a dubious claim. Especially so, when we realize how much Derrida did not wish to be caught within the webs of any grand systematic thinking. No doubt he would have wryly observed how much easier it is to summarize and categorize a thinker once he or she is dead. His death in 2004 now opens the door to considerations of his legacy, his place in the development of philosophy – everything that threatens to reduce a living work into another paragraph in the history of ideas.

However, I do think it is possible to trace the lines of continuity in what preoccupied Derrida, always aware that this entails a risk of recruiting him to a narrowly defined cause or position. I take a cue from some words he wrote in 1990 in the preface to a very early work of his, written in fact as a student in 1953–1954, and only just then being published.

Of course, Derrida himself is not fool enough to think that an author is always the best interpreter of his work, or that he can tell the reader how they should go about reading him. He does nevertheless attempt to notice the questions and problems that have been persistent in his work even from these student days. He writes: 'It is always a question of an originary complication of the origin, of an initial contamination of the simple, of an inaugural divergence that no analysis could *present, make present* in its phenomenon or reduce to the pointlike nature of the element, instantaneous and identical to itself' (PG, p. xv).

There is a huge amount packed into those few words: about origins, and how they are never simple; about presence and what appears to our consciousness; about time and identity. For this very reason, they provide a useful starting point, one that does respond to the concerns of Derrida's texts. It is a question of the 'originary complication of the origin'. Here is the paradox that will haunt Derrida's writing, which will lead some to accuse him of not believing in any truth or values at all. But for others, there will be the hint of new questions for religious and theological thought. After all, theologians too are interested in origins.

Deconstructing itself

At first glance, the work that brought Derrida to international attention in the 1960s does not look very promising from the point of view of theology. In fact the word 'theology' is often used dismissively, or associated with an essentially oppressive, systematic philosophical approach. However, things are not quite what they seem.

One of the moves for which Derrida is best known is the manner in which he questions the way Western metaphysics has privileged speech over writing as a bearer of meaning. In various texts, he argues that there has been a big assumption that when I speak, my meaning is immediately present in my words, and thus reaches the other person in the face-to-face encounter with the minimum of delay and distortion. In contrast, writing drifts free of its original author and context. It loses immediacy, and becomes open to multiple interpretations.

There is an echo of this approach in Pauline dictum that the letter kills but the Spirit gives life. The written word, so the image implies, is essentially lifeless. Its signs are grave markers. In contrast, the voice is alive with breath and spirit. Derrida traces this association through Plato, through Egyptian mythology and through a variety of modern philosophies. The model of meaning that is assumed in much Western philosophy of language is of ideal meaning. Ideas pre-exist in the mind; they are then wrapped in language for delivery to another mind. The wrapper is accidental to the inner truth being conveyed.

By way of contesting this position, Derrida argues that writing offers the best clue as to how meaning is made and communicated. The idea that speech delivers a pure and ideal meaning is an illusory ideal. Meaning does not pre-exist language in an ideal realm of thought. The very idea that it does is something that is formulated in words. Any spoken utterance depends upon a prior existing language. And language only works as a system of differences, in which one word, term or phrase is only defined in relation to others. There is no getting away from context and contexts are never completely determinable. That is, we can never know with absolute clarity what the boundaries of any relevant context might be. Even if a speaker feels absolutely sure of their meaning and the words chosen to express them, they are entering into a pact with a language that preceded them, and with multiple future contexts they cannot control. They cannot fully anticipate how their message will be received, or what new contexts will reshape it.

Difference, then, becomes a key to understanding how language works. And so does time. Even if I am speaking to you directly, face to face, it takes time to say what I am saying: time to formulate it, to speak, time for you to hear and interpret. The ideal model of meaning would like to do away with time. Meaning is simple, pure, eternal. But time interrupts this longed for eternity. Meaning takes time, and that is the only meaning to which we have access.

Derrida puts it like this:

> An interval must separate the present from what it is not in
> order for the present to be itself, but this interval that
> constitutes it as present must, by the same token, divide the
> present in and of itself, thereby also dividing, along with
> the present, everything that is thought on the basis of the
> present, that is, in our metaphysical language, every being,
> and singularly substance or the subject. (M, p. 13)

According to Derrida, drawing on Heidegger, the Western philosophical tradition has been dominated by the idea, or ideal, of presence. In this tradition, the true nature of being itself is characterized by presence. Truth claims are judged according to whether or not they correspond to and convey that presence. This way of understanding being and truth is persistent and pervasive.

What Derrida and others have called deconstruction follows on from this. Deconstruction is related to what Heidegger previously called *Destruktion*.[1] Heidegger believed that in Western philosophy, the question of Being – the most basic question about what there is – had been forgotten or suppressed. Being had been treated like just another object in the world: more solid, more exalted, but essentially a fixed foundation, timeless and isolated. The question of Being needed to be reopened and this was only possible through the dynamic care and concern of those beings who had the ability to ask the question for themselves. Heidegger's term for such a being was *Dasein*. It is difficult to translate this word, because it does not refer simply and straightforwardly to a human being, but to human being insofar as it is not swallowed up by the forgetful, unthinking existence of the anonymous mass man, but appropriates its own existence and orients itself towards the question of Being.

In order to do this, the philosophical tradition had to be destroyed. This does not mean that philosophy is wholly dismissed or torn to shreds, but that it is laid bare, opened again to what it had forgotten. We have to put ourselves in a position to strip away the layers that covered Being and experience it in a primordial way for ourselves.

Deconstruction is perhaps less optimistic about this continuing mystical dimension in Heidegger's thought. But it shares the ambition of a radical questioning of philosophical ideas. Deconstruction is not so much a technique that an individual can master and employ. It is more an inherent dynamic of language and meaning. It is something that happens, and that reading and writing and acting engages with, without us ever fully grasping it. Reading deconstructively means something like being attentive to an event, an unexpected arrival, that interrupts, contradicts and dislocates what appeared to be settled and fixed. It is important to note that deconstruction does not simply create this event, as if it were a matter of projecting our own wishes and fantasies upon a text. The event, the other, what is happening or being testified to or announced in a text, these have a certain priority in provoking the response of deconstruction. In this sense it is absolutely right to see deconstruction as *threatening*, because it is inhuman, no longer in the control of a human subject. Indeed, it calls into question the violent acts of exclusion that have gone into making such a subject intelligible and coherent.

Derrida clarifies this in his 1983 'A Letter to a Japanese Friend' in which he reflects on the nature of deconstruction and how it might be translated in contexts very different from his own. He writes that 'deconstruction is neither an analysis nor a critique . . . It is not an analysis in particular because the dismantling of a structure is not a regression toward a simple element, toward an indissoluble origin'.[2] Deconstruction is distinguished from a 'method', an 'act', an 'operation', all of which assume a technique under the control of a knowing subject, when it is just this notion of original power that deconstruction calls into question.

The strange paradox is that deconstruction has a life (and death) of its own. It is an unpredictable event:

> Deconstruction takes place, it is an event that does not await the deliberation, consciousness, or organization of a subject, or even of modernity. It deconstructs itself. It can be deconstructed. [*Ça se deconstruit.*] The 'it' [*ça*] is not here an impersonal thing that is opposed to some egological subjectivity. It is in deconstruction (the Littré says, 'to deconstruct itself [*se deconstruire*] . . . to lose its construction'). And the 'se' of 'se deconstruire', which is not the reflexivity of an ego or of a consciousness, bears the whole enigma.[3]

Deconstruction is a response imposed by the dangerous otherness that is woven through all texts. For instance, in reading literary or philosophical works, Derrida sets out to notice the ways in which the apparent surface meaning is suspended or crossed by other interpretations; how there are blind spots in any system of thought. Any system, any totality, any absolute starting point must always try to absorb all otherness. It can't leave anything out. It must be its own beginning, its own end, its own source of life. But this ambition is constantly defied by the nature of language and meaning making.

A good piece of early deconstruction is the one-page demolition of Descartes by Nietzsche.[4] Descartes made a typical metaphysical move: he sought after the one sure starting point for knowledge that could not be doubted, and concluded that one could not doubt the fact of one's own thinking and therefore the existence of a thinking self – I think, therefore I am. Nietzsche points out that this seemingly obvious statement is full of hidden assumptions, simply by virtue of it being expressed in language. How can one get from one end of the sentence to the other without having assumed a whole language of subject and predicate, of the nature of rational argument and self-evidence, of the nature of the 'I'? Nietzsche insisted that interpretation was essential to meaning, not secondary. The 'I' becomes a construct, a fiction (even if a necessary one).

Deconstruction therefore does not assume a given self or basis of knowledge, but invites us to notice that we are always already in the middle of secondariness, interpretation and flux. Derrida's take on this is influenced by his own immediate philosophical background, including especially the complex approach that goes under the name of phenomenology. In order to orient our investigation into Derrida's relevance for theology, it is necessary to look a little more deeply into these philosophical engagements. Phenomenology is particularly important, because it shows Derrida from his very earliest publications set on a course that will complicate the whole notion of *origins*. What was said earlier about deconstruction may seem programmatic and obscure unless Derrida's own complex beginnings are called into play.

Older than presence: different origins

That student text of the 1950s took as its theme the problem of *genesis* in the writings of the phenomenological philosopher, Husserl: how does objective truth come into existence for us? In answering this question, Husserl sought to avoid the twin perils of formalism and psychologism. To understand this division, we need to reach back a little into the history of ideas.

Immanuel Kant had argued that the mind is not merely a passive receiver of truths imprinted upon it from the outside world. Rather, the world only becomes ordered and knowable because it is organized by the forms and categories imposed upon it by our own sensibility and understanding. We shape the flux of experience into a cosmos. However, for Kant, this is not just an arbitrary procedure. There is one and only one set of ordering categories, universal to all knowing minds. Knowledge is therefore at the same time constituted by us and objective.

Kant wanted to overcome the split he inherited between empiricism and rationalism. The former attempted to found knowledge on sense impressions alone, but it ended in scepticism, unable to assure us of the objective validity of the most basic ideas such as causality, or even of mathematical truths. Rationalism looked instead to innate ideas within the mind as its starting point, but Kant thought that this led to unbridled metaphysical speculation. He insisted that reason could not give us theoretical knowledge of things of which we had no experience. Kant's famous formula – 'concepts without intuitions are empty, intuitions without concepts are blind' – expresses his own solution: the understanding needs the stuff of experience on which to do its work, but experience is mute and unformed unless shaped by the mind.

Kant's resolution proved unstable. The dualism between understanding and experience he had sought to heal was reintroduced into the working of the mind itself. Kant drew a distinction between our empirical, everyday self and the universal, formal self that lay beneath all our knowing and perceiving: the transcendental ego. The latter could not itself become an object of knowledge or intuition, since it was a priori. The transcendental ego made intelligible experience possible in the first place.

The price paid for this was that the origin of knowledge became obscure. Followers of Kant in the latter part of the nineteenth century essentially accepted this situation, arguing that knowledge could only be considered objective as the application of formal a priori rules. There was no way of looking beyond or behind those rules, because this would just lead to ungrounded speculation, precisely what Kant wanted to avoid. Briefly, formalism insisted that the kind of ideal and objective truth possessed by mathematical, logical and geometrical theorems could never be derived from empirical experience.

Opposition to neo-Kantianism came from 'psychologists' such as Carl Stumpf, who insisted that truth had to be truth for someone, for a thinking person. Formal rules were not enough. The psychological process that led to the formation of, for example, mathematical truths had to be understood. Initially, Husserl followed this approach. However, he came to believe that it was an inadequate account of the objectivity of mathematics and logic.

Phenomenology was born as an attempt to do justice to the objectivity of knowledge, while remedying Kant's neglect of the way it came into being for the knowing ego. For Husserl, the transcendental ego was to become the key object of intuition, but only as a result of a radical change in our natural attitude towards the world and the self. Knowing-oneself-knowing in this purified sense would be the phenomenologist's route to reach the Holy Grail: the origin of truth and therefore of the world itself.

The importance of phenomenology for Derrida cannot be understated. It formed his intellectual milieu and the starting point for his own distinctive investigations into language, identity and difference. For so many of the most influential philosophers in the continental tradition – Heidegger, Sartre, Merleau-Ponty and Levinas, to name a few – it provided an indispensable stimulus for thinking.

Phenomenology was in a sense the modern heir to Descartes (one of Husserl's major works is the *Cartesian Meditations*).[5] Descartes' philosophical project was one of universal doubt, a search for a beginning for knowledge that was self-evident and clear. His method was to turn inwards, to identify what properly belonged to the self when all contingent accretions were stripped away.

Husserl too wanted to think back to a sure foundation, and so overcome the divisions between objectivity and subjectivity, realism and idealism that still plagued philosophy. His roots were in the philosophy of mathematics, but, as we have noted, he became dissatisfied with the 'psychologism' of his early attempts to account for mathematical and logical knowledge. For Husserl, the doctrine that logic can be wholly accounted for by understanding the workings of the mind through empirical observation was wholly unsuited to establishing the kind of objective truth to which logic aspired. It led to the absurd position that mathematical laws would be better founded if we understood the psychological mechanisms that enabled us to use them. Husserl objected that logic and mathematics sought ideal truth, not truths dependent upon the contingent and subjective workings of the human mind.

His method was therefore to attend simply to 'phenomena', to what actually appeared to consciousness, while bracketing out all natural assumptions about the existence of an external world; then to abstract away from all empirical content of thought to the ideal essences that lay within each contingent appearance or experience; and finally to grasp what it was that made this ideal truth possible in the first place. Husserl concluded that there is a transcendental ego: an experiencing, perceiving 'I' that stands behind and before every appearance. This 'I' exists not in ordinary passing time, but in the living present of pure certainty. It could be intuited, known immediately, once all that was inessential was laid to one side.

Derrida's early studies of Husserl focus upon the question of origins, because here lay a basic tension within phenomenology.[6] On the one hand, logic and mathematics should have ideal and timeless truth. On the other, the transcendental ego must be the absolute origin, constituting the knowable world, and this ego must itself be experienced in this pure form. The questions flowing from this seemingly abstract dilemma are crucial. Is truth a given, or something made? Is the consciousness of the ego purely self-contained and self-founding, or is it always open and responsive to something that precedes it? In the experience of time within the transcendental ego Husserl seeks to exclude merely empirical, worldly time. But there is still an experience of retention and protention, a past and a future that are integral to the present, and without which it could not experience or articulate truth for itself. The further question arises: does time flow from the self, or is the self already situated within the time of the world?

In his student dissertation, Derrida notes that for Husserl, we can only understand the beginnings of science by starting with its development in the present day, and working back to 'reactivate' the original birth of the ideas. Husserl refers to this as a 'zigzag' method, as we move between the origin and the present to clarify each of these terms. Derrida notes that 'If this zigzag method is essential and indispensable, it is because at the moment when we get to the most originary constituting source, the constituted is already there' (PGH, p. 164). In other words, the pure origin always escapes consciousness, and Husserl's method is 'indefinite' (PGH, p. 165).

If, as Husserl insists, history is not just a falling away from or covering up of ideal certainties once given, then some account has to be given of time and otherness at the very origin of consciousness. The absolute, transcendental ego begins to look rather less than absolute: it is constituted, dependent upon moments and relations that precede it.

Derrida therefore notes that Husserl still needs to give an account of how the inner 'I' can gather together time and otherness. Husserl is not unaware of this issue, which is what makes him so fascinating for those pursuing a fully non-dogmatic philosophy. He values language as the means by which we are liberated from this or that contingent event, and ideal truth is passed from person to person and generation to generation.

Derrida's introduction to Husserl's short *Origin of Geometry* shows the dawning realization of just how unsettling this shift in focus towards time and language will be, not only for phenomenology, but for the whole Western metaphysical tradition that stands behind it. Husserl argues that geometrical truth is ideal and objective. It doesn't depend upon the contingencies of empirical experience. However, that ideal meaning must be discovered at a particular point in time. Then, in order to be communicated and so freed from its mute isolation, it must be transmitted in language. This language makes a history of truth possible. Genesis becomes story.

However, Husserl insists that this is not history in its ordinary factual sense. It is an ideal history that must be animated by the breath of the conscious ego, reactivating ideal meanings, freeing them from all their empirical distractions. Language is the wrapper, delivering pure meaning unscathed through time. But this makes Husserl's project unstable. Language and time, as we have seen, introduce an essential undecidability, an uncertainty, a plurality into the way meaning is made and communicated. The living present is always haunted by something else: by absence, by death. In fact, rather than the living present being the condition of possibility for everything else, Derrida maintains that presence is a construct, something that is itself dependent upon difference. It is no longer possible to draw a hard and fast distinction between merely empirical history and the pure internal time experienced by the ego; or between an ideal language transmitting objective meaning, and the natural language, which always exceeds the boundaries of pure, gathered, self-present consciousness.

It becomes difficult to find solid ground, a place to begin without presuppositions. History is made possible by language, which is made possible by history. The pure ideality of meaning is made possible by time and words, the very things that wreck the possibility of pure and ideal meaning. The ideal and the real find themselves bound up together, contaminating one another: 'the origin and possibility of this ideal omnitemporality remain marked by a factual contingency, that of the reality intended by the judgement or that of subjective acts' (IOG, p. 73). Husserl declares that the essence of objective truth exceeds language. It is purely ideal, and comes to birth in the silence of the soul of the one who 'invents' it. However, in order to become a truth available and intelligible to all, it requires incarnation in the 'flesh' of language (IOG, p. 76). As much as Husserl seeks to keep this flesh unstained by merely worldly bodies, flesh is always vulnerable, mortal, changing. When the word becomes flesh, the scandal of impurity has already begun.

Husserl attempts to resolve this problem by projecting the idea of absolute meaning as a 'telos', a goal towards which history aims. For Derrida, however, this is a step beyond the purely present intuition that is supposedly at the heart of phenomenological certainty. Ideally, the pure 'logos' or primordial expression of truth will move towards a final telos to achieve perfect clarity. In this sense, 'the *Absolute is Passage*', a movement through time to unity (IOG, p. 149). However, for Derrida, this passage is anything but guaranteed. Sense can be lost along the way. Meaning can wander far from its source: 'This movement is also *Danger(ous) as the Absolute* [*l'Absolu d'un Danger*]' (IOG, p. 149). We are driven to ask what it is that makes the dream of pure meaning possible, at the same time as the absolute seems to be shattered in its original unity, exposed to an interpretation and questioning for which we must take responsibility.

In *Speech and Phenomena*, we can see this argument worked out in greater detail, and it is here that the complication of origins takes a radical new step: in the darkness of Genesis, it is the word that makes (and unmakes) the ideality of the world.

Derrida identifies the phenomenology's 'source and guarantee of all value, the "principle of principles" i.e., the original self-giving evidence, the present or presence of sense to a full and primordial intuition'. He goes on to ask whether it is possible to see 'the phenomenological critique of metaphysics betray itself as a moment within the history of metaphysical assurance' (SP, p. 5). Derrida is raising the question of whether, for all its rigorous devotion to the pure givenness of appearances, there is not at work in phenomenology an underlying, highly traditional set of metaphysical assumptions. According to Derrida, Husserl's view is that 'The ultimate form of ideality, the ideality of ideality, that in which the last instance one may anticipate or recall all repetition, is the living present, the self-presence of transcendental life' (SP, p. 6).

The word 'transcendental' is important here. In the philosophical tradition stretching back to Kant and beyond, something is transcendental if it is a condition for knowledge to be possible at all. It is a priori, something presupposed and given before all empirical knowledge. It is what allows appearances to appear to a consciousness. For Husserl, the reductions that suspended our natural empiricist outlook led to the consequence that the transcendental ego (not our everyday sense of self) was the necessary condition of all knowing.

Phenomenology strives to free itself from the prejudices of both common sense 'natural' attitudes and dogmatic metaphysics by returning to the experience of 'the things themselves', without presuppositions. However, the very division of the contingent and empirical from the necessary and ideal is a classic metaphysical move. Derrida argues that this move is vulnerable once we begin to question the ideal of self-presence and pure identity that govern it.

An initial clue comes in the way Derrida describes Husserl's distinction between the task of psychology and the scope of transcendental phenomenology. The former is an investigation of the empirical life of the mind. The latter, transcendental approach asks for the absolute conditions that make that empirical life possible. However, we have to begin with empirical experiences, for where else do we discover the things that will reveal to us their conditions? It is thus difficult, argues Derrida, to see any real difference in content between empirical psychology and phenomenology proper and yet there must be a radical difference between the two if Husserl's philosophy is to get away from description of merely contingent events and experiences.

Derrida thus writes of 'a difference which, without altering anything, changes all the signs, and in which alone the possibility of a transcendental question is contained. That is to say, freedom itself. A fundamental difference, thus, without which no other difference in the world would either make any sense or have the chance to appear *as such*' (SP, p. 11). The very possibility of phenomenology depends upon us being able to draw this line between empirical experience and what makes that experience possible, a line that alters nothing in the world, but that sets up an ideal of pure meaning and subjective freedom.

For Husserl, the mistake would be to set up this interior ideal as just another part of the world or aspect of our mind. That would fail to account for anything, fail to found knowledge or meaning in any significant way. However, in the search for the pure source of ideal meaning, Derrida claims that language inevitably breaks down into conflicting metaphors. He comments that

> it is at the price of this war of language against itself that the sense and question of its origin will be thinkable. This war is obviously not one war among others. A polemic for the possibility of sense and world, it takes place in this *difference*, which, we have seen, cannot reside in the world, but only in language, in the transcendental disquietude of language. Indeed far from only living in language, this war is also the origin and residence of language. Language preserves the difference that preserves language. (SP, p. 14)

This striking passage shows Derrida getting a little ahead of his own argument. At this early stage of his career, he is already suggesting that the line between empirical reality and pure ideality is an unstable one. Even to try to draw this line unsettles and disjoints language in a violent way. And this 'war' is no accident: only because of it can the possibility of sense emerge.

It is tempting to draw a parallel here with the difficulties that face any attempt to account for the origin of language. If language is supposed to emerge 'naturally' from a non-linguistic background, we are unable to account for the leap from meaningless gesture to significant sign. On the other hand, if language is supposed to be a supernatural gift from the outside, as it were, we are unable to account for how it was recognized as meaningful by its first recipients. From within language, we are driven to think its origins as a paradox: for only if we have language already could we ever invent or receive it. What makes language possible is in turn made possible by language: a very Derridean complication.

How does this complication of the origin of sense and meaning play itself out in Derrida's analysis of Husserl? This is where we need to go a little deeper into the nature of signs.

Husserl distinguishes two modes of how signs work. In indication, the sign is contingently and empirically associated with an external entity. A particular sound or mark is associated with a referent, but the association is conventional rather than necessary. Another sign would have done just as well if it had been agreed upon. The sign is associated with the reality of an object.

However, there is another way in which signs convey meaning: expression. Unlike indication, in expression, meaning is immediately present to the speaker. This is the touchstone for truth: despite the arbitrariness of signs and their relation to the external world, they express something in the internal world of consciousness that is ideal, purified of chance and change.

In real life, expressions are always caught up in communication, which means they are always interwoven with indications. However, expressions can be (and, for Husserl, must be) distinguished in principle from indications. They can work in our solitary interior life too, where they continue to express something without having any physical existence and without being offered as communication. Signs possess this possibility of pure, inward meaning, alive in the solitary self. However, as Derrida points out, this purity of meaning is always caught up in indication and 'Caught up is the same as contaminated' (SP, p. 20).

The paradox for Husserl is that language is most expressive when it is least related to anything *outside* the solitary life of the self. But even in this interior realm, expressions still function as *signs*. For Husserl, this can be admitted as long as it is clear that the meaning intention of expressions is directed towards an ideal object, that is, one that remains essentially within consciousness.

Derrida points out that Husserl is replicating a classic division between body and soul, with the life of the soul remaining qualitatively distinct from and unaffected by material reality:

> The opposition between body and soul is not only at the center of this doctrine of signification, it is confirmed by it; and, as has always been at bottom the case in philosophy, it depends upon an interpretation of language. Visibility and spatiality as such could only destroy the self-presence of will and spiritual animation which opens up discourse. *They are literally the death of that self-presence.* (SP, p. 35)

We can begin to see why it is both correct and misleading to view Derrida as primarily a philosopher of language. Language and signs are central for him, but only insofar as they are interwoven with the basic distinctions philosophy has always operated with. In the essay under discussion, Derrida has already noted the link between Husserl's project and the fundamental themes of metaphysics. We now find him drawing on terms that are also at home in a religious thematic: body and soul, mortality and immortality, purity and impurity, the death of the letter and the life of the spirit. In each case, Derrida is beginning to question our assurance that we can create a stable polarity or hierarchy between the terms, such that one is foundational and essential and the other merely contingent and passing.

According to Husserl, expression alone is able to fulfil the idea of pure self-presence, as long as it suspends all communication with others and with an external world. As Derrida puts it, 'Pure expression will be the pure active intention (spirit, *psychē*, life, will) of an act of meaning (*bedeuten*) that animates a speech whose content (*Bedeutung*) is present' (SP, p. 40). An analogy suggests itself here between Husserl's analysis of ideal meaning and the thoughts that exist in the mind of God prior to or apart from creation. For God, there is expression: a pure presence to self, a unity of will and intention. But there is no obligation laid upon God for his Word to give external form and existence to a created, empirical, temporal reality. As we will see, Derrida's critique of Husserl is also an unravelling of this theological scheme.

Expression is pure, but because it is still a sign, it represents. In the end, what it represents is not some accidental factual content, but the presence of the self: 'In monologue, nothing is communicated; one represents oneself (*man stellt sich vor*) as a speaking and communicating subject' (SP, p. 49). Derrida argues that it is not possible rigorously to distinguish representation from reality, however. He goes further: 'it doesn't help to say that this happens *in* language; language in general – and language alone – *is* this' (SP, pp. 49–50).

Why? Derrida returns to the basic nature of any sign. A sign must be open to the possibility of repetition. Otherwise, it would just be a once off event, with no ability to carry meaning across time: 'A sign which would take place but "once" would not be a sign; a purely idiomatic sign would not be a sign. A signifier (in general) must be formally recognizable in spite of, and through, the diversity of empirical characteristics which may modify it' (SP, p. 50). It is important to note the unavoidable irony at work here. The very distinction Husserl makes between ideal meaning and empirical reality is only possible because signs can be repeated, thus making the pure, self-presence of ideal meaning unattainable. Difference, time and non-presence are built into the sign. *What the sign makes possible – an ideal of presence – it also makes impossible.*

Derrida does not think that this is merely a local difficulty for Husserl's arguments. He claims that it is a fundamental instability affecting the whole history of metaphysics, 'the adventure of the metaphysics of presence' (SP, p. 51). However, there can be no simple taking leave of metaphysics, because there can be no account of meaning that escapes these problems. The clamour to abandon all metaphysics for a pure land of direct encounter with reality – whether it be empirical science or mystical intuition – is itself a classic metaphysical move. Hence, those who question the tradition 'will only be capable of working over the language of metaphysics from within' for some time (SP, pp. 51–52).

For Derrida, then, 'the presence-of-the-present is derived from repetition and not the reverse' (SP, p. 52). Again, we note a paradox: the beginning is not identity but repetition. How can we begin with repetition, with what is secondary? This complication of the origin of meaning runs through Derrida's later work and is key to understanding his critique of the philosophical tradition and his engagement with questions of religion. According to Derrida 'the universal form of all experience . . . and therefore of all life, has always been and will always be the present' (SP, p. 53). Only in the present is identity safe and sound. It is worth quoting what follows at length, as it touches on key elements of our developing theme:

> The present alone is and ever will be. Being is presence or the modification of presence. The relation with the presence of the present as the ultimate form of being and of ideality is the move by which I transgress empirical existence, factuality, contingency, worldliness, etc. – first of all, *my own* empirical existence, factuality, contingency,

worldliness, etc. To think of presence as the universal form of transcendental life is to open myself to the knowledge that in my absence, beyond my empirical existence, before my birth and after my death, the present is . . . The relationship with my death (my disappearance in general) thus lurks in this determination of being as presence, ideality, the absolute possibility of repetition. The possibility of the sign is this relationship with death. (SP, p. 54)

The philosophy of presence, which identifies presence with being itself, is haunted by death. Only if signs can survive in the absence of their maker can meaning be preserved. But this means that signs must be able to survive apart from the full intuition of meaning that is supposed to anchor them in presence and therefore in being.

Derrida draws out the consequences of this for the self: 'the appearing of the *I* to itself in the *I am* is thus originally a relationship with its own possible disappearance. Therefore, I am originally means *I am mortal. I am immortal* is an impossible proposition' (SP, p. 54). But the self of phenomenology, as we have seen, could be read as a secularized version of the selfhood of God. If the self cannot be immortal, does this also apply to God? Is Derrida ruling out the possibility of God, the possibility of one who escapes the contamination of time?

Let us explore the logic of this position a little further in relation to the 'I'. The famous argument 'I think, therefore I am' is only as valid as the philosophical presuppositions that underlie it, despite the Cartesian aim to do away with all such presuppositions. As mentioned earlier, Nietzsche calls into question the concept of 'immediate certainty', a pure given outside of time and language. Only in language, in an act of interpretation, can such a project be formulated. It always therefore bears within it a temporal dimension and a reference to what is other than itself, including a reference to the possibility of its own disappearance, its own death.

In an obvious but important sense, it takes time to say anything, including the *cogito*. And all language is tensed, in a way that raises the question of how past, present and future relate to one another. In addition, language always involves difference (words only make sense in combination and distinction from one another), rules (using words to mean anything depends upon grammar and convention) and therefore otherness. Implicit in the heart of the *cogito* is a temporal and spatial difference that cannot be contained within pure self-presence, the pure identity of the 'I' with itself. Referring to the idea of the pure moment – Husserl's German term *Augenblick* literally translates as 'the blink of an eye' – Derrida writes that 'There is a duration to the blink, and it closes the eye. This alterity is in fact the condition for presence, presentation' (SP, p. 65).

We can begin to see why Derrida's early investigations of Husserl's phenomenology led him towards the importance of time and difference. Husserl, by bracketing the indicative mode of language with its reference to external realities, seeks a purely inward form of speech and expression that, in a sense, communicates nothing except itself. The body of the sign has to be set aside, leaving the breath or spirit that alone animates it. A principle of pure life is discovered.

However, such a securing of presence depends upon a process of differentiation: the transcendental ego has to be distinguished from what lies 'outside' it. In speaking to itself, it assures itself of its own persistence and identity. But Derrida asks whether such a purely inward speech is in fact a self-contradiction. It is intrinsic to the nature of the sign that it can be repeated across time and context. Only this possibility of repetition makes it possible for us to pass judgements about the identity of meaning which a sign expresses. Similarly, it is only in relationship to what is outside the self, to what is other and absent, that it makes sense even to talk of self-presence. Without these dimensions of time and difference, without repetition and absence, there would only be pure silence without speech: a nothingness that could hardly be a foundation for knowledge.

Presence has to be *re-presented* if it is to persist and come into its own. Representation – the necessity of the sign to secure identity – introduces an externality, an otherness into the heart of the self. Pure speech cannot exist without embodiment, and even expression implies that meaning goes out of the inner sanctum of the ego and is interwoven with the world outside. As Derrida puts it 'the presence of the perceived present can appear as such only inasmuch as it is continuously compounded with a nonpresence and nonperception, with primordial memory and expectation (retention and protention)' (SP, p. 64).

Difference and time break open the closed circuit of pure meaning. Derrida coined the word *différance* to gesture towards this. *Différance* combines the French terms meaning to differ and to defer, to delay. *Différance* is the structure of temporal delay and spatial difference without which meaning is impossible. Derrida refers to this structure as 'the possibility of re-petition in its most general form, that is, the constitution of a trace in the most universal sense' and goes on to add 'Such a trace is – if we can employ this language without immediately contradicting it or crossing it out as we proceed – more "primordial" than what is phenomenologically primordial' (SP, p. 67).

The course we have followed so far enables us to see more clearly why Derrida questions the privilege given to the spoken word that he detects in the philosophical tradition. For Husserl, the voice offers the best approximation to pure meaning. We are immediately present to the meaning we utter as we hear ourselves speak. There is an 'auto-affection' at the heart of speech. But even this minimal difference – speaking to oneself as if to another – is crucial. It shows that even the inner voice depends upon difference if it is to work, a difference that it cannot account for or produce, and that refers the self to everything Husserl had hoped to exclude from pure expression, including the outside world and the body. *Différance* is at work 'at the origin of sense and presence' (SP, p. 82). Writing, the external sign that survives in the absence of its author, is not added on to speech. It is coiled in the heart of speech from before the beginning (SP, p. 97).

Identity is therefore in fact secondary to a temporal and spatial structure. Put like this, it might seem at first that what Derrida is doing is replacing one transcendental, one condition of possibility with another. According to this line of thinking, *différance* or the trace would become a new foundation for thinking, an overarching framework making sense and meaning possible. In fact, something more complex is going on: the troubling of a whole series of metaphysical oppositions between same and other, presence and absence, life and death, oppositions that phenomenology has not subjected to a sufficiently radical critique.

Language about the primordial nature of the trace has to be erased as soon as it is offered, because there is no question here of uncovering some absolute beginning. The trace is always crossing itself out, always deferred, never at one, never home. The trace is therefore not only a condition of meaning but of unmeaning too. It prevents meaning being gathered into pure self-presence and so fulfilling its philosophical destiny. There is no pure interiority, because the inner voice 'is the irreducible openness in the inside' (SP, p. 86). It is quite correct to note, as many commentators have done, that the relationship to the other plays a vital role in Derrida's thinking. However, it must be noted that this 'other' does not come ready-made with a positive ethical or theological meaning. It is wounding, threatening and evasive, partly because it does not come upon a self that is already established and centred. It is there before the beginning, before there is any self, before there is anything remotely 'human'. If this is theological, it is theology of a very unsettling kind.

Derrida can make it sound as though *différance* is an alternative kind of origin, perhaps even a substitute creator. After all, the subject, the person who can say 'I', is shown to be derivative, a product, of a force that preceded them: 'This movement of dif" ferance is not something that happens to a transcendental subject; it produces a subject . . . It produces sameness as self-relation within self-difference; it produces sameness as the nonidentical' (SP, p. 82). However, the relationship described here is not like that traditionally envisaged between God and creature, or even between a philosophical rule or principle and its particular example or use. There is no pre-existing timeless identity being unfolded here. There is no subject, not even an infinite subject, controlling the process. Temporality and non-identity come first, which makes it nonsense to speak of coming 'first' at all. 'The living present springs forth out of its nonidentity with itself and from the possibility of a retentional trace. It is always already a trace' (SP, p. 85). The origin is always temporal and spatial, which means that it never coincides with itself.

Clearly, *différance* does not exist like a prime mover, outside of time and change. It is the process of time and change. It is not an origin in a simple sense. The paradox is this: that the supplement, the secondary are what come first. They are the condition for all meaning for any idea of stability, origin or foundation.

The final chapter of *Speech and Phenomena* is entitled 'The Supplement of Origin'. The title captures something of the queer logic to which Derrida is calling our attention. Repetition comes first, the 'origin' is a secondary supplement, life depends upon the death within it: 'The strange structure of the supplement appears here: by delayed reaction, a possibility produces that to which it is said to be added on' (SP, p. 89). We have always already begun, and cannot appeal to a timeless starting point.

As we saw, Derrida argues that mortality is necessary for me to be able to say 'I'. As he explores this argument further, he appears to rule out any confusion of *différance* with an infinite and therefore divine life:

> Only a relation to my-death could make the infinite differing of presence appear. By the same token, compared to the ideality of the positive infinite, this relation to my-death becomes an accident of empirical finitude. The appearing of the infinite *différance* is itself finite. Consequently, *différance*, which does not occur outside this relation, becomes the finitude of life as an essential relation with oneself and one's death. (SP, p. 102)

Différance is not a local phenomenon, a temporary problem to be solved by further research, or a unique intuition. It is a constant and inescapable structure. In one sense, therefore, it has no limits, it is not this or that particular being or aspect of being. As we will see, this will lead some to consider it a reflection of the God of negative theology. However, Derrida denies any positive infinity to *différance*. It is an infinite *process* that is always finite, always mortal, always passing. If it is constant, it is also unstable. If it is a structure, it is also a ruin.

No wonder Derrida calls for '*unheard-of* thoughts' as he looks to a philosophy that can break the grip of the dream of absolute knowledge. What seemed to come second, to be contingent and look for the absolute and original as its ground now appears to be 'older' than presence, older in a sense that knocks time out of joint (SP, p. 103). There is something before the first time, there is something deeper than the foundation, which is not another foundation, but something different.

Something wild

We can begin to see how Derrida doesn't just debunk phenomenology (SP, p. 82). He radicalizes it by pushing it towards and beyond its own self-imposed limits. In its quest for the absolute origin of the world, phenomenology is prepared to dismantle not only the assumptions of our everyday natural beliefs, but also the narrow perspectives of critical philosophy. Husserl sought a perspective that went to the very roots of how the world comes into being. To do so, he could not retain the picture that set the limited thinking self over against a world of objects, which is the core of the natural attitude. After Kant, philosophers were prepared to explore the ways in which the mind was not merely a passive receptacle of impressions, but was active in shaping and ordering the flux of experience into a meaningful, knowable order. Nevertheless, even this critical advance did not get to the absolute standpoint that could experience the actual coming into being of world and mind together.

There is something transcendent, one might even say theological, about phenomenology's quest for the creation of the world. However, we must be clear about what this entails. Husserl was deeply critical of the kind of metaphysics that set the absolute up as a separate being, about which it then made dogmatic pronouncements, ungrounded in any self-evident experience. If he did have a use for God, then it was potentially as the unifying ground of knowledge, the ideal observer who could guarantee the truth of a shared world. Nevertheless, even this stripped down metaphysics seems to betray the strict principles for knowledge laid down in phenomenology.

In the essay '"Genesis and Structure" and Phenomenology', published in 1965, but whose initial version was presented at a conference in 1959, Derrida returns to the issue of genesis, which preoccupied him as a student. There is a tension in phenomenology, between describing static structures of appearance on the one hand, and giving some account of the absolute origin of those structures. He argues that Husserl does this only by transgressing his own method, introducing an account of purpose and development into his philosophy of knowledge that steps beyond the bounds of pure description of what is given to intuition. Husserl, we might say, invents a theology to ground his descriptions. For Derrida, this teleology allows Husserl to master the origin, the 'untamed genesis' that threatens the purity and stability of phenomenology (and indeed all philosophy) (WD, p. 157). The French phrase rendered by 'untamed genesis' is *une genèse sauvage*, which could also be translated as 'savage genesis'. There is a wildness at the origin of any structure. It is a disruptive upsurge; as the origin of structure, it is not part of that structure. It follows no pre-given rule, and it escapes domestication in all conceptual knowledge. The savage genesis is the opening of history and its ruin. It is therefore also the possibility of a real future and genuine otherness. That future and that otherness will, however, remain resistant to domestication. They do not come to complete us.

Whether phenomenology can offer valid descriptions of religious experiences or intuitions that answer to religious truth claims is a matter of sharp dispute.[7] In the case of Husserl himself, it seems clear that he was not asserting the existence of any parallel supernatural world apart from the one that can be known by unaided reason, because it is also constituted by the transcendental ego we all share. If his phenomenology has a theological dimension, it is a matter of its inner spirit and direction, rather than any turning towards a world above or transcendent sources of revelation.

Derrida's critique shares and disrupts this spirit. Following the question of origins, he unlocks a savage genesis and a wandering word that cannot be held in check by philosophy, which must therefore be unsettled, shaken by the approach of its non-philosophical other to which it responds and upon which it depends. However, Derrida is in no way opening the door to a restatement of dogmatic metaphysics. He points to a radical temporality and difference that dispute any notion of pure beginnings or final ends, that cannot be gathered under a single, simple master name. Even that of God.

Is that the end of theology, then? By no means. Humanism and secularism are also the faces of a dogmatic metaphysics which is called into crisis by its repressed and inhuman genesis. Derrida's unheard-of thoughts find themselves touching again and again on a strange 'theological' dynamic that is neither theistic nor atheistic. The following chapters will trace this uneasy passage more closely.

Chapter 2

In the Beginning was
the Word: Repeat

What comes first? Nothing. For orthodox Christian theology, God's word is spoken into a void. Creation is called forth from pure nothingness by the breath of the divine voice. At least, so we have come to assume.

Of course, the reality of the text of Genesis is rather more ambiguous than this polished doctrine supposes. God's name echoes with plurality ('Let us . . .'), and the world, far from being a blank slate or emptiness waiting to be filled, is seething with potential. The writers of the Bible had no use for creation from nothing. There is always something there, waiting to become.

Catherine Keller has put the case most powerfully for a recovery of this ancient tradition, as a point of constructive resistance to the domineering and patriarchal theologies of creation that have demeaned if not dispensed with the material and the maternal.[1] So what comes first? No *thing*: there is no 'first', only a dialogue of creativity without beginning or end. A fluidity, in which there is no absolute origin, because difference and repetition have always already begun.

This revisioning of Christian theology might seem a world away from Derrida's concerns. However, as we have seen, the way he troubles the question of the origin of the world in phenomenology is intimately bound up with an emerging philosophy of language. Complicating the origin, for Derrida, means that the relationship between words and meaning, form and content, the ideal and the real all have to be re-thought. This is the basic ground upon which the philosophical project has always defined itself from the start. It is also close to the heart of theology, particularly in the Islamic, Jewish and Christian forms, which drew much of their conceptual architecture from Greek metaphysics.

The doctrine of creation out of nothing implies a connected series of normative philosophical positions. Matter is nothing in itself, and the world depends for its intelligibility upon the pure, spoken spiritual word of God. That word pre-exists all finite being, identical in its essence with the divine nature. It is pure form, pure creativity, lacking nothing, timeless and invulnerable to change. It is life unshadowed by death. As eternal and divine, the word does not go astray, or fail to achieve its end. It is an absolute point of departure, principle of life and standard of truth. The word of God stands erect forever.

In the light of this, we can see that changing one's philosophy of language is not merely a theoretical shift. Derrida seems to emphasize writing and difference at the expense of living speech and the immediacy of meaning. For some, this means that he has abandoned the theological foundation necessary for language to be anchored to what is true and abiding. He has set us adrift in a shifting sea of meanings, with no centre, no safe port in view.

As I suggested in the introduction, Derrida's most famous statement, 'there is nothing outside the text', has taken on a life of its own. It is used to confirm the suspicions of those who argue that Derrida simply traps us within the bounds of language. There is no longer any reference to a truth beyond our words. Texts mean what we want them to mean, since there is nothing outside them that constrains their words or our readings. The word has taken aimless flight from its divine source and we are left spinning fictions in the dark. Relativism and nihilism are at the door: everyone does what is right in their own eyes.

However, setting up the problem in this way – theology and truth versus free play and nihilism – means we have already accepted the terms laid down by dogmatics. Keller and others suggest there is more to theology than such dualisms. Perhaps we can find in Derrida, if not a new theology, at least a thinker who provokes us to consider the possibility of doing theology otherwise.

The previous chapter took us from the question of genesis to the growing importance of language for Derrida's developing thought. We can now look in more detail at his work on writing, texts and contexts, continuing to bear in mind the theological issue: how does the word begin the world?

Making it up: beyond structuralism

If Derrida does not simply break with phenomenology, but pushes it to its limits, the same could be said for structuralism. Ferdinand de Saussure wrote his *Course in General Linguistics* before World War I, and this became the seedbed for structuralist thinking.[2] In it, he made the point, to which we've already referred, that language is a system of differences, in which each term refers to others. He argued that there are no positive terms in language, by which he meant that there are no words or phrases that leap out of language and hook up in some unambiguous way with reality. For Saussure, the signifier was the word or sign used and the signified – that to which it referred – was a mental concept rather than an object in the so-called real world. The structure of language comes first. The way language is organized and governed by rules, contrasts and oppositions is what makes it possible for us to make meaningful statements. There is no 'key', no central point from which language can be decoded. We are always caught up within the web of its differences. This applies to both signifiers and signifieds. Language was not merely a copy of an external order, but was the means by which experience became possible in a structured form. Word and world belong together.

Structuralism became applied to all sorts of literary and anthropological and religious studies. Scholars sought to expose the basic structures that made discourses and complex practices work, whether they were myths, rituals, kinship structures, novels or wrestling matches. Derrida inherits this trend but again pushes it across its settled boundaries. He notes that the structures discovered by this method seek to be timeless, with a 'fundamental immobility and reassuring certitude' (WD, p. 279). Against this, he argues that structures come into being in specific ways and have a contingent history. Chance and discontinuity play an irreducible part in their construction.

There is a connection here with his previous critique of phenomenology, which is brought out in the early essay 'Genesis and Structure', to which we have already referred. Here, Derrida argues that Husserl aims to hold together two philosophical directions. The 'structuralist' demand wants to account for truth as a totality, an interrelated system, timeless and universal. The 'genetic' project, on the other hand, looks for the absolute origin of the structure. According to Derrida, it is the inevitable failure of the attempt to hold these two goals together that drives phenomenology (WD, p. 157).

According to Derrida, however much Husserl tries, he can never complete or close his structures. This is not accidental. There is a 'structural impossibility' (WD, p. 162) at work here: what makes it possible to unify our grasp of truth at the same time makes it impossible for us to make that grasp complete. The content of thought (what Husserl called the *noema*) cannot be simply identified with our acts of thinking (*noesis*). Something always remains other, and this has to be the case if thought is to connect with an objective truth. In addition, the thinking ego always remains passive at a crucial moment of thought, because it always finds itself thinking within time.

Thought must always be thinking what is other than itself, and time has always already begun. No system can account for its own possibility, for its own point of view. The purity of the structure is thus infected by the accidents of genesis from before the beginning: 'the transcendentality of the opening is simultaneously the origin and the undoing, the condition of possibility and a certain impossibility of every structure and every systematic structuralism' (WD, p. 163). Neither the otherness of the world nor the nature of time can become the object of pure, self-evident present knowledge.

Husserl tries to shield his philosophy from this by drawing a distinction between merely worldly origins, time and language, and their purified transcendental versions. Derrida is unconvinced: the very openness and incompleteness that we find in the most purified structures of truth shows that such distinctions are unstable at best. At worst, they lead us back into dogmatism. We might even suggest that they result in a form of idolatry: taking as timeless and absolute what is secondary and contingent.

Of course, idolatry is a loaded word. It suggests a true God and true worship against which the false, all-too-human varieties can be judged and found wanting. Derrida offers no such reassuring resolution. In the well-known lecture that brought him initial notoriety in the English-speaking world, Derrida seems to embrace the dissolution of all structuralist ambitions towards certainty. Instead, he turns to the 'play' of the chance and the inventive, the open-ended and mobile metaphors that frustrate our systematic desires for totalizing knowledge. However, we need to catch the nuance of what Derrida in fact says:

> Play is the disruption of presence . . . Play is always play of absence and presence, but if it is to be thought radically, play must be conceived of before the alternative of presence and absence. Being must be conceived as presence or absence on the basis of the possibility of play and not the other way round. (WD, p. 292)

Note how Derrida is himself playing with terminology: he is denying any timeless, absolute origin of truth, but he can only do so by using similar language: that play is a 'basis' (the French *à partir de* suggests a point of departure), that it comes first, that difference is an origin and so on. He is well aware of the paradox, and does not attempt to resolve it. Thinking and decision making, politics and faith, all depend upon keeping this paradox alive, upon not coming down on one side or the other.

Derrida argues that the history of metaphysics in the West has always depended on the idea of structured knowledge, which is given order and unity by a centre, 'a point of presence, a fixed origin' (WD, p. 278). The centre gave stability and discipline to the structure, making it clear what could and could not be done and said within it. In other words, it put a limit on play (the cases of Plato expelling the poets from his ideal Republic, or the ban on theatre and dancing instigated by puritanical reformers through history being only the most obvious and external examples of this phenomenon). However, this means that the centre must be distinguished from, separate from the structure that it governs. It must be entirely beyond the 'play' in order to master it.

The centre took on a variety of names in the history of ideas, among which Derrida includes 'transcendentality, consciousness, God, man and so forth' (WD, p. 280). We should note how 'God' here simply lines up alongside many other philosophical master names, all of which have been used to try and keep meaning in check and truth well-founded. What matters, it seems, is not the particular name privileged, but the logic of the system.

For Derrida, this system is disrupted when structuralism, pushing the idea of the ordered system to its limits, shows us that the structure has no centre at all. This happens when we no longer take language for granted, as if words were merely a neutral medium that delivered truth to us ready made. Thinking of language as a system of differences with no centre, leads us to a situation in which there is no longer a centre, a master name. Derrida offers a roll call of thinkers and moments that have led us to this point: Nietzsche, Freud and Heidegger, all of whom have called into question the ideas of self-presence lodged at the heart of metaphysics.

However, the next step is crucial, for Derrida maintains that there is no way in which we can simply wash our hands of metaphysics. All the earlier mentioned thinkers disputed inherited philosophical answers in the name of better answers and more secure truths, however radical and counter-intuitive these truths might have appeared. Even the concept of the sign itself, which Derrida sees at the heart of the turn to language, has an ancient metaphysical history that has always distinguished between the signifier and the signified, the sign and that to which it refers. The idea of stable, objective truth, of a division between the sensible and the intelligible, is built into the very idea of the sign. If we forget this, then we end up naïvely entangling ourselves in unconsciously held philosophical dogmas, exactly the problem into which Derrida believes empiricism falls. Those who forget the history of metaphysics are condemned to repeat it.

The analysis of the structuralist anthropologist Claude Lévi-Strauss, which takes up much of the rest of the essay, demonstrates this ambiguity in detail. Derrida takes as a guiding thread the classical opposition between what is natural and what is cultural.[3] He argues that making this distinction is one of the founding acts of philosophy. Nature is the counterweight to law, politics, technology, freedom, art, education and so on. It is with reference to a contrast with nature that philosophers have defined what is properly human. In this sense, it is what makes thinking and philosophy possible at all. The stakes are that big.

In contemporary thinking, Derrida notices that the critique of the metaphysical tradition goes hand in hand with a rejection of ethnocentrism, the assumption that European ways of thinking have a kind of universal cultural validity. However, Derrida argues that we cannot simply walk away from the assumptions embedded in European metaphysics. We will always be using ideas such as presence, universal truth, law and so on, even when denouncing the particular parochial forms those ideas have taken in the West (WD, p. 282). Derrida is posing the question of how we inhabit the language we have inherited, conscious of its limits and potential for prejudice and abuse, but without the naïveté that presumes we can leap out of our skin and into a new language.

In his study of mythologies, Lévi-Strauss himself wants to overcome the old division between nature and culture. The key fact around which he disputes the validity of the distinction is the incest prohibition, which seems to be both universal to all societies, and therefore natural, but at the same time is still a prohibition or law, and therefore cultural.

Derrida believes that two choices face the theorist, once the line between nature and culture has become blurred. One path is to try to suspend and criticize all such 'founding' concepts and divisions, an enormously difficult task, since it is 'the beginnings of a step outside of philosophy' (WD, p. 284). Derrida notes wryly how many have assumed they could take that step with 'cavalier ease' only to be swallowed up by metaphysical ideas once more.

The second path is the one that Lévi-Strauss chooses. He rejects the idea that the nature/culture distinction has any absolute validity, but continues to use it as an interpretative tool. To illustrate this, he introduces the famous idea of the *bricoleur*. Unlike an engineer, who designs and builds a whole creation from scratch, the *bricoleur* just uses the bits and pieces that lie ready to hand, even though they are not specifically designed for the job in mind. Derrida points out that the concept of the engineer is of one who is 'the absolute origin of his own discourse', a creator out of nothing, the creator of the 'verb', the possibility of action and creativity itself. The engineer is therefore a 'theological idea' and a myth (WD, p. 285). And since myths are the ad hoc inventions of the *bricoleur*, the engineer–creator is in fact a fictional product of *bricolage*.

Derrida is arguing that the ideal of the engineer, of the absolute origin and creator, is itself secondary, produced by the much more arbitrary, contextual, supplementary work of the *bricoleur*. This gives us a clue to one of the primary claims of Derrida's early work. God (who lies behind the engineer's disguise) is supposed to be the absolute origin and centre of meaning, the one who creates by the active power of his word alone. However, Derrida is suggesting that all such theological ideas are in fact secondary effects of the workings of language, which has no centre, no first word.

As a result of this insight, structuralism faces something of a dilemma. If we accept that the engineer is itself a mythological idea, then *bricolage* is essentially all there is. There is no way out of the secondariness of language into a pure, literal or absolute statement of truth in itself. 'Making do' in a very pragmatic and empirical way is the best we can hope for. However, structuralism does not want simply to make do. It wants to move beyond a mere assemblage of facts to expose the systematic organization of a whole field of discourse. But how is this possible, if there is no divine engineer's timeless view?

Lévi-Strauss acknowledges that a total mythological pattern is unattainable. Derrida argues that he gives two reasons for this. One is that there is simply too much data to be gathered. If we consider the wealth of mythological stories and themes the world over, no single system could hope to take account of all that information. However, there is a second, more radical reason why totalization is impossible: not just because there is too much information (the field is too large), but because the system itself breaks down, cannot be closed off, finalized or given an absolute foundation. Because structuralism is a reflection of language upon itself, it cannot account for its own origin, cannot catch its own tail. Language is caught up in supplementarity: signs refer to and substitute for one another. There is no first mover in language, which sets everything else in motion. Language is both finite and impossible to limit.

This is why Derrida identifies play as a key theme of Lévi-Strauss's writings. Play is not necessarily frivolous. It is made possible by a commitment to rules. However, the rules never determine what will happen in the field of play, in which an unlimited number of events is possible. For Derrida this idea of play leads to two instructive tensions in structuralism.

First, play is in tension with the idea of history. Lévi-Strauss sets history to one side in order to explore the structures that govern myths. In doing so, he also sets aside the metaphysical view of history as linear, moving from an absolute beginning to a final destination, from one full presence to another. This risk, according to Derrida, is that this leads him into an ahistorical and abstract view of myth (and of language), which assumes that the truth must be separated out from the changes and chances of time. However, this is to fall back into metaphysics, which has always valued timeless Being over the contingent world of decay and death. The result is that structuralism can give no account of why a structure arises and disappears, or how one gives way to another. It is driven to embrace ideas of chance and rupture, of discontinuity.

Consider the issue of the origin of language. From before the eighteenth century, theorists have debated whether language arises out of 'natural' precursors – inarticulate cries, instinctual gestures – or whether it must be attributed a supernatural source, because it marks the distinctiveness of human beings over and against nature. This is a particularly vivid form of the nature versus culture division.

The structuralist tries to overcome this division by focussing, not on origins, but on language as a system, viewed as static and timeless. When we consider this more closely, however, we get caught in paradoxes. If language emerges from nature, we have to explain how inarticulate sounds and movements ever get turned into a system of abstract communication, without presupposing the existence of such a system in the first place. How does brute fact become meaningful sign, without assuming that we already have an idea of meaning a priori? Nature, it seems, requires a break with 'nature' in order to produce language. The naturalistic argument thus appeals to something arbitrary and catastrophic, a view that is not very different from the idea that language is a supernatural gift. At any rate, it seems to fly in the face of the scientific spirit of structuralism.

The second tension Derrida identifies is that between play and presence. It is in this context that the passage we quoted earlier appears, in which Derrida writes of play as a disruption of presence. We have already seen how Derrida's early work on Husserl led to a critique of the idea of a founding, transcendent moment of presence. However, he recognizes that just as it is impossible to escape from metaphysics with a simple gesture, so the idea and ideal of presence cannot just be shrugged off. He argues that Lévi-Strauss is still nostalgic for this lost centre, origin or foundation, as is shown through his idealization of societies that are archaic, and therefore closer to the pristine founts of myth.

Derrida closes the essay by positing two possible attitudes towards the loss of presence. There is the negativity, guilt and nostalgia exemplified by a thinker such as Rousseau, who laments our alienation from founding truth. On the other side lies the celebration of play that we find in Nietzsche, an affirmation of becoming that no longer yearns for a lost centre (WD, p. 292).

Derrida claims that there are thus 'two interpretations of interpretation': one seeks an origin beyond the play of the world. The other affirms that play of difference and becoming. It passes beyond the notion of fixed presence and foundations around which both humanism and ontotheology revolve (WD, p. 292).

A number of crucial ideas come together here. First, there is the contrast between the search for origins and foundations and a form of interpretation that abandons that search, which affirms what Derrida calls 'the seminal adventure of the trace'. Second, the metaphysical search for foundations beyond the world is associated with ontotheology, Heidegger's term for the identification of God with the Supreme Being, the first principle and ground of all reality.

In *Identity and Difference*, Heidegger writes of the 'ontotheological constitution of metaphysics' in which 'The Being of beings is thus thought of in advance as the grounding ground'.[4] This general characteristic of metaphysics – seeking the ground or foundation of beings – becomes ontotheological when God is identified with Being. God is represented as the *causa sui*, the One whose cause of existence is not outside of himself, the One whose existence is necessary in order to support all other contingent beings. God, the highest being, accounts for all other beings as their supreme cause.

For Heidegger and those who followed him, this turned Being into a static, fixed foundation and it could not account for time, difference and language, the conditions under which we question and discover Being. God, meanwhile, becomes a function within a causal system, the kind of foundation for thought whose role could equally well be taken by another impersonal principle. Heidegger comments that 'Man can neither pray nor sacrifice to this god. Before the *causa sui*, man can neither fall to his knees in awe nor can he play music and dance before this god'.[5] However, he goes on to suggest that there is a 'god-less' thinking that, having abandoned this inert god of philosophy, might be more open to the 'divine God'.

Derrida shares this questioning of ontotheology. However, in Heidegger's case at least, this does not close off all thinking of the divine in other terms. Moreover, humanism, the idea of the essence of man, is also being shaken. Replacing the God of ontotheology with a human essence made in God's likeness is still a way of playing the metaphysical game.

Remember Derrida's claim that 'Being must be conceived as presence or absence on the basis of the possibility of play and not the other way round'. In other words, it is not a matter of declaring that God or Being is dead, gone and buried, and then setting up an atheistic humanism in its place. Presence is not simply replaced by absence, because the two terms reflect one another. They are both metaphysical names for the absolute (and we recall that both God and man were cited by Derrida as possible titles for the centre). Rather than simply directing us towards relativism, nihilism or even atheism, Derrida is suggesting that the difference between presence and absence (and between theism and atheism) needs to be re-thought in a new way.

Therefore, it should not surprise us when Derrida closes the essay, not with a celebration of free play, but with a refusal to choose between the two attitudes to play or the two ways of interpretation. The search for origins, truth and a centre of meaning cannot just be abandoned. Those who proclaim the death of God or relativism as a new truth or point of departure only show they are caught in the web of metaphysics without being aware of it.

There is no abandonment of critical rigour or of truth in this essay, despite the notoriety that surrounded it. Instead, Derrida pictures himself sharing in the anticipation of a birth, without knowing what form of life will emerge from its gestation. He speaks of this new life as 'the unnamable', 'the formless, mute, infant, and terrifying form of monstrosity' (WD, p. 293).

Something unsettling is arriving, and it is as unsettling for humanism as it is for theism. The other comes as a monster.

Are there hints here for a theology to come, a theology that does not sit easily within the constraints of metaphysics and the construal of God as an absolute presence and foundation? Is the monster sacred in a way not yet named? We will explore this possibility more fully in future chapters. For now, we need to note that Derrida is not simply taking a position for or against theology, but uncovering some of its classical presuppositions, just as he is uncovering the presuppositions that underlie humanism, empiricism and the naïve affirmation of a non-metaphysical, purely scientific truth. If we always find ourselves caught up in the language of metaphysics, then philosophy must engage with theology. It cannot simply be wished away. Nor, we might add, can its own metamorphosis be prejudged.

For Derrida, philosophy is always obsessed with its 'other'. Thought always wants to think through, make transparent or even assimilate what appears outside of itself. In phenomenology, this presented itself as a way of thinking that tried to do without all accidental features in order to grasp the absolute origin of the world for consciousness. Husserl recognized that such a thought could only remain lifeless and mute without language to give it universal and objective form.

Language, however, proves a tricky medium. It does not deliver the kind of founding origin or still centre demanded by systematic philosophy. The very signs that make truth and objectivity available and intelligible also threaten its very essence. The sign can only work by presupposing time and difference. Words can only mean anything if they can be repeated apart from their original context or author, a condition that calls into question any idea of an origin or first creator:

> For there is no word, nor in general a sign, which is not constituted by the possibility of repeating itself. A sign which does not repeat itself, which is not already divided by repetition in its 'first time', is not a sign. The signifying referral therefore must be ideal – and ideality is but the assured power of repetition – in order to refer to the same thing each time. (WD, p. 246)

Language has always already begun, and any sense we have of stability or finality is woven in and through its play of differences. As Derrida points out, 'My own presence to myself has been preceded by a language' (D, p. 340).

Of God and grammatology

In *Of Grammatology*, Derrida begins by claiming that 'the problem of language has never been simply one problem among others' (OG, p. 6). Here, in the mid-1960s, he is aware of the fashionable nature of focussing upon language, such that the sign is inflated to encompass everything worthy of study. He reads this as a symptom of the crisis in metaphysics, which has always depended upon anchoring the play of signs on a transcendent reality. Without this anchor language at once becomes limitless in its play, but also strangely finite again, cut adrift from 'the infinite signified which seemed to exceed it' (OG, p. 6).

Is language, then, just playing with itself? Is it cut off from all reference to a world beyond itself? Are we trapped in signs that point to nothing but each other?

As the book proceeds, Derrida explores the ways in which the priority of speech has been displaced in our understanding of what language essentially is. Speaking, as we have seen, implies that the speaker is immediately present in his or her words. There is no gap between intention and expression. The voice 'has a relationship of essential and immediate proximity with the mind' (OG, p. 11). Writing was disparaged because it lacked this living connection with meaning.

Derrida's argument is that the supposedly distinctive and negative characteristics of writing are in fact built in to *all* signs: 'The secondary that it seemed possible to ascribe to writing alone affects all signifieds in general, affects them always already, the moment they enter the game. There is not a single signified that escapes, even if recaptured, the play of signifying references that constitute language' (OG, p. 7). The crucial point is that language cannot remain on the inside of thought: pure, transparent and at rest. All language uses signs that are repeatable and temporal. Meaning does not exist in a perfect and untroubled interior space before being expelled into the external world where it becomes subject to misunderstanding and decay. No: that exteriority, that ambiguity, that death is lodged in the heart of the sign, even the ones we breathe to ourselves in the loneliest night. Derrida summarizes his argument by saying 'that there is no linguistic sign before writing. Without that exteriority, the very idea of the sign falls into decay' (OG, p.14).

In troubling the link between signifiers and some infinite signified, Derrida is therefore not turning language in on itself. Quite the opposite, in fact. Language is now inextricably turned towards otherness, because the possibility of resolving all differences down into a knowledge or intuition of pure timeless presence looks increasingly like a doomed metaphysical dream. Just as Derrida called into question the possibility of an all-encompassing structure, so here he rejects the possibility of the 'book', his image for the desire of metaphysics for a closed and finished knowledge that would leave nothing out: 'The idea of the book is the idea of a totality, finite or infinite, of the signifier; this totality of the signifier cannot be a totality, unless a totality constituted by the signified preexists it, supervises its inscriptions and its signs, and is independent of it in its ideality' (OG, p. 18).

Two points needs to be made here. First, Derrida is using words such as 'sign' and 'writing' in the context of explaining and undermining the claims of metaphysics. Their importance goes beyond actual spoken or written words; they become clues to the way in which all life is structured and ruptured by difference and time. Second, Derrida is using this generalized idea of writing to stand in contrast to the totalizing, systematic pretensions of the 'book'. In doing this, he is pointing out a paradox: the appeal to the infinite signified, the absolute origin or creator, seems to point us to the outside of the system. In effect, however, it confirms that we are trapped within a pre-existing structure, which reduces difference to sameness and time to the punctuality of the eternal present. In contrast, 'writing' carries us to an irreducible exterior.

Can this otherness have any theological connotations, however? *Of Grammatology* seems to take a consistently negative attitude towards theology, always associating it with totalization, the dream of mastery and the suppression of writing, interpretation and play. Note the use of specifically theological, indeed,

Christian language in Derrida's description of the way metaphysics presumes that the signifier must refer to an ideal signified. Modern structuralist semiotics still replicates this signified–signifier distinction, even when it thinks it has broken with metaphysics. It still demands

> reference to a signified able to 'take place' in its intelligibility, before its 'fall,' before any expulsion into the exteriority of the sensible here below. As the face of pure intelligibility, it refers to an absolute logos to which it is immediately united. This absolute logos was an infinite creative subjectivity in medieval theology: the intelligible face of the sign remains turned toward the word and the face of God. (OG, p. 13)

A little further on, Derrida again refers to the 'transcendental signified' as 'the condition of the very idea of truth' and associates it with the medieval transcendentals, the fundamental principles of reality that were interchangeable with one another as the very essence of God in his simplicity: being, truth, goodness, unity (OG, p. 20).

It may come as no surprise, therefore, to find Derrida asserting that 'The sign and divinity have the same place and time of birth. The age of the sign is essentially theological. Perhaps it will never *end*. Its historical *closure*, is, however, outlined' (OG, p. 14). That final couplet should give us pause for thought before we rush to conclude that Derrida is done with theology once and for all. For one thing, he says that 'it is not a question of "rejecting" these notions' of the sign and of God (OG, p. 13). We still need them to think with and against. They lie in wait at the very root of our ideas of truth, ideality, the sensible and the intelligible. In addition, the end of theology and its closure are two different things. Perhaps there is a certain closing of an era in which the theological ideas underlying our view of language were taken for granted. However, theology does not end, anymore than the sign and truth come to an end. It has an afterlife. What that afterlife consists of still remains to be determined.

If Derrida does not simply reject theology, is his own approach theological in some way? It might look as if he is swapping one

foundation – summed up by the ideals of speech, the logos, fullness of presence and the absolute origin or centre – for another,
in which 'writing' becomes the key to unlocking the meaning and
nature of language and truth. Statements such as 'language is a
possibility founded on the general possibility of writing' could be
taken to confirm this suspicion (OG, p. 52). Writing becomes the
new starting point and origin, the new transcendental signified.

However, things are not so straightforward. For one thing,
Derrida is clear that he is not just trying to exchange one foundation for another: 'It is not a question of rehabilitating writing in
the narrow sense, nor of reversing the order of dependence when
it is evident' (OG, p. 56). We need to underline the fact that
Derrida is drawing on the idea of writing in a particular way, so
that we notice how meaning and life are made possible by the
irreducible movement of differences. No starting point or foundation can account for this movement. Writing 'in the narrow
sense' gives way to what Derrida calls 'arche-writing', the difference that always precedes and makes possible any presence to self,
any truth, any stability, any beginning. There is an irony here: this
writing is 'arche', not because it comes first, but because it is older
than the origin. It throws into question any idea of first and
second. As Derrida puts it elsewhere, 'perhaps difference is older
than Being itself' (M, p. 67).

A certain ambiguity remains, however. Writing, in this enlarged
sense, is what makes everything else possible, and it does not
belong to the system that it sets in motion. It is hardly surprising
that it can look very much like the transcendental signified:

> It is because arche-writing, movement of differance,
> irreducible arche-synthesis, opening in one and the same
> possibility, temporalization as well as relationship with the
> other and language, cannot, as the condition of all linguistic
> systems, form a part of the linguistic system itself and be
> situated within a field. (OG, p. 60)

What then is the difference between writing and the logos, with
its face turned towards God?

Derrida articulates the idea of arche-writing through the notion
of the trace. The trace evokes the graphic marks, the external signs

that are necessary for writing to work. Again, Derrida's point is that such marks are not secondary to a fully internal and immediate meaning. They are implicit in all language, in all signs and therefore in all meaning.

The trace makes language possible, but it does so not as an unmoved mover or divine plenitude, but as a movement of difference and time, never at rest, never captured, never one with itself. Derrida refers to it as the 'originary trace'. In the context of another discussion of Husserl, he spells out how the trace is the inescapable mark of time and difference:

> Without a retention in the minimal unit of temporal experience, without a trace retaining the other as other in the same, no difference would do its work and no meaning would appear. It is not a question of a constituted difference here, but rather, before all determination of the content, of the *pure* movement which produces difference. *The (pure) trace is differance.* It does not depend on any sensible plenitude, audible or visible, phonic or graphic. It is, on the contrary, the condition of such a plenitude. Although it *does not exist*, although it is never a *being-present* outside of all plenitude, its possibility is by rights anterior to all that one calls sign ... (OG, p. 62)

The trace might sound a little like God (and, as we will see, Derrida was accused of flirting with negative theology and mysticism). However, the self-cancelling, ironic and mobile nature of the trace is never forgotten:

> *The trace is in fact the absolute origin of sense in general. Which amounts to saying once again that there is no absolute origin of sense in general. The trace is the differance* which opens appearance and signification. Articulating the living upon the nonliving in general, origin of all repetition, origin of ideality, the trace is not more ideal than real, not more intelligible than sensible, not more a transparent signification than an opaque energy and *no concept of metaphysics can describe it.* (OG, p. 65)

Derrida has no choice but to multiply paradoxes. He has already admitted that one cannot just choose to do without the metaphysical language of real and ideal, form and matter and so on. These distinctions make it possible for us to talk about truth. However, what he is describing makes that metaphysical and theological language possible, without amounting to anything like a divine fullness or solid foundation. As Derrida states, 'The trace is *nothing*, it is not an entity, it exceeds the question *What is?* and contingently makes it possible' (OG, p. 75). In another context, he writes 'There is no trace *itself*, no *proper* trace' (M, p. 66).

Repetition, we have stressed, comes first, and so throws all talk of the first time into confusion. The only way of approaching this thought, however, is through the metaphysics that is its effect. Deconstruction, which follows the paradoxes of meaning produced by the attempt to suppress writing, time and difference, must 'inhabit' metaphysics 'in a certain way' (OG, p. 24), consciously and critically. Inevitably, deconstruction will 'fall prey to its own work' because there is no way of even addressing issues of truth and reality without borrowing from metaphysics. The point is to expose the internal instabilities, the blind spots, the repressed otherness that are necessary to any system or totality. Any foundation is an act of sovereign exclusion. However, deconstruction is always at work within what is so founded.

Derrida writes that 'Originary differance is supplementarity as *structure*. Here structure means the irreducible complexity within which one can only shape or shift the play of presence or absence: that within which metaphysics can be produced but which metaphysics cannot think' (OG, p. 167). The other or outside of metaphysics is always on the move within it. But if this other is never a presence, never a first cause, cannot even be said to exist, can it be anything but the destruction of theology's claims? However much deconstruction still lives in the house of metaphysics, hasn't it deprived the owner and builder of the house of all his proprietary rights?

Of Grammatology consistently argues that metaphysics represents the suppression of difference, absence and death. Theology, entangled with metaphysics, becomes the vehicle to deliver this dream, for 'God's name holds death in check'. Derrida goes on:

'Only infinite being can reduce the difference in presence. In that sense, the name of God, at least as it is pronounced within classical rationalism, is the name of indifference itself' (OG, p. 71). The pure and unadulterated life of God, beyond change, perfectly at one with itself is ironically indistinguishable from death. By immobilizing the movement of difference, the name of this God leaves no room for life.

As Derrida makes clear, this is not a theological veneer on a basically philosophical problem. The theological is at the heart of this way of thinking, from Plato to Hegel, and we still live within its grasp. Theology is not a passing or accidental set of beliefs, it is the inner dynamic of metaphysics: 'the logos as the sublimation of the trace is *theological*' (OG, p. 71). God, through the pure creativity of the word, neutralizes all difference.

Derrida's aim, then, is to re-open the exposure of philosophy to its other, in a way that will not define otherness in advance as just one more philosophical concept, already mastered and assigned its place in a system of thought that helps us define our human distinctiveness. With this in mind, we need to underline the fact that the God who smothers difference is the God of classical rationalism, of totalization and dominance. Could it be that another God is possible, one who opens us to the encounter with the other and undercuts facile humanism as much as theological dogmatism?

Derrida does not develop this thought, but he does at least leave the door open to a more constructive theological alternative. He makes it clear that to abandon the metaphysical God of indifference is not the same as to embrace the total absence of the divine. There is not a simple choice between the theological and the atheistic or the religious and the secular:

> That the logos is first imprinted and that that imprint is the writing-resource of language, signifies, to be sure, that the logos is not a creative activity, the continuous full element of the divine word, etc. But it would not mean a single step outside of metaphysics if nothing more than a new motif of 'return to finitude,' of 'God's death,' etc., were the result of this move. It is that conceptuality and that problematics that must be deconstructed. They belong to

the onto-theology they fight against. Differance is
something other than finitude. (OG, p. 68)

Something other than finitude, but something that does not result
in the kind of 'infinitist' metaphysics that Derrida sees running
through the Western tradition. Derrida invites us to think the
limitless play of language without coming to rest on a 'positive' or
fully actual infinity. This would be a thinking that takes seriously
the reality of death, not just as the limit to mortal life, but as the
condition for life to be possible.

The outside in the text

We are now in a better position to understand Derrida's claim that
'there is nothing outside the text' (OG, p. 158). It is made in the
context of introducing a reading of Rousseau. Derrida argues that
Rousseau's writing, especially on the origin of language, is caught
in a contradiction. Rousseau idealizes human beings in a state of
nature, seeing civilization as a work of artifice that alienates us
from ourselves. However, 'nature' only becomes valuable for
Rousseau's human beings because they are able to reflect, imagine
and so become self-aware. In other words, the condition for their
blessedness is also the condition for their fall.

The same applies to language. Rousseau derives language from
natural gestures and cries. However, it is only because language
breaks with this instinctive repertoire that it can articulate any
idea of nature and goodness. Rousseau's nostalgia for a natural
immediacy of self-present meaning is constantly undone by the
necessity for artifice and culture to make that meaning available to
us. This is no accidental lack of consistency on Rousseau's part. It
is a symptom of the inherent tensions and paradoxes that inhabit
the metaphysical assumptions on which he draws. Deconstruction
is already at work in what he writes.

As he prepares for this reading of Rousseau, Derrida describes
his double method of critical interpretation. On the one hand,
he takes seriously the classical need to uncover the author's
intentions in what is written. This rigorous attention to the text is
needed to protect against the risk of just attributing any and every

fanciful reading to it. At the same time, Derrida rejects the idea that there is a pure and ready-made meaning just waiting out there on the other side of the text.

We can understand this as an extension of his critique of the idea of presence. Meaning is always produced by the interaction of differences. It always occurs in time. There is no absolute origin or foundation. This system of traces, this *différance*, is what Derrida has called arche-writing or (in this passage) 'writing in general'. So when Derrida says that there is nothing outside the text, he is not making the absurd claim that language is all that there is, or that words refer only to themselves. Rather, he is saying that there is no truth, no reference that is not constituted by the movement of differences, by the weave of traces. The original French is 'il n'y a pas de hors-texte', which might better be translated as 'there is no outside of the text', a rendering that perhaps conveys better that Derrida is discussing the conditions that make all life and meaning possible, and that we cannot rise above without contradicting ourselves.

In the texts collected in *Limited Inc.*, which represent Derrida's dispute with the philosopher John Searle, the idea that this position implies relativism is confronted head on. Derrida states that his work in no way denies that language refers to realities outside itself, or that he has no use for the idea of truth: 'the value of truth and all those other values associated with it) is never contested or destroyed in my writings, but only reinscribed in more powerful, larger, more stratified contexts' (LI , p.146). He goes on to clarify the statement that there is nothing outside the text, which he earlier re-words as 'there is nothing outside context' (LI, p.136). Derrida maintains that this is in fact a way of affirming the possibility of meaning:

> That does not mean that all referents are suspended, denied, or enclosed in a book, as people have claimed, or have been naïve enough to believe and to have accused me of believing. But it does mean that every referent, all reality has the structure of a differential trace, and that one cannot refer to this 'real' except in an interpretive experience. The latter neither yields meaning nor assumes it except in a movement of differential referring. That's all. (LI , p.148)

However, there is no disguising the potentially unsettling aspect of this approach to reality and truth. What remains unsettling for theology in particular is the sense of slippage: meaning is no longer anchored in the simplicity of an absolute origin, a first time, because the word is always divided and wandering from itself. Derrida refers to this as a 'dissemination' of meaning beyond any secure and exhaustive context.

In the book *Dissemination*, he continues his analysis of the role played by writing in diverse works of Plato, Freud and Mallarmé. In each case, a notion of writing troubles and displaces any quest for absolute self-evident meaning. Derrida follows the ways in which Plato's dialogues seek to assign writing a secondary place. Socrates calls writing a *pharmakon*, a Greek word that means both cure and poison. In the dialogue *Phaedrus*, Socrates turns to myth to explain the origin of writing (although he earlier distinguished myth from the proper business of philosophy). He tells of the god Theuth, who presents writing to the father and king of the gods as a remedy for forgetfulness. The king responds by condemning writing as a substitute for true knowledge. Writing produces only the semblance of truth. It is true forgetfulness.

For Derrida, the irony is that Plato's Socrates resorts to metaphors of a writing within the soul in order to describe and secure a more self-evident and ideal truth than the one preserved in mere writing. For Derrida, the oscillation between writing as good and evil, gift and curse, internal and external represents an unstable attempt to define and limit writing in the name of authorized meaning. The king, the father of the gods, stands for the name of the father in general, the one who keeps meaning in limits. A generalized writing, in which presence is always contaminated by absence and death, dethrones the king. The father is killed and replaced by the son, the logos.

This death of the father–god opens up the possibility of meaning. But this is not a meaning that can be wholly preserved and protected against what threatens all meaning. There is no theological guarantee. Thus 'dissemination *affirms* the always already divided generation of meaning. Dissemination – spills it in advance' (D, p. 268).

As we have seen, the disruption of any pure origin that founds the system of truth is an opening of philosophy towards its other, towards what makes thought possible, but that cannot itself be thought. Thinking remains incomplete. The structure of reflection can never be closed off. *Dissemination* itself suggests that this form of thinking could have dire consequences for theology.

For theology, the question becomes irresistible: does this incompleteness permit an opening to or for God? Or is God merely a pale reflection of a more elusive 'truth', a remnant of the father–king who must be expelled from his kingdom? If 'dissemination interrupts the circulation that transforms into an origin what is actually an after-effect of meaning' (D, p. 25), then is all theological talk about God as the source of being and life made redundant? Is God no more than an 'effect of the trace' (WD, p. 108)?

To approach these questions, we need to examine in more detail Derrida's understanding of the relationship between the 'other' of philosophy and what it is that 'God' names.

Chapter 3

The Other, the Thief, the Great Furtive One: Saving the Names of God

According to Rodolphe Gasché, Derrida's philosophy is best understood as a heterology, a radical thinking of otherness.[1] Gasché identifies reflection as one of the key central themes of all Western philosophy. Reflection is not merely considered or rational thought, but a self-conscious decision to think about what makes knowledge and thought possible in the first place. In the modern era, following Descartes, reflection turns inwards. Descartes makes the reflecting subject into the source and foundation of knowledge. Kant pursues a transcendental reflection that brings to light the conditions within our own minds that order the world and make objective knowledge possible.

The philosophy of reflection tries to do two things at once. It wants to guarantee knowledge by demonstrating that our thinking mirrors the world, while also reflecting upon itself, upon the process of knowing. The problem is how to relate these two aspects of reflection, to produce a unity of thought.

Hegel argued that Kant failed to reconcile the split between the thinking subject and the world. The resolution lay in the realization that the world is not a merely external other, but the subject's 'symmetric Other', 'a representation of its alienated self'.[2] Self and other belong to one another, and the goal of reflection is to secure their harmonious unity. The self recognizes in the world its own passage into difference and otherness, in order that it may return to itself, enriched and self-aware.

Hegel's absolute or speculative idealism is the attempt to synthesize self and other through the unfolding narrative of Spirit's journey from immediacy through alienation towards reconciliation. The trinitarian structure of this dialectic is explicitly acknowledged by Hegel, for whom Christianity is the most perfect possible religious representation of the absolute philosophical ideal. God the Father's relationship to the world is mediated by the Son, who suffers death and alienation from God in order to achieve a unity of the divine and the human. This unity cannot remain a one-off historical fact, however. Therefore, the Holy Spirit is poured out on all flesh, making the divine-human life available universally. From Creation to Good Friday to Easter and Pentecost, the Christian story is one of the self or Spirit moving from isolation and opposition to the world towards a fully realized unity of subject and object, real and ideal, infinite and finite. No unknowable beyond, no recalcitrant 'other' must remain outside the totality of reflection.

The power of Hegel's philosophy is that it seems to anticipate and include within itself all possible objections. Any assertion of a reality that seems to elude the resolution of difference into harmony can be shown to be partial, ungrounded and arbitrary. Only speculative idealism can grasp both subject and object as they belong to and complete one another, and so give unity to thought and world. Criticisms are still moments of reflection, attempts to think the truth of the whole and our relation to it. Their very nature shows that they are in search of the grounding and wholeness that only absolute reflection can supply.

The alternative, 'heterological' move is therefore to argue that reflection is not the original generator of all knowledge, but a derivative phenomenon, made possible by what is non- or pre-reflective. Thus, when Heidegger talks of *Dasein*, he does not have in mind the self-conscious knowing ego, but an existential reality that is always already related to a world before all reflection. *Dasein*'s 'identity' is not internal to thought, but is bound up in its temporal relationships with the being of the world in which it finds itself. Gradually, Heidegger moved even further, from the thought of *Dasein*, with its connotations of a residual humanist subjectivity, towards the thinking of Being. Self-consciousness is a reductive and narrow manifestation of Being. It is Being that makes reflection possible without being caught between its mirrors.

Derrida's thinking radicalizes this notion of an otherness or alterity prior to all self-conscious reflection. *Différance*, the moving network of time and difference, is not itself an object of reflection or a ground upon which a totality could be erected. Like other terms used by Derrida, such as the trace, the supplement, or writing, *différance* is not the hidden essence of truth, but what limits and destabilizes all essences even as it makes them possible. It is not in the service of unity, of the simplicity of the One.

As Gasché puts it, 'The alterity that splits reflection from itself and thus makes it able to fold into itself – to reflect itself – is also what makes it, for structural reasons, incapable of closing upon itself. The very possibility of reflexivity is also the subversion of its own source'.[3] Reflection 'opens itself up to the thought of an alterity'. This otherness is neither the mirror image nor the negation of thought. Either of these options would allow thought to recapture and domesticate it in a speculative embrace. Derrida offers us an otherness that is not merely the other of the same, one half of a matching pair.

Derrida writes of literature that it is 'A part that within and without the whole, marks the wholly other, the other incommensurate with the whole' (D, p. 56). Deconstruction, he claims 'thinks only on the level of the impossible, promises through its prohibition, an other thinking, an other text, the future of another promise' (MP, p. 135). It is a thinking that can no longer be calculated, but answers to 'the incalculable order of a wholly other: the coming or the call of the other' (MP, p. 137).

Does the 'wholly other' resonate with the divine? Or is it something else?

God, *différance* and the theatre of cruelty

In the introduction to *Margins of Philosophy*, Derrida writes that 'Philosophy has always insisted upon this: thinking its other. Its other: that which limits it, and from which it derives its essence, its definition, its production' (M, p. x). Philosophy wants to define and therefore contain its other in advance, to keep it safe at home. It wants 'mastery over the limit' by thinking its other, but, as Derrida argues, 'In thinking it *as such*, in recognizing it, one misses it' (ibid.).

Derrida is well aware that ideas such as otherness or alterity do not automatically escape the clutches of philosophical speculation. There is a need for 'an other which is no longer *its other*' (M, p. xiv), a radical alterity that resists being pressed into the service of absolute knowledge. But what could possibly lie beyond philosophy? Derrida answers that there is no pure absence or void outside the margins of knowledge, but something much stranger: 'beyond the philosophical text there is not a blank, virgin, empty margin, but another text, a weave of differences, of forces without any present center of reference' (M, p. xxiii).

The first essay in *Margins* is perhaps the fullest exposition Derrida gives of the notion of *différance*, and it is striking how it constantly approaches the themes of otherness and of theology. Titled simply 'Différance' it originally appeared in 1968, the year following the publication of *Speech and Phenomena*.

At the outset, Derrida makes it clear that there is something strangely uncanny about the notion of *différance*. It 'is literally neither a word nor a concept' (M, p. 3), and it 'is never presented as such' (M, p. 6). We are also quickly led into the radical implications of this anti-concept for the notions of truth, totality – and theology. Anticipating the discussion of the father–king of the gods in *Dissemination*, Derrida states that *différance* is 'not far from announcing the death of the tyrant' (M, p. 4). It gives us no 'absolute point of departure' for 'no transcendent truth present outside the field of writing can govern theologically the totality of the field' (M, p. 6).

It is at this point that Derrida makes one of his most famous allusions to negative theology. We are already familiar with the point that *différance* eludes the language of ontology and existence. Indeed, we seem only to be able to approach it by saying what it is not. Some commentators had concluded from this that Derrida was engaged in a revival of negative theology, with *différance* merely masquerading for the hidden divinity who could only be reached by the mystic prepared to strip away all positive predicates and enter the cloud of unknowing. Derrida's reply to this interpretation is worth quoting at length:

the detours, locutions, and syntax in which I will often have to take recourse will resemble those of negative

theology, occasionally even to the point of being indistinguishable from negative theology. Already we have had to
delineate *that différance is not*, does not exist, is not a
present-being (*on*) in any form; and we will be led to
delineate also everything *that* it *is not*, that is, *everything*; and
consequently that it has neither existence nor essence.
It derives from no category of being, whether present or
absent. And yet those aspects of *différance* which are thereby
delineated are not theological, not even in the order of the
most negative of negative theologies, which are always
concerned with disengaging a superessentiality beyond the
finite categories of essence and existence, that is, of presence, and always hastening to recall that God is refused the
predicate of existence, only in order to acknowledge his
superior, inconceivable, and ineffable mode of being . . .
Différance is not only irreducible to any ontological or
theological – ontotheological – reappropriation, but as the
very opening of the space in which ontotheology –
philosophy – produces its system and its history, it includes
ontotheology, inscribing it and exceeding it without return.
(M, p. 6)

Derrida recognizes that his language can look very similar to
that employed by negative theologians. However, he maintains
that his aim is very different, Negative theology remains very
much a part of metaphysics and ontotheology. It is steeped in
Neo-platonic thinking, in which the transcendent purity of the
One, the Good, can only be approached through an ascent away
from the world of time, change and difference, culminating in
a pure mystical intuitive union with the divine. Words fall away,
but they do so in order to clear the ground for a direct encounter
with the God who is so fully pure, simple and present that ordinary predicates of existence and Being seem inappropriate. This is
not the end of metaphysics, but its apotheosis, as it outbids itself in
attributing supremacy to the One.

Différance should not be assimilated to this mystical metaphysics.
It is not a present being, however ineffable or superior. It is not an
essence beyond all other essences. The experience of *différance* is
not one of timeless union, but of the irreducibility of time and

difference, in which the self is never fully gathered and transparent to itself. Recalling our earlier discussion of the complication of origins, Derrida writes that '*Différance* is the non-full, non-simple, structural and differentiating origin of differences. Thus, the name "origin" no longer suits it' (M, p. 11).

Unlike the God who has mastery over the work of his hands,

> *différance* is not. It is not a present being, however excellent, unique, principal, or transcendent. It governs nothing, reigns over nothing, and nowhere exercises any authority. It is not announced by any capital letter. Not only is there no kingdom of *différance*, but *différance* instigates the subversion of every kingdom. (M, p. 21–22)

Différance, structured by a 'radical alterity' (M, p. 21), leaves no sovereignty unshaken. It is therefore not God, or at least God under any description known to us from metaphysics and therefore from much of theology too, even if that theology takes the way of negation: 'This unnameable is not an ineffable Being which no name could approach: God, for example. The unnameable is the play which makes possible nominal effects, the relative unitary and atomic structures that are called names' (M, p. 26).

Ontotheology desires an illusory stability produced within the movement of differences. For Derrida, by contrast, the name of God can be translated or substituted as much as any other name.[4] He ends the essay with a very positive appraisal of the loss of any origin or centre of Being that is entailed by *différance*. Here at least, he rejects any nostalgia for the 'unique name' that would ground or gather all truth, and calls his reader to affirm the play of *différance* 'in a certain laughter and a certain step of the dance' (M, p. 27).

Ontotheology and philosophy dream of gathering all things into unity, back to the security of the origin, which is also the end of all things. But difference cannot be so captured. Any actual instance of unity is always dependent upon the differences out of which it is forged; it is always dependent on contingencies, always questionable and always subject to a future it cannot fully predict, much less control.

Nevertheless, Derrida does not advocate a purely immanent philosophy in any straightforward sense. That is, Derrida does not claim that deconstruction must be purely secular, this-worldly, renouncing all ideas of transcendence. We should not forget that it is in the name of the other, in response to the other, that deconstruction seeks to expose the limits of any system. Philosophy is broken open in its very heart to the other that goes before it: 'A radical trembling can only come from the outside' (M, p. 134). It would be too hasty to equate otherness or *différance* with God, and Derrida resists such a reading himself. But we cannot assume that the relationship between these terms is one of a pre-judged incompatibility or hostility. God can be seen as the foundation and limit of all difference, as pure presence. At the same time, God is also the name or trace of an otherness that defies comprehension by systematic knowledge, and even by the categories of being.

Take the essay 'La parole soufflée', where Derrida discusses how Antonin Artaud's radical approach to theatre was driven by a desire for immediacy, in which words and actions would no longer be separated. His 'theatre of cruelty' was to be a theatre of spontaneity and absolute creation, not inauthentic, second-hand repetition. It would be a pure incarnation, in which the body would no longer be subject to the spiritualized authority of the spoken and written word.

Derrida's interest in Artaud is that he pushes the desire for immediacy to such limits that he is able to understand the workings of language all the better. Artaud sees that language always disrupts my presence to myself, stealing away my words and separating them from the immediacy of my own life and expression. Interestingly, Artaud associates this stealing away with God.

God appears in two related guises in 'La parole soufflée'. He is the dominating author or director, the one who writes the script and tells the actors what to do and say. Artaud's rebellion against this God echoes many other atheistic rejections of supernatural authority. However, God also appears in another guise. As Derrida puts it, 'The Other, the Thief, the great Furtive One, has a proper name: God' (WD, p. 180). God is furtive, and furtiveness 'is thus the quality of dispossession which always empties out speech as it eludes itself' (WD, p. 177). This is a very strange God – fleeting, thieving, deceptive, below our radar: 'God is thus the proper name of that which deprives us of our own nature, of our own birth; consequently he will always have spoken before us, on the sly.

He is the difference which insinuates itself between myself and myself as my death' (WD, p.180).

This is a God very different from the images of the absolute creator or Lévi-Strauss's engineer. Derrida associates this God with the demiurge, the one who forms a world out of ready-made materials rather than creating out of nothing. He follows this thought all the way to its heretical end. This God

> is the thief, the trickster, the counterfeiter, the pseudony-mous, the usurper, the opposite of the creative artist, the artisanal being, the artisan: Satan. I am God and God is Satan; and as Satan is part of God's creation . . . God is of my own creation, my double who slipped into the differ-ence that separates me from my origin, that is, into the nothing that opens my history. What is called the presence of God is but the forgetting of this nothing, the eluding of elusion, which is not an accident, but the very movement of elusion . . . (WD, p. 182)

God is not where we would expect God to be. Therefore, God is even associated with excrement, the abject leftover of life sepa-rated from me. An image of betrayal, death and impurity.

Such language might appear shocking and absurd. It is impor-tant to note that Derrida is commenting closely on Artaud's own words. As in many of his essays, the line between commentary and a direct statement of his own views is perhaps impossible to determine. What is significant, however, is that Derrida is prepared to explore the otherness of God in a way that does not tie the divine down to ideals of presence. There are, in effect, two Gods. One is the reassuring God of presence who allows me to forget the difference, the nothingness that throws me into a life in time. The other God is the furtive one, the dispossessor, the elusive difference that separates me from myself. This God is not an abso-lute creator, but is perhaps creativity itself. Without dispossession and separation from pure presence, nothing new could ever come into being. The trickster God is inseparable from what the 'I' rejects or represses in order to establish itself.

Artaud's desire to overcome the God of controlling power depends upon his acknowledgement of this other God. The theatre of cruelty is caught in this tension: if it really achieved its goal of pure immediacy and the end of language, it would have nothing to say or do. All would be silence. Without God, I cannot be a creator.

This duality is shown again in a second essay on Artaud from the same work. Derrida argues that 'The theater of cruelty expulses God from the stage', but it does not do this in order to enthrone an atheism that would 'proclaim the death of God'. This radical theatrics does something different, it makes truth differently, producing 'a nontheological space' (WD, p. 235) that neither theism not atheism can define. He goes on to explain that the space of the theatre is theological when it is dominated by the voice, by a 'primary logos' that controls and orders the theatre from the outside. In Artaud's theatre, there will no longer be any dictation or dictatorship of a divine author–creator.

Crucially, this nontheological space is distinct from one that is simply atheistic. Artaud advocates a return to the language of gestures, before the separation of soul and body, God and humanity: 'This is the event of the origin of languages, and of the dialogue between theology and humanism whose inextinguishable reoccurrence has never not been maintained by the metaphysics of Western theater' (WD, p. 240).

One one level, Derrida is pointing out that Artaud's rejection of God and metaphysics is still caught up in a highly metaphysical desire for primordial presence. However, this is not an exercise in discrediting Artaud, since the dialogue to which he bears witness, a dialogue between theology and humanism, is inextinguishable. For Derrida, the truth does not lie in rejecting one pole of this opposition, still less in resolving them into some higher harmony, but in maintaining the creative difference between them. The shadow of God is never finally expelled from the stage.

I am not claiming that Derrida is endorsing an alternative theological approach, even one as strangely heterodox as the one suggested here. However, his work does open possibilities for theological imagination that are not shut down by his suspicion of the God of pure presence. In the difference between God and God, there may be no resolution, but the coming of something unexpected, the return of a repressed sacred that is both creative and inhuman, inviting and repulsive.

Writing and Difference contains a number of other texts that contribute to a fuller understanding of this other God. Before we examine them, it is worth exploring a little further how the name of God relates to the disorderly non-origin that is *différance*.

Getting the drift: God and the trace

Derrida affirms the inescapability of interpretation. But he is also denying that interpretation can be laid to rest to by a particular kind of reference, one that takes us out of the movement of differences towards a pure intelligibility.

In the essay that set in train his dispute with John Searle, Derrida contests the assumptions underlying speech–act theory. J. L. Austin's famous work *How to Do Things with Words* drew attention to the way in which language is used, not merely to describe the world, but to bring about effects within it.[5] Through linguistic acts such as promising, apologizing, forbidding, passing sentence, together with a host of less explicit examples, speakers aim to perform an action, and not just state a fact.

According to Derrida, speech–act theory demands a strong link between the meaning of what is said and the intentions of the speaker who says it. Although it enriches our understanding of language as performative and not merely descriptive, it still privileges the ideal of meaning as immediate presence in the mind of the speaker, which can then be communicated to others. It also relies upon the claim that the ambiguities surrounding the interpretation of a speaker's intentions can be largely eliminated by taking full account of the context in which the words are spoken.

Derrida raises the question 'are the conditions of a context ever absolutely determinable?' (LI, p. 3). Drawing upon his notion of a generalized writing, Derrida argues that signs only work because they can be indefinitely repeated in ever new contexts, and in the absence of their original author or speaker. He writes that 'My communication must be repeatable – iterable – in the absolute absence of the receiver or of any empirically determinable collectivity of receivers' (LI, p. 7). He also notes 'the logic that ties repetition to alterity' (ibid.). In other words, signs can only be available to others if they are not tied to a present meaning immediately contained within my own mind. Language, which has always preceded my sense of self, requires that 'I' am structured by difference and time from before the beginning. For Derrida, this means that 'there is no experience consisting of pure presence but only of chains of differential marks' (LI, p. 10). It is important to note that he is making a point about *all experience*, not just a technical claim about the way in which language works.

In his reading of Austin, Derrida draws attention to the way in which speech–act theory tries to respond to these issues by making distinctions between serious and non-serious or parasitical acts. The latter might include making statements in quotation marks, or as part of a joke or a theatrical production. They are distinguished from proper speech acts because they are not 'meant' in the same way. However, Derrida argues that it is never possible once and for all to exclude the possibility that 'serious' speech acts are also partly artificial, quoted, dramatized, mentioned rather than used. This possibility is not an unfortunate accident, it is integral to the working of language. The word is always divided by the possibility of repetition. That's what makes it work. The idea of pure presence within the speaker is a secondary one. Even the signature, the unique mark of a text's author, is still a trace, readable in the shadow of its creator's absence, even of her death.

In his further contributions to the debate initiated with Searle, Derrida underscores the connection between repetition and the contamination of presence: 'Iterability alters, contaminating parasitically what it identifies and enables to repeat "itself"; it leaves us no choice but to mean (to say) something that is (already, always, also) other than what we mean (to say)' (LI, p. 62).

Significantly for our purposes, Derrida also draws out a striking theological corollary of this claim. He points out that, in his original article 'Signature Event Context', the section concentrating on Austin is titled 'Parasites. Iter, of Writing: That It Perhaps Does Not Exist'. This is a playful reference to the fifth of Descartes' *Meditations* whose Latin title is *De essentia rerum materialum; et iterum de Deo, quod existat* [*On the Essence of Material Things; And Likewise of God, That He Exists*]. Derrida notes that Descartes added the second part of the title, acknowledging that he felt it necessary prove the existence of God once more, even though he seemed to have given a satisfactory proof in the second meditation.

Derrida asks about the significance of multiplying and repeating proofs of God's existence, when God is the 'ultimate guarantee (being unique, irreplaceable, beyond all substitution both *absolutely repeatable* and *unrepeatable*) of all certitude, all proof, all truth?' (LI, p. 83). God is repeatable because He is timeless, unlimited by any context, always present, always true, always the same. But this also makes God unrepeatable, because He is unique, absolute, self-same. Derrida's substitution of 'writing' for 'God' in his re-working of the title might suggest that he sees writing as the new bearer of this paradoxical theological significance.

His own explanation leaves such questions hanging. He claims to be

> drawing the name of God (of the infinite Being) into a graphematic drift [*dérive*] that excludes (for instance) any decision as to whether God is more than the name of God, whether the 'name of God' refers to God or to the name of God, whether it signifies 'normally' or 'cites', etc., God, being here, *qua* writing, what at the same time renders possible and impossible, probable and improbable oppositions such as that of the 'normal' and the citational or the parasitical. (LI, p. 83).

In a sense, writing does play the role classically given to God. But Derrida is also raising the question of what we are doing when we speak of God anyway. Is theology using the name of God or just mentioning it? Does it speak for God, of God, to God? What context would determine the answer to such questions?

In any case, Derrida is not simply rejecting or reducing theology as the naming of God. There is no alternative secular language into which God-talk can be translated without remainder, for the simple reason that there is no master language or absolute ground available to us. Theology can still reveal – despite or beyond its own intentions – the instability of its own attempts to name the unique God. In the process, it can call into question its own captivity in ontotheology.

Derrida says of writing that it lies

> outside the authority of ontological discourse, outside the
> alternative of existence or nonexistence, which in turn
> always supposes a simple discourse capable of deciding
> between presence and absence. The rest of the trace, its
> remains [*restance*] are neither present nor absent. They
> escape the jurisdiction of all ontotheological discourse
> even if they render the latter at times possible. (LI, p. 83).

If there is a cross-contamination between writing and God, theology may have to reckon with the possibility of a God no longer defined by metaphysical being, simplicity and presence.

This is not a matter of rejoicing in ambiguity or uncertainty for the sake of it. Ambiguity can also be a mask for a way of thinking that gives pride of place to presence and the ineffability of a Supreme Being. If we are returned into time, difference and secondariness, then the need for conceptual rigour is even more important. Derrida insists on this in his disagreement with Searle: any conceptual distinction has to follow the logic of 'all or nothing' as far as it can go. In other words, it is only by being as precise as possible that we are able to distinguish an idea of difference that is truly disruptive to the dominant philosophy. Derrida implies an ethical dimension to this approach, which 'is better for thought and for the relation to the other, the two of which I do not separate here: neither from one another, nor from the "experience" of différance' (LI, p. 117).

Otherness has a weight that is both rationally subversive and ethical, but it cannot be left as a rather vague and comforting ideal of relationality. Its cutting edge leaves our settled notions of truth and power wounded. The other comes as the thief and dispossessor. Our question remains: is there any sense in calling this other God? Is the act of naming God in this way descriptive, performative or something that cannot settle between either option?

Writing and the dissonance of God

The essays collected in *Writing and Difference* come from the period 1963–1967. They precede the publication of 'Différance' and Derrida's own worry about being polluted by the stain of negative theology. They are perhaps therefore more open to exploring the different layers and possibilities of theological language. We have already seen Derrida's striking commentary upon Artaud's 'furtive' God, and there are other rich resources here for exploring the tensions and contaminations that bring together writing, difference and the divine. Derrida, it seems, cannot leave God alone.

All through the essays, Derrida is exploring the possibility of thinking otherwise than in metaphysical categories that privilege presence and eternity, even in the dynamic and historical form given to them by Hegel. Derrida, commenting again on Artaud, invokes a different sort of dialectics, one that would not be tied to the 'philosophical or Christian idea of pure origin', that would be 'the indefinite movement of finitude, of the unity of life and death, of difference, of original repetition, that is, of the origin of tragedy as the absence of a simple origin' (WD, p. 248). Why tragedy? Because such a dialectics will not close over the wounds of existence, the inevitable dimension of risk that haunts our living.

The opening chapter, 'Force and Signification', makes the by now familiar point that 'Meaning must await being said or written in order to inhabit itself, and in order to become, by differing from itself, what it is: meaning' (WD, p. 11). This differing of meaning from itself spells the end of 'the theological certainty of seeing every page bind itself into the unique text of the truth', the book of all truth dreamed of by philosophers. Modernity has lost this certainty, this 'divine writing', with the result that divine creation becomes disseminated into human poetic creativity.

The Romantics idealized human poetry as itself a sacred origin of meaning. Derrida acknowledges that the loss of belief in an absolute divine origin of the world puts the work of creating meaning into our hands. However, it is never simply ours to have and control. Meaning can no more be gathered and grounded by the will of the creative poet or genius than it can be dictated by God. It spills out and over, for meaning cannot now 'absolutely precede writing'. Creation is a risk, it is equivocal, because it opens us to the best and the worst possibilities of life. Still, without this slippage of meaning into writing, time and difference there could be no creation. Writing is 'inaugural' and therefore risky. It stands at the absent 'origin' of creation, yet it has no idea where it is going, and no knowledge maps out its path in advance. Its future is open (WD, p. 11).

Human creativity is therefore not an act of Promethean self-definition, as we take over the functions formerly reserved for God. Writing exposes us to the other, not just the other person, but to the wholly other that subverts our mastery and divides our human essence. It opens us to an unpredictable future, a constitutive inhumanity. Just as we think that Derrida has done with God as the lost anchor of a failed theological certainty, we read this: 'Is not that which is called God, that which imprints every human course and recourse with its secondarity, the passageway of deferred reciprocity between reading and writing?' (WD, p. 11). God is not just the absolute origin or presence who arrests all meaning and reduces all difference. God is also the name of that which makes every act of creation 'already a response', of the otherness that is not transcendent in the sense of separate, but that is 'imprinted' within the movement of language. If there is a divine writing, if God too is compelled to write or be written, then there is a sacred text that escapes 'the theological simultaneity of the book' (WD, p. 24). Without a simple origin, there cannot be a clean break with God. God and writing, it seems, do not stand apart from one another. Each infects the other.

Again, therefore, Derrida underlines the fact that one cannot simply make a brand new start and walk away from what philosophy has inherited. It must be reckoned with, and it may be that within metaphysics we find the traces of a difference that it cannot master (WD, p. 20).

This dislocation of the system is signalled in another famous essay in this collection, 'Cogito and the History of Madness', in which Derrida offers a critique of Foucault's work on insanity. The division between the two thinkers centres on their interpretation of the famous *cogito*, the 'I think' that becomes the foundation for knowledge in Descartes' philosophy.

According to Derrida, Foucault sees the *cogito* as the deliberate exclusion of madness. Reason grounds itself by rejecting, defining and silencing its insane other. Foucault's genealogical approach to such acts of exclusion is aimed at letting madness re-emerge, speaking for itself and troubling the power of reason's ordered language.

Derrida's objection is that one cannot simply separate out reason and madness in this way. At the heart of the *cogito* is a hyperbole, an extreme act of self-founding. If the ego founds itself, it can appeal to no rational law other than itself, its own act. There is no reason without this moment of madness at its heart, a moment unsanctioned by any self-evident rule. By the same token, one can only protest against the excesses of rational order and its exclusions by drawing on reason. There is no pure madness outside the bounds of reason, which can liberate us from its clutches. Reason and madness contaminate one another. If this is not acknowledged, Foucault's history of madness runs the risk of just setting up another 'pure' foundation, simply inverting the value placed on reason and madness. That would be just to repeat and confirm the metaphysics from which he wishes to break.

The *cogito* is excessive, a zero point. It makes thinking the totality of existence possible only by escaping that totality. Even if the world disappears, even if I am gripped by deception or madness, I still think. Madness is its very possibility. For Derrida, the *cogito* is anything but a reassuring foundation. It is 'not human' but rather 'metaphysical and demonic' (WD, p. 56). It 'opens and founds the world as such by exceeding it' (WD, p. 57). Here again, at the origin of the world we find, not the self-transparent consciousness of phenomenology, but a consciousness always derived and divided in itself.

This inhuman madness is necessary for thought to get going. If it is not acknowledged, even by those wishing to stand up for the victims of history's exclusions, then we risk erecting a totalitarian structure, with all the potential for violence that that entails (and we should note this early ethical concern of Derrida's). This refusal of what is other, this reduction of everything to one, worldly level 'makes possible all straitjackets' (WD, p. 57). However, Derrida wants to make it very clear that he is 'not invoking an *other world*, an alibi or evasive transcendence' (ibid.) that would only promote further violence and oppression.

What does Derrida mean here? He wants to acknowledge an otherness at the heart of thinking, an otherness that sets it in motion, but cannot be defined as a prime mover, or located in some otherworldly realm. His rejection of transcendence as an alibi and evasion is illuminating. A purely this-worldly materialism can be in league with supernaturalist dogmatism. Both can claim to possess the key to understanding the world in its totality, reducing the world to a flat, immanent plane that can be interpreted, manipulated and controlled by the guardians of orthodoxy. Derrida seeks a more troubling and uncontainable sense of alterity.

In the final pages of this essay, Derrida discusses the role played by God in the founding of reason. Although Descartes wishes to establish a pure and self-contained starting point for thought, stripping away all that can be doubted, he is nevertheless unable to avoid compromising his aims. He needs to prove the existence of God in order to make the transition from the *cogito* to an ordered world. God rescues the self from vertigo and madness that haunt its origins (WD 58).

Derrida leaves open the possibility of reading this intervention of God in two ways. On the one hand, God's reassuring authority and presence is what normalizes reason, protects it from its other. On the other hand, God is the ever open (dangerous) passage between reason and madness, between order and what escapes it. God is the spacing, the difference that enables us to live and communicate, but that always eludes domestication. And this is so, not because God lives in an other world, but because God is imprinted within this one, keeping it unsettled and alive to what exceeds it. This God lives in the difference between madness and reason.

This reading is perhaps given more credence by the appearance at the head of 'Cogito' of a quotation from Kierkegaard: 'The Instant of Decision is Madness'. For Kierkegaard, of course, the decision was also the leap of faith in a God indirectly and paradoxically revealed in the 'text' or 'spacing' of existence.[6] It is Kierkegaard who will be one of Derrida's main interlocutors in *The Gift of Death*, another work that links madness, decision and responsibility with the name of God.

I have been suggesting that Derrida is walking a line that evades the opposite choices of theism and atheism, theology and humanism. It does this in two ways. First, Derrida exposes the underlying metaphysical assumptions that shape and unite both ends of this spectrum. Second, he is at least prepared to explore the possibility that language about God might do something other than posit a pure and indifferent foundation of truth. It is from within the text of metaphysics that Derrida seeks to dislocate the whole, and God is also the name of a fleeting, furtive difference that no structure can enclose.

One of the most important essays in *Writing and Difference* can help us to clarify what this might mean. 'Violence and Metaphysics' is one of Derrida's most sustained engagements with the work of Emmanuel Levinas. Levinas was also a student of phenomenology, and, like Heidegger, wanted to break with its concentration on the knowing human subject as the centre and origin of the world. However, Levinas was also deeply critical of Heidegger's attempt to recast our understanding of existence though a focus on the question of Being.

Heidegger argued that the distinction between particular beings and Being as such had been forgotten and obscured in the philosophical tradition. Ontotheology reduced Being to a given entity, a fully present being. It was incapable of thinking the difference between beings and Being. The early Heidegger argued that in order to uncover that difference, we had to analyze the being for whom Being itself was a question: *Dasein*. As we stressed earlier, *Dasein* is not mere factual human being, but an existential possibility or state. *Dasein* is the privileged site from which the question of Being can be asked. It is not an isolated monad of pure consciousness. It is temporal and existential, always interrelated with a world, rooted in a pre-reflective comprehension of Being.[7]

This short sketch shows that Heidegger wished to break with the reflective philosophy that had given centre stage to pure consciousness and abstract knowledge of beings. For Levinas, however, Heidegger's thought is still bound to a conception of Being that closes us off from a genuine encounter with difference. He advocates an experience of otherness that is first and foremost ethical. The 'I' is not self-grounding, but summoned into being by the ethical demand embodied in the face of the Other. Ethics is the true first philosophy, not metaphysics as it has been understood since Aristotle, not even Heidegger's existential ontology. Ethics is what breaks us out of totalizing systems of thought that imprison us within sameness and indifference.[8]

Derrida's reading of Levinas is sympathetic yet critical. Perhaps most surprising, given all that we have seen of his work so far, is Derrida's reluctance to let go of the language of being.

Levinas represents a radical move to break with the inherited Greek tradition of philosophy. He calls us to a 'dislocation of our identity', moving from the Greek site towards a 'prophetic speech' (WD, p. 82). The clear Jewish undertones of Levinas's thought are already being heard. Prophecy promises deliverance from the oppressive structures legitimated by 'the Greek domination of the Same and the One' (WD, p. 83). Ethics inaugurates a nonviolent relationship with the infinitely other, and so opens a space of liberating transcendence.

There is much here that is in accord with the spirit of Derrida's own turn to alterity. This is confirmed when Derrida distinguishes Levinas's thought from any kind of theology or Jewish mysticism. It cannot be identified as 'a dogmatics, *a* religion, nor as *a* morality' (WD, p. 83). In other words, Levinas is not basing his ethics upon a divinely ordained source, scripture or institution, nor is he claiming that it flows from any self-evident intuition or union with God. His transcendence is rigorously ethical. It does not transport us out of the relationship with the human other.

For Derrida, Levinas appeals not to authority but to experience as 'the passage and departure toward the other; the other itself as what is most irreducibly other within it: Others' (WD, p. 83). Levinas is shown to reject the privilege given to the light of (Greek) reason, a privilege that persists in Husserl and Heidegger. Instead, the other must remain beyond presence if she is to lead us beyond the confines of a reason that comprehends everything according to a single measure. The other resists being categorized or understood in advance. She calls us to respond.

The relationship to the other is what makes time possible as an opening to the unpredictable future event, rather than the unfolding of a preordained end. Derrida says this future is beyond history, but again, we should not interpret this beyond as pointing to another world, to a time after time. This future 'is *present* at the heart of experience. Present not as a total presence but as a trace. Therefore, before all dogmas, all conversions, all articles of faith or philosophy, experience itself is eschatological at its origin and in each of its aspects' (WD, p. 95). We are directed to an otherness we cannot master by a religious terminology whose content and dynamic are themselves dislocated.

Levinas calls the face-to-face relationship with the other 'religion', but given what Derrida has just said about the absence of dogma and any idea of full presence, this is a religion that escapes codification in an institutional tradition. Derrida calls it 'Not *a* religion, but *the* religion, the religiosity of the religious' (WD, p. 96). It is neither theoretical knowledge nor dogmatic theology, in the sense of the mediation of defined, authoritative teaching. It takes the bare form of a supplication, prayer and address to the other.

The infinite, that which surpasses and breaks any totality of thought and being, does not take a merely conceptual form. It is incarnated in the vulnerability of the face of the other. There is an irreducible play of presence and absence, proximity and distance involved in this experience. The face can never become an object or theme of knowledge (WD, p.103). The face is not of the world, it is 'the origin of the world'. It is absolute in its difference.

It is here that Derrida's hesitations about Levinas's project begin to emerge. The face-to-face relationship is not one between equals. It is not symmetrical. The Other commands me (even if I choose to ignore or disobey that command). This inequality, this commanding nature of the Other, could be used as a justification for the worst forms of oppression and injustice. Levinas's way of avoiding this is by stressing that the Other is not part of a finite totality, but is infinite. The infinite is not part of the world, seeking to subject everything to its rule. It commands in its nakedness, without mastery.

For Derrida, this implies that there is a kind of appeal to God lodged at the heart of Levinas's ethics. God is the name of the infinite Otherness, making the truly ethical relationship possible. A paradox emerges here. On the one hand, without this God there would only be the violence that reduces others to being parts of a whole and means to an end. On the other hand, without this God, there could be no ethics, no face of the Other – and therefore no violence and war (since there would be no Other to oppress).

Derrida concludes that 'War supposes and excludes God. We can have a relation to God only within such a system' (WD, p. 107). We do not live in a world of pure peace and harmony. There is war: this is the difference between the face and the world without a face. Our experience of war, of difference, of the play of absence and presence is what makes possible the thought of God: 'Only the play of the world permits us *to think the essence* of God' (ibid.).

Derrida pushes this idea further by examining the resemblance Levinas asserts between the Other and God. Levinas claims that language, our address to the Other, is lifted up to be an address to God. He is careful to avoid the position that language enables us to participate in God (mysticism), or describe God (theology) (WD, p. 108). The asymmetry between myself and the Other must be preserved.

For Derrida, however, the tensions in Levinas's thought are strengthened at this point. The relationship with the Other is at once the 'very presence of God' and yet we exist only in the 'Trace of God' (WD, p. 108). In other words, Levinas is trying to hold together two thoughts. The first is that God is a positive infinity, who alone can break the shackles of totalizing systems of philosophy and allow ethics to come to birth. The second states that God can never appear as such, never be present, only exists as a trace, as difference. This leads Derrida to suggest again that perhaps the reality of God is secondary, a product of the play of the world and of difference: 'and if God was an *effect of the trace*?' (WD, p. 108). It is unclear whether Levinas is overcoming the inner logic of ontotheology even as he tries to break with it. Derrida's displacement of God is also the displacing of Levinas's ethical hierarchy, which determines and absolutizes the Other.

A key element of Derrida's critique of Levinas is therefore to question the compatibility between the classical idea of God as positive infinity and any kind of infinite ethical alterity: 'The infinitely Other would not be what it is, other, if it was a positive infinity, and if it did not maintain within itself the negativity of the indefinite' (WD, p. 114). The infinite, in other words, only has any meaning in relation to the finite, which it negates. If there is no such relationship, if the infinite is *wholly* other, then it becomes unrelated indifference, unspeakable and without any effect in the finite world.

Derrida's disconcerting claim, therefore, is that 'The other cannot be what it is, infinitely other, except in finitude and mortality (mine *and* its)' (WD, pp. 114–15). A positive infinite would be utterly disconnected from finite life. Recalling Derrida's point in *Speech and Phenomena* that to say 'I am' is to say 'I am mortal', we could not even say that this positive infinity were alive in any sense.

Derrida insists that if the face is body, is vulnerable, then it must be mortal. This is where the ethical demand comes from, the demand to respect and not to murder the other. Death is part of what it means to live, just as presence is dependent upon its relation to non-presence. It is worth quoting Derrida's elaboration of this point at length:

> Infinite alterity as death cannot be reconciled with infinite alterity as positivity and presence (God). Metaphysical transcendence cannot be at once transcendence towards the other as death and transcendence towards the other as God. Unless God means Death, which after all has never been excluded by the entirety of the classical philosophy within which we understand God both as Life and as the Truth of Infinity, of positive Presence.
>
> But what does this *exclusion* mean if not the exclusion of every particular *determination*? And that God is *nothing* (determined), is not life, because he is *everything*? and therefore is at once All and Nothing, Life and Death. Which means that God is or appears, *is named*, within the difference between All and Nothing, Life and Death. Within difference, and at bottom as Difference itself. This difference is what is called History. God is *inscribed* in it. (WD, pp. 115–16)

This passage weaves together the different values and meanings that Derrida assigns to the name of God. First, God is Life, conceived as pure, positive presence. There is nothing in God that is imperfect or unrealized. God has nothing to do with death or evil, which are not themselves positive entities, but merely the privation of being. Second, however, God is Death, in the sense that this pure positive presence lacks the conditions that make life possible. Beyond all difference, beyond all limitation, God is indistinguishable from Nothing, from the darkest night of non-being.

Third, God is both life *and* death, everything and nothing, being and non-being at once; or, rather, God appears in the difference between them, even as Difference itself. Difference and time (history) come first, and only in time and language do we formulate ideas of infinite presence and purity. But these ideas are always contaminated by their origins in the movement of difference. For Derrida, it seems, God can name both our reactive, doomed attempt to stop that movement, and also the creative, risky life of that movement itself.

The reason Levinas is open to such readings, which go against the grain of his intentions, is that he does not make the classical move of disdaining language, and appealing to a foundation or certainty beyond signs. There is no thought before language for Levinas. He has accepted the need for truth to be stated within time and words, and so denies himself the strategies of mysticism. Negative theology can inhabit language as foreign medium 'spoken in a speech that knew itself failed and finite' (WD, p. 116) while aiming at mystical communion. But Levinas excludes this possibility. For him, speech is more righteous than mystical communion; it refuses assimilation with the other and preserves the distance necessary for ethics to work.

The consequence is that there is no pure nonviolence, no ultimate resolution of difference into harmony. One can only fight light with light in order to avoid the worst violence (WD, p. 117).

This also means, however, that Levinas's attempt to secure a purely ethical nonviolent discourse untainted by philosophical concepts such as 'being' must always be compromised. Indeed, Derrida argues that this must be the case if ethics is to survive. In a way analogous to his discussion of God's infinity, Derrida maintains that the other must always be the other of the same. Otherness is never pure and absolute. It has meaning only in relation, else it is simply a mute nothingness. Levinas wanted to reject Husserl's view that others appear to me as alter-egos. For Husserl, because I have no direct access to the inner life of others, I understand them as selves by comparing them with my own experience of selfhood. Levinas thought that making others into alter-egos reduced them into mirror reflections of me, imprisoning them within a metaphysics of sameness.

However, Derrida counters that Levinas misses the radical nature of what Husserl is saying. In phenomenology, the ego is the productive origin of its world. To see others as alter-egos is to recognize in them that same creative function. An alter-ego is not just a reflection of me, it is an origin and an end in itself. This is in fact the origin of ethics, for without it, others could just be seen as things, available for me to use at will.

Derrida is of course far from endorsing all that Husserl says about the nature of the ego, but in this case he believes that there are nuances that are being missed by Levinas. The result is that the latter's ethics are too idealized, too cut-off from the actual experience of otherness as we encounter it. For Derrida, there is no ethics without that relationship of sameness-in-difference between me and my other. Only this relationship can be the basis for me to desire the other's well-being. The corollary of this is that the possibility of violence can never be wholly eliminated from the world. There is no absolute peace or absolutely nonviolent ethics, only an 'economical' ethics that tries to make the 'most peaceful gesture possible' (WD, p. 128). It is always possible for me to reduce the other to the status of an object, because I can never experience otherness pure and simple. There is a 'transcendental violence' that makes ethics possible. Difference, limitation and all the risks of misunderstanding are inevitable features of our finitude. Infinite otherness is indistinguishable from indifference, absolute sameness. The dream of perfect peace is also a nightmare in which every disharmonious voice is suppressed.

If all otherness must appear to an ego, can only ever appear to me within 'my world', and if this is ironically the only way it can be truly other to me, then the same applies to God. For Husserl, God is always God for me; my idea of God is my own conscious production. Husserl is careful to underline the point that this does not mean that I am the creator of God, or that God's transcendence is my invention. However, as Derrida points out, God must still mean something to an ego, must still be God for me (WD, p. 132). Without this safeguard, the danger of impersonal totalitarianism would emerge. If God as infinitely other could simply impose himself upon me, there would be nothing left for me to be, no relationship with God worth speaking of. There would only be the triumph of absolute presence, devoid of any relationship to what exceeds it.

The final part of the essay focuses upon the question of Being. For Levinas, Being was the ultimate abstract, totalizing category that robbed the other of his otherness. Derrida argues that, however valid this might be as a critique of cruder forms of ontology, it does not get to the heart of Heidegger's thought. Levinas's critique is directed against the oppressive anonymity of Being as a general category that swallows up any experience of genuine difference. Derrida counters that, in Heidegger's work, the thought of Being does not work in this way. It is not a pre-existing abstract unity to which all reality is subject, nor is it merely a theoretical concept (WD, p. 139). It precedes all concepts and categories, any ideal of presence. It only emerges in and through time and existence, making difference possible (WD, p. 140). This recovery of a thought of elusive, fleeting Be-ing is not the static foundation Levinas takes it to be.

With this in mind, Derrida claims that the thought of Being is necessary to preserve the irreducibility of existence, otherness and responsibility. Being only emerges in and as language, time and difference, without ever being equated with this or that particular being. If Being gets frozen in that way, then it has been lost and forgotten, and we are left with a world of brute facts that we try to master by imposing our concepts upon them.

Because Levinas does not appreciate the subtlety of Heidegger's thinking of Being, he rejects it as one more expression of a failed philosophical tradition. As a result, he is at risk of falling back into the kind of metaphysical humanism from which he is trying to escape. It is because man is an essence, a substance, because man resembles God in his positive infinity, that man can be the face, the other that ethics demands. The analogy between God and man is a way of securing man's essence with reference to the being who supremely is. Ontotheology and humanism are here united in this search for a Supreme Being that would act as the controlling ground for all truth. Derrida even takes a side swipe at 'atheistic humanism' that does not dispute the logic that we are searching for the timeless essence of things, but merely inverts the order of priority between man and God (WD, p. 143).

Derrida is arguing that the thought of Being precedes our determination of God, man and their relationship. It does not do so as a general, abstract concept, but as the dynamic emergence of difference and possibility. Being becomes neither a substitute nor a foundation for God (WD, p. 143). In a footnote, Derrida argues that speaking of God as an 'example' of what Being as difference produces is neither inherently reductionist nor blasphemous. Being (in this dynamic and non-foundational sense) permits us to think of God without making God into an object (WD, p. 318). If God is an 'example' of difference, then we are invited to think the sacred as dispersed from any centre or controlling point of reference. This is not the same as the abolition of the sacred or the simple death of God.

These difficult ideas lead us back to the ambiguity inherent in the name of God. God, as infinitely other and absolutely One, is both the supreme 'example' of the trace and the instance of its arrest and death into pure presence. Derrida is not reducing God's otherness or transcendence, but arguing that these are only possible as effects of a play of differences. Once we understand that Being is not the timeless foundation desired by ontotheology, we can get some distance between Being and beings, and also between Being and God. This distance or difference is what makes life and meaning possible.

Derrida is not simply opting for atheism, if that atheism uncritically leaves the idols of metaphysics in their niches. His thought is a more difficult one, which still leaves open the possibility of a relationship to the sacred Other. The thought of Being is not one of settled foundations. It is bound up with the idea of promise, a theme that we will see re-emerge in Derrida's later work. The promise opens a relationship to the other that is temporal and risky, but without it, that relationship dies. This is not a merely humanistic ethic, however. Thinking Being as promise is an experience of the sacred, 'the essential experience of divinity or deity', before those ideas are captured by theology and religious traditions, and solidified into the presence of God (WD, p. 145). Being comes before God, not as foundation, but as the emergence of life and difference within which the idea of God can do its work.

However, these distinctions – between Being or divinity and God, between the sacred and the theological – are surely unstable.

Derrida can only hold to a thinking of Being in his critique of Levinas because of the transformation or recovery of its meaning by Heidegger. In other words, the meaning of Being also has a history. The same could be said for God. God has already appeared in Derrida's writings, not only as positive infinity and pure presence, but as the furtive other, the difference between life and death, the passage and trace of a sacred writing. Is Derrida staying too close to Heidegger, for whom the thought of Being had to be rigorously distinguished from theology? What makes such a distinction absolute?

Derrida acknowledges that negative theology can appear to approach the thought of this Being, this divinity that precedes the definition of God as supreme being. Meister Eckhart is cited as an example, for whom there is a radical distinction between God and the 'Deity of God' (WD, p.146). However, Eckhart still encloses this deity within a dogmatic Trinitarian scheme and still attributes to God a more elevated Being, now understood as presence. The result is that negative theology remains tied to ontotheology.

Derrida's queasiness about negative theology will be qualified in the later texts we will read in the next chapter. For now he insists that 'transcendence toward Being, permits, then, an understanding of the word God, for example, even if this understanding is but the ether in which dissonance can resonate' (WD, p. 146). The thought of Being makes language and the relation to the other possible. It is the closest we can come to nonviolence, given that Derrida believes pure and absolute nonviolence to be a contradictory idea. Ethics and otherness are only possible because Being differs from itself. There is no primordial peace, no golden age from which we fall (hence Derrida's suspicion of nostalgia). We could let nothing be itself, we could not even have a life in time, without this complication of the origin (WD, p. 147).

The origin is always absent, Being is always veiled, since that is the only way in which they can appear. The temptation such language provokes is to desire the unveiling of Being, as if there were a pure and pristine truth somewhere out there beyond the play of differences. But the fulfilment of that desire would be indistinguishable from death. In the name of such desires, indeed, the most horrific violence has been unleashed upon the world.

The thinking of Being as difference leads Derrida to close the essay by wondering how far Levinas and Heidegger really are from one another. For the latter, Being is the thought of the other, which does not reduce difference to a fixed homogenous abstraction. Levinas, however, represents the possibility as an alternative thinking of God, a God who would be another name for Being, the opening of life and difference, not merely one other being within the world: the ether in which a dissonance can resonate. The suggestion is that Derrida's earlier critique of Levinas perhaps did not tell the whole story.

There is a strange alliance between the thought of Being and the thought of God, once neither is reduced to an abstract foundation or static presence. Indeed, it might even be that it is the actually existing God who opens our access to Being, to difference, to the other. But this implies in turn that only some idea of what it means to 'be' can lead us to God. Levinas's renunciation of the question of Being leaves his idea of infinite otherness cut adrift from the world. Only in the difference and dialogue between God and Being can the other be saved.

Derrida refers to this as the confrontation between a Greek thought on unity and being and a Jewish thought of the infinitely other. Greek philosophy needs to take account of otherness at the very heart of being. Jewish faith needs to recognize the philosophical question of being at the heart of what it means to talk about God's otherness. We live in the difference between these conflicting approaches (WD, p. 153).

'There is no simplicity in God'

The introduction of a Jewish motif into Derrida's discourse leads us to the final essays we will consider from *Writing and Difference*. In 'Edmond Jabès and the Question of the Book', Derrida meditates on the poet Jabès's imagery of the end of the Book, and of the writing that wanders away from any gathered centre. In the process, he also considers the nature of Jewishness as bound up with writing (WD, p. 64).

According to Derrida, Jabès's poetry exposes the way in which origins are always broken open by the adventure and the passion of writing. The Jew and what the Jew proclaims is 'always elsewhere', never gathered into a place of exclusion (WD, p. 66). The poet often invokes a Jewish kabbalistic tradition of God, and reflecting on this, Derrida writes 'God separated himself from himself in order to let us speak, in order to astonish and interrogate us. He did so not by speaking but by keeping still, by letting silence interrupt his voice and his signs, by letting the Tables be broken' (WD, p. 67). The fullness of God's presence must be split apart if we are to have our chance to be free and to live. Such ideas stand in stark contrast to the classical metaphysical assertion of God's unity and simplicity: 'If God opens the question in God, if he is the very opening of the Question, there can be no simplicity of God' (WD, p. 68).

This self-differing of God from his own essence is experienced by the poet as a kind of absence. Direct revelation from God is not available. The voice falls silent, but it does so in order to allow us to speak: 'God no longer speaks to us, he has interrupted himself: we must take words upon ourselves' (WD, p. 68). God can only bring otherness into being if God is alienated from Godself, for 'separation can emerge only in the rupture of God – with God' (WD, p. 69). Derrida acknowledges this to be unthinkable by classical rationality. But is it unthinkable by theology? Is the way we conceptualize God tied to this fixation on pure origins and absolute ends? Is God simple?

There is a kind of self-humbling undergone by God, which is analogous to the work of the poet. The poet must deny her own presence in order to let the story be told, let language speak. Creation involves a letting-go and letting-be, rather than a continuing domination and control. God awaits and needs the response of humanity, or in words of Eckhart quoted by Derrida, 'God becomes God when creation says God' (WD, p. 71).

To use a quasi-mythical image: only in the secondariness and repetition of writing can meaning be freed from its isolation. Meaning is only possible if there is a response: 'The other originally collaborates with meaning' (WD, p. 71). The oscillation between God and Being, which was so much a part of Derrida's reading of Levinas, is here too: 'Whether he is Being or the master of beings, God himself is, and appears as what he is, within difference, that is to say as difference and within dissimulation' (WD, p. 74)

That is the truth that 'tradition' – the literal meaning of cabal – carries within itself. Tradition exists because meaning is not pure. And 'traditionality is not orthodoxy' (WD, p. 74). Derrida cites the chain of heterodox readings of scripture that lie behind Jabès's work: from the Cabbala itself, through the mysticism of Jakob Böhme, through romanticism, Hegel and beyond. Jabès has an ambiguous relationship with his Judaism, one that had resonances for Derrida himself. Judaism embodies in its history the split between the pure origin of law and revelation and the endlessness of scripture and commentary upon scripture that gives it continuing life.

This ambiguity is played out in the idea of the book, which here again refers to the possibility of collecting all truth, decoding the world, divining its inner meaning. Faith in this book, Derrida says, can precede and survive any particular dogma or belief in the Bible. In contrast to this complacent belief in the unity of meaning, Derrida invokes a Being outside the book, a 'radical illegibility' (WD, p. 77) that makes all language and reason possible. Literature such as Jabès's *Book of Questions* is the nearest writing can get to making such illegibility appear to us. It gives a chance for life to be creative, as difference is creative: 'Life negates itself in literature only so that it may survive better. So that it may be better. It does not negate itself any more than it affirms itself: it differs from itself, defers itself and writes itself as difference' (WD, p. 78). In this sense, life and God are close to one another, and Derrida closes by referring to Jabès's phrase that God is 'an interrogation of God' (ibid.). The essay is signed 'Reb Rida', a playful, but also affirmative, sign of Derrida's own questionable belonging to Judaism, to which we will return.

So far, we have come across a number of references to negative theology. The most well-known of these came in the essay 'Différance', in which Derrida took pains to deny that his project bore anything more than a superficial resemblance to negative theology. The latter worked with the paradoxes of trying to say the unsayable, but its aim was fundamentally different to that of deconstruction. It is rooted in Neoplatonic philosophy, and its God is simply another version of the God of metaphysics: perfect, eternal, absolute presence. It leads the believer towards a wordless mystical union with God. Language, for negative theology, is just a ladder that gets kicked away in the end.

However, in the course of exploring other of Derrida's texts from this early period, it has become apparent that this is not the last word on either negative theology or God. For one thing, Derrida has no desire to advocate a straightforward atheism, or what he calls the 'negative atheology', which is the mirror image of negative theology. Such an atheology celebrates the absence of God at the centre of things. Derrida wants us to move beyond such obsession with the centre, to affirm the joy of becoming and play, although, even here, he doubts whether we will ever be done with the lure of presence and foundations (WD, p. 297).

There is more to Derrida's theological engagement than merely this ghost of God, however. The language of the Cabbala, Hegel's thinking of difference and negativity and Heidegger's though of Being suggest approaches to the question of God that are not just continuations of the search for foundations, authority and certainty. If it is possible for Heidegger to reclaim the language of Being in a thinking that does not suppress the time and world of existence and passion, why should the language of God languish in its unreformed state? Already we have seen how Derrida is willing to allow God and Being to question and contaminate one another, and to suggest that it is in God's difference from himself that creation comes to be.

It is not surprising, therefore, that Derrida returned to a discussion of negative theology and of the relationship between the thought of Heidegger and theology. In the next chapter, we will examine some of Derrida's later writings in which this interrogation is sustained and extended.

Chapter 4

How to Void Speaking: Derrida and Negative Theology

Derrida's negotiations with negative theology are not straightforward. The antipathy we found in the essay 'Différance' never entirely went away. However, Derrida's return to the question showed a willingness to engage with layers of the mystical tradition that could not just be written off as ontotheology.

In this sense, the writings on negative theology offer an example of Derrida's dealing with theology as a whole. In the books and essays we have looked at so far, the 'pure' philosophical meaning of the metaphysical God is always being contested by other voices. The otherness of God is staged by Derrida. In writing 'about' God and Artaud's theatre, Jabès's poetry or Levinas's encounter with the face of the Other, the texts perform a dissonant reading of theology.

Derrida's later writings on negative theology are also staged, because it is never certain whether God's name is being used or 'only' mentioned. As we will see, this indirectness is part of what Derrida wants to draw out as the promise of the negative way.

The promise and the desert

'How to Avoid Speaking: Denials' was a lecture given by Derrida in Jerusalem in 1987. He begins by once more noting the 'family resemblance' that obtains between negative theology and any discourse that (like that of *différance*) works by denying that its theme can be identified with this or that concept or entity. At the same time, by associating negative theology with the approach to a silent intuition with God, who is a Being beyond being, he draws our attention to the dissimilarity between its God and *différance*.

However, this time Derrida wants to explore further just what it is that makes negative theology such a haunting presence in his own project and anything else that resembles it. He notes that reactions to this presence often take the form of accusations that the thinker is really saying nothing. Derrida identifies three different types of this attack.

The first simply accuses the thinker in question of being a nihilist who affirms nothing, and so undermines knowledge, theology and even atheism, conceived as a rational theory. The second accusation is that the thinker speaks for nothing, or, rather speaks just for the sake of speaking. Finally, the most interesting suspicion is that when Derrida, for instance, denies that he is a negative theologian, he is betrayed by his own words. His adoption of the techniques of negation raise the possibility of 'the becoming-theological of all discourse' since 'Every negative sentence would already be haunted by God or by the name of God, the distinction between God and God's name opening up the very space of this enigma' (HAS, p. 76). God would be the reality that set in motion all negativity. Nothing, Derrida admits, could disallow such an interpretation.

In the light of this, Derrida revisits his earlier response to the charge of doing negative theology. He identifies two stages in that response. The first says simply 'No, what I write is not "negative theology"' (HAS, p. 77), because the latter always seeks a hyper-essentiality, a Being beyond being. Despite the sophistication of this type of theology, which goes beyond conventional theism and atheism, Derrida feels compelled to state that *différance* is not a unified name or concept, a presence or even a Being beyond being. It is true that *différance*, like any other word, can get caught up again in the system it seeks to destabilize – 'the onto-theological reappropriation always remains possible' – but it is no less true that *différance* points to the fact that ontotheology's 'ultimate failure is no less necessary' (HAS, p. 79). The presence or union with God that is promised by the negative way privileges a full-ness of vision and intuition that will always be suspect in the blurred eyes of deconstruction. *Différance* offers no such immediate, timeless union with the ineffable.

The second stage of Derrida's response is more constructive, for it suggests that the blanket term 'negative theology' obscures a reality that is highly complex. Perhaps there is something within it that is 'hidden, restless, diverse, and itself heterogeneous' (HAS, p. 82). If negative theology conceals such a promise, then Derrida's promise has been that he would one day return to study it with greater attention.

The reference to promising is not accidental. It leads Derrida to reflect on something that is fundamental to our experience of language. He suggests that prior to all language 'there is necessarily a commitment or a promise' (HAS, p. 82). In other words, every act of communication is already an act of promising oneself to the other, asking for their trust, implying that one will be faithful to one's word. Derrida connects this with his topic when he says that 'The experience of negative theology perhaps holds to a promise, that of the other, which I must keep because it commits me to speak where negativity ought to absolutely rarefy discourse' (HAS, p. 14). Negative theology is also a logos, a word offered to the other. What it seeks is not necessarily a supernatural being on the far side of language, but the dynamic structure of faith and commitment that sets language in motion. As Derrida asks, 'Why can't I avoid speaking unless it is because a promise has committed me even before I begin the briefest speech?' (ibid.).

The promise is spoken of in a way that previously was reserved for concepts such as *différance*, the trace, writing, where the emphasis was on rupturing, delay, death and difference. The transition to the language of promise does not deny what has gone before, but lends it a very different tonality: 'The promise of which I shall speak will have always escaped this demand of presence. It is older than I am or than we are. In fact, it renders possible every present discourse on presence' (HAS, p. 84). The promise is not secure foundation, since it is vulnerable to dislocation, misunderstanding and failure. Betrayal is always a risk. Thus, Derrida is now inscribing a structure and experience of *faith* at the origin of the world. However, that structure is always open, the origin is never simple. The experience of the promise and of faith is therefore irreducible and yet impossible, in the sense that it can never be fully present for us.

In reflecting on the title he chose for this lecture, Derrida notes that the French *Comment ne pas dire?* can mean both 'how to be silent, how not to speak?' but also 'how to avoid speaking incorrectly, how to speak well?' The impossibility and the necessity of speaking are implied. One cannot not speak (even silence has a meaning only within language), but how to avoid betraying the reality of which one speaks? This is surely a primary impulse of theology, and not only in its negative mode.

Derrida develops this thought by considering what it means to have a secret. Negative theology is often associated with the keeping of secrets in esoteric societies. Derrida quotes Pseudo-Dionysius, who advises his follower not to disclose his teachings to those who are entangled with the world of beings, and who, as a result, reduce God to the level of any other thing in the universe. There is an undoubtedly political dimension to this distinction between insiders and outsiders.

However, Derrida's interest in the secret is not in some bit of knowledge that may or may not be disclosed. Rather, the secret is that there is no secret: there is no key of absolute knowledge that will make everything clear and explain all the loose ends. The secret names what defies presence, what cannot be reduced to the concept or forced into the light of day, however bright that light.[1] The secret is not something that exists, but is the inherent incompleteness of knowledge. It opens knowledge and being to the other, to the movement of the promise and the possibility of faith. The secret is there for all to see, but it cannot be seen: 'There is no secret *as such*; I deny it' (HAS, p. 95).

Derrida does not deny that the theological 'insinuates' itself into this secret, but 'this does not mean that the secret itself is theological' (HAS, p. 95). Elsewhere, the correlation between the secret and apophatic theology is noted, but the secret is never simply caught within any determinate theological programme. Theology, in this limited sense, is always a response to a secret that has gone before it and set it in motion (ON, p. 24).

The secret denies, or better denegates itself (*Denégations* is the French subtitle of the lecture). It does not remain pure and self-enclosed. As soon as it is formulated as a secret, it has already begun to manifest itself; but as soon as it manifests itself, it is dissembled once more, because there is nothing to tell. The secret cannot be worked into the smooth dialectics of Hegelian philosophy, in which negation exists to serve a positive synthesis, a higher clarity and harmony. This secret is inextinguishable.

Derrida argued against Levinas that it was only with reference to my own ego, my own singularity that a genuine relationship with the other could be maintained. The same could be said of the secret. Only if there is this secret (which never exists as such, present and legible), only if there is something that ruptures our communion can we really communicate. And we have always started communicating. We were already promised to the other before ever we spoke a word: 'Such a reference to the other will always have taken place. Prior to every proposition and even before all discourse in general – whether a promise, prayer, praise, celebration. The most negative discourse, even beyond all nihilisms and negative dialectics, preserves a trace of the other' (HAS, p. 97).

From the perspective of a Christian mystic such as Pseudo-Dionysius, this means that God is prior to all our speech about God. Derrida translates this belief to say that God names the origin of speech, an origin that is not simple or present, but a trace: 'This is what God's name always names, before or beyond other names: the trace of the singular event that will have rendered speech possible even before it turns itself back toward – in order to respond to – this first or last reference' (HAS, p. 98). We always come on the scene too late to catch our own beginning, which has occurred in a past that was never a present: 'Language has started without us, in us and before us. This is what theology calls God, and it is necessary, it will have been necessary, to speak' (HAS, p. 99).

Derrida goes on to develop a more detailed analysis of three stages of apophatic theology: the Greek, the Christian and the Heideggerian. Each one is shown to be complex, and yet promising for an alternative thinking of transcendence.

In the Greek stage, Derrida identifies two contrasting impulses, both deriving from Plato. The first is the description of the Good as 'beyond being' (*epekeina tes ousias*). The Good transcends all notions of being, and yet, because it is still seen as the source of all that is, of light and intelligibility, it is still linked to being. The second approach to what lies beyond being comes in the dialogue *Timaeus*. Here, Plato refers to the *khora*, the receptacle or matrix in which eternal forms or essences of things are impressed by the demiurge. As Derrida reads it, this strange space is neither being nor non-being. It precedes and is radically foreign to all concepts or discourses. The *khora* is the spacing, the pure difference, within which any sort of ordered cosmos is made possible, but it is not part of that cosmos.

For Derrida, the *khora* resists being appropriated by any positive or constructive theological language. It is 'Radically nonhuman and atheological . . . it neither creates nor produces anything . . . It gives no order and makes no promise' (HAS, p. 106). The *khora* represents a singular point of resistance to any straightforwardly theological reading of ideas such as *différance*. It is always a possible way of naming the beyond of being that sets nothing positive in motion. It therefore stands in tension with Derrida's turn to the language of promise. If *khora* promises nothing, how do we reconcile this with the sense that the promise has always already begun? Do we have to choose between these interpretations of *différance*? Derrida implies not: the two are always possible, and it is in the tension between them that we are freed to experience the otherness of *différance*.

However, a contradiction remains here: is the structure of language one of promise and response, or is its relationship to its 'outside' one of pure alienation? Surely there is a danger here that the *khora* becomes a figure of the old God: unrelated and indifferent in its otherness? The turn to the language of promise does not imply any settled theological interpretation of *différance*, but it does offer an irreducibly ethical dimension to it, one that provokes not merely theoretical questioning, but questioning as a form of faith and responsibility to the other. The *khora* does nothing, it gives rise to no promise, no event. Isn't that exactly what *différance* comes to displace?

One reason Derrida invokes the notion of the *khora* is to keep a distance between his thinking and the Christian *via negativa*. Derrida locates the difference in the prayer that opens and guides the mystical path. In order to avoid saying just anything in the desert of language, cut off from all stable references, prayer is an essential address to the other. Prayer keeps faith with the other and keeps the negative theologian on track.

Derrida identifies two aspects of this prayer. First, it contains 'an address to the other as other; *for example* – I will say, at the risk of shocking – God' (HAS, p. 110). We have come across the exemplary use of God's name in previous texts. Derrida uses it to signal an otherness that comes before any theological definition, and that makes possible the thinking of God.

The second aspect of the prayer is the encomium, the celebration or praise of God. For Derrida, it is this aspect that defines and determines the direction of the prayer in a specifically theological and Christian direction. It identifies a God who is beyond being but also Trinitarian in nature. The distinction between prayer as address, and prayer as a determination of the addressee, is crucial for Derrida, because it allows him to think 'prayer in itself' as 'nothing other than the supplicating address to the other' (HAS, p. 111).

The prayer, thought separately from the encomium, is an appeal and a response to an otherness not yet defined by this or that orthodoxy. Without it, theology could not define itself, but it always resists total comprehension in any discourse. The inherent openness and ambiguity of the prayer means that Christian negative theology is both an act of deconstruction but also an attempt to arrest the play of differences in a moment of union with God. The most radical denials of God's being and essence (such as those contained in the writings of Eckhart) are both beyond and within the bounds of the theological.

The last of the three stages of negative thinking is associated with Heidegger. Derrida focuses on the text *What is Metaphysics?* and particularly the role played by anguish in opening us to an experience of negativity. This in turn allows us to experience the strangeness of Being.[2]

For Heidegger, Being is wholly other, but it is not a separately existing entity. Its transcendence is experienced by *Dasein* as a question about the Being of beings: what does it mean to be? Why is there anything rather than nothing? No merely factual or worldly answer can be given to this question, but this does not imply that there is an answer in another world apart from this one.

We have already seen that, for Heidegger, Being is dynamic, self-differentiating, dispersed in existence. It is therefore used in a very different way from the role it plays in ontotheology. However, Derrida discusses two places where Heidegger notes how problematic it still is to use the language of being.

In the first, Heidegger proposes to use the word being only 'under erasure', writing it with a cross drawn through it. The word is still legible, but it cannot be spoken in any simple way. The cross disrupts the conventional idea of being as divided into subjects and objects, captured in a philosophy of reflection. It also signals the irreducible differences (what Heidegger called the 'fourfold') that constitute reality and the point at which those differences can be gathered once more, especially in the language of poetry.

The second case of distancing himself from being comes when Heidegger suggests that if he were to write a theology, the word being would not occur within it. God and Being are kept apart, and God requires a response of faith that goes beyond philosophy. At the same time, it is through the experience of Being that we can be open to the possibility of a particular revelation. In other words, the thinking of Being gives us access to 'revealability' (*Offenbarkeit*), the condition for revelation (*Offenbarung*) to come to us and be received by us. This distinction between revealability and revelation will be important to Derrida in his later writing on religion.

Being, even in the sense given to it by Heidegger, continues to be problematic. But Heidegger's attempts to distinguish God from Being remain unstable. Even if God's essence is not thought on the basis of Being, it is only through the thinking of Being that we can encounter God.

The detailed readings of these three stages – Greek, Christian, Heideggerian – can seem obscure, and Derrida makes no systematic conclusions from them. For one thing, he is highly conscious that the lack of any consideration of Jewish and Islamic mysticism is a huge gap in what he is writing. Nevertheless, an important thread binds the stages together. Each one is divided in itself: between the notion of Good as beyond, but still linked to being, and the idea of the *khora* as foreign to all being, goodness and promise; between the prayer that is open to the other before all determination, and the encomium that determines the prayer in a specifically theological direction; between the desire to cross out or suspend the thought of Being, and the recognition that even an encounter with God still needs to move within the dimension of Being. Openness and closure, otherness and identification constantly meet and repel one another in different but related ways in these discourses.

That interminable dialogue is staged in a number of ways in Derrida's texts. One worth noting comes at the close of another examination of Heidegger, in the light of the latter's involvement with Nazism.

Spirit in flame and water

Following a number of publications in the 1980s, including the re-issuing of Heidegger's pro-Nazi Rectoral Address from 1935, it became difficult to be associated with his thought, especially as Heidegger never unambiguously disowned his Nazi connections. Derrida, as someone who clearly drew much from Heidegger's work, but who was suspected of nihilism himself, came under the microscope.

In truth, Derrida was never an uncritical devotee of Heidegger. He became increasingly concerned about the residual metaphysical humanism in the latter's work, and ways in which this could be allied to a dogmatic nationalism and even to racism. *Of Spirit: Heidegger and the Question* takes another tack: Heidegger's use of the notion of *Geist*, a concept rich in associations from Germany's philosophical past. For Derrida, Heidegger in his Nazi period abandons the subtleties of his thinking of Being, adopting an idea of Spirit that flies too close to mystical nationalist ideals of German destiny.

However, Derrida does not accept that the enormous potential of Heidegger's thought for thinking the difference of Being should all be tarred with the same brush and thrown out. In particular, he sees in Heidegger's suggestive idea of 'Spirit-in-flames' a way of thinking Spirit as always different and disseminated, owned by no one, always burning beyond itself.

At the end of the book, we are offered an unresolved conversation between a voice representing Heidegger's thinking of being and Christian theologians. The first voice proposes a 'spirituality of promise' foreign to Christianity (OS, p. 107). Echoing what is said about the promise in 'How to Avoid Speaking', such a spirituality would be a response to the experience of what is given in and through Being. As Derrida writes a little earlier, 'The call of Being – every question always already responds to it, the promise has already taken place wherever language comes' (OS, p. 94). This spirituality of the promise would be 'Origin-heterogeneous' (OS, p. 107). In other words, it would not seek to identify the source of the call and promise in any defined entity, such as God. Indeed, any such identification would undermine the radical nature of the call, bringing it back to a foundation that would annul time and difference.

The theologians respond that this spirit is not foreign to Christianity, but is its very essence. The themes used in Heidegger's philosophy hardly succeed in veiling their roots in Christian ideas of call, promise, sin, fall and resurrection. The God of 'flame and fire writing in the promise' (OS, p. 111) is none other than the God who is praised by Christians (and possibly Jews and Muslims too): a God who is not domesticated or subdued under abstract categories, a God who falls under no essence or ownership, a God who opens the future to its possibility.

Derrida imagines that Heidegger would reply that he does not mean to oppose Christianity, but 'to think that *on the basis of which all this is possible*' (OS, p. 111). This condition of possibility is not yet thinkable, not yet named in any determinate religion. It remains 'to come'. Religious ideas of God and Spirit come after the thinking of 'flame' in all its untamed risk. This mystical and poetic language of Heidegger opens out on to something unthought: not a new content, but another *way* of thinking Being as entirely other to all definable content.

Derrida gives the theologians the final word. They deny that they want something else than what Heidegger is after: the entirely other. But, crucially, they propose that the dialogue needs to keep going. The truth, we might say, lies in not letting the conversation end, not imposing upon it an arbitrary final destination, when the theme of the conversation is actually something other than a resting place or answer of that sort: 'it's enough to keep talking . . . It's enough not to interrupt the colloquium, even when it is already late. The spirit which keeps watch in returning [*en revenant*, as a ghost] will always do the rest. Through flame or ash, but as the entirely other, inevitably' (OS, p. 113). The book ends as the dialogue continues. Derrida himself forces no resolution on it.

Once again, we are brought back to the thinking of the origin that impels Derrida's work. It is striking how often the themes and dislocations of negative theology are associated with the rupture of all pure origins. Two brief examples from divergent texts can illustrate this.

In an essay on the writer Paul Valéry, Derrida discusses a text entitled 'In Praise of Water', and he comments 'To be cut off from the source, as predicted finally by "In Praise of Water," is to let oneself be multiplied or divided by the difference of the other; to cease to be (a) *self* (M, p. 277). Derrida states that his reading will emphasize the birth of language and literature from this otherness, 'a certain heterogeneity of the source: and first, there are sources, the source is other and plural' (ibid.).

Later in the essay, Derrida writes of Valéry's postulation of the pure 'I' as the source of all meaning and presence, the defining reality that depends on nothing outside itself. However, this pure 'I' is known only by its disappearance. It can never present itself: 'This source therefore has no proper meaning' (M, p. 281), it is 'always disseminated far from itself' (M, p. 283). Derrida links this explicitly to the excess signified by negative theology:

> this source is nothing, almost nothing. It would be experi-
> enced, if it were experienced, as the excess of everything
> that can be related to it. A relation of nothing to nothing,
> this relationship is barely a relationship. Imagine the God of
> negative theology attempting by himself to describe
> himself, to catch himself in the grid of a determining
> discourse: he will almost annihilate himself. (M, p. 282)

The meaning of the source is never identical with the source 'itself'. It is likened to a 'threatened God, impoverished and impo-tent by virtue of its very originality and its independence from the source' (M, p. 284).

These reflections on the origin of literature are striking and curious. They echo in advance the description of religion without religion as a 'relation without relation'. And although God is men-tioned only in passing, perhaps this is significant. If 'the Absolute is Passage', here God is known in the failure of absolute meaning, emptied out and wandering far from any unified source. The threatened God is the creative non-power of this self-annihilation. God passes out and passes on, leaving only a trace.

Memoirs of the Blind – a meditation on drawing and blindness, on the truth that escapes vision – is another text that links the trace to negative theology. Nothing belongs to the trace, nothing is assembled there. Art is a disfiguring, refusing to make present what must remain unseen.

The text is also staged as a dialogue or colloquium, no one voice able to state directly what is seen in the work of art.

One voice asks if it is by chance that we are reminded of 'The withdrawal of the One whom one must not look in the face, or represent, or adore, that is, idolize under the *traits* or guise of the icon? The One whom it is even dangerous to name by one or the other of his proper names?' (MB, p. 54). The 'God-memory' of this kind of drawing 'is theological through and through, to the point, sometimes included, sometimes excluded, where the self-eclipsing *trait* cannot even be spoken about, cannot even say itself in the present, since it is not gathered, since it does not gather itself, into any present' (ibid.). Here too, the theological wears different guises. It is the discourse of presence and authority that excludes the heretical and fixes God's image or being. It is also the medium of the trace that eclipses itself, disperses itself to the four winds.

Art, no more than speculative philosophy, can produce the perfect meaning or vision of truth. The self-portrait, apparently the most immediate and truthful of all, reveals itself as a fiction, always dependent upon a moment of blindness, the separation of self from self, which can never close its own circle of meaning. With regard to the self portrait, Derrida writes that 'In the beginning, at the origin, there was ruin. At the origin comes ruin; ruin comes to the origin, it is what first comes and happens to the origin, in the beginning. With no promise of restoration' (MB, p. 65). This ruin does not lead to the death of art. On the contrary, it is what enables art to appear. The disfigured and divided figure is all we have of the image of God.

Is there a promise here, where the promise of restoration is exhausted? Does something offer itself to be saved in the self-annihilation and withdrawal of God?

Saving the name

'Sauf le Nom' is written in dialogue form between two otherwise unidentified voices. The text explicitly draws attention to its form at the outset:

> – . . .
>
> – Sorry, but more than one, it is always necessary to be more than one in order to speak, several voices are necessary for that . . .

 −Yes, granted, and par excellence, let us say exemplarily,
 when it's a matter of God . . . (ON, p. 35)

The text begins with a hiatus. It is as if we are coming into a conversation that has already begun. Language requires more than
one voice, and the language of negative theology in particular is
plural: 'The voice multiplies itself, dividing within itself: it says one
thing and its contrary, God that is without being or God that (is)
beyond being' (ON, p. 35). The text is not content with describing
this plurality; it performs it.

Apophatic theology is riven with contradictions. It cannot help
but be divided in this way, since it is not a discourse that obeys the
laws governing statements about particular things within the
world. Such is its paradoxical nature that it 'at times so resembles
a profession of atheism as to be mistaken for it'. It announces the
'end of monologism' (ON, p. 35).

Sauf is itself a divided word.[3] It can mean 'except', 'save' (with
connotations of rescuing, religious salvation), 'safe'. Saving the
name of God might mean rescuing it from oblivion, or leaving it
aside. It might mean redeeming it by treating it as an exception to
ordinary language. The duality plays itself out through the voices
of negative theology.

In one register, apophatics is prepared to abandon all positive
predication, to let go of all the names of God precisely in order to
save God from being reduced to the level of other entities. In the
process, God is elevated to a higher degree of being. However, this
project always flirts with godlessness, the dispersal of God into
nothingness.

Consider an exchange from near the beginning of 'Sauf le
nom'. One of the voices asks 'If on the one hand apophasis inclines
almost toward atheism, can't one say that, on the other hand or
thereby, the extreme and most consequent forms of dedicated
atheism will have always testified to the most intense desire of
God?' (ON, p. 36). The answer given is 'yes and no'. Apophasis can
be identified with the desire of God, and given direction and
definition by that desire. Or it can remain 'foreign to all desire, in
any case to every anthropotheomorphic form of desire' (ON,
p. 37). In other words, by addressing the wholly other, the negative
way could break the link between God and humanity, leaving

nothing that could be desired. The first voice replies that this tension is not an either/or; it is built into the nature of desire as it reaches out to the other. Such desire must also renounce itself to avoid diminishing or capturing the other in false categories.

The dialogue continues with an exploration of the ambiguity of the phrase 'desire of God': is it my desire for God, or God's desire for me? The origin and end of this desire is undecidable. Crucially, it is argued that we have no self-definition, no self-awareness before this desire; it is always at work in us.

As we follow the conversation, the sense unfolds that negative theology is a matter of testimony and prayer and this means that it must always have non-knowledge or unknowing at its heart. That unknowing is radical and disturbing, because it cannot guarantee the outcome of desire, or that God's name will remain 'safe'. The witness turns both to God and to the recipient of the witness, and it is no longer absolutely certain that God and the other person can be clearly distinguished. Prayer or testimony is offered to the other without determining in advance who that other may be. Recalling Augustine's *Confessions*, we read that 'Confession does not consist in making known – and thereby it teaches that the transmission of positive knowledge is not essential' (ON, p. 39). Something other than knowledge is at stake in this form of religious language, something noncognitive, but not merely a projection of human desire.

The text continues by commenting upon the poetical writings of Angelus Silesius, a seventeenth-century German mystic. Silesius pushes the paradoxes of the negative way as far as they can go, stating that '*To become Nothing is to become God*'. The proximity between God and Nothing, between becoming oneself and becoming God is an impossible thought. And yet it is seen as 'strangely familiar to the experience of what is called deconstruction' (ON, p.43). As we have seen, deconstruction is distinguished from any programme, method or technique. Rather it is 'the very experience of the (impossible) possibility of the impossible, of the most impossible, a condition that deconstruction shares with the gift, the "yes," the "come," decision, testimony, the secret, etc. And perhaps death' (ibid.).

This list of names for the experience of the impossible contains some already familiar to us from Derrida's work and some that we will look at in more detail in the following chapters. What is important is the thread that binds them together. Deconstruction is bound up with affirmation, singularity, otherness, not simply as an intellectual reflection or method of interpretation, but as a witness to an experience that defies knowledge and mastery. From this point, taking into account all the reservations Derrida has expressed about the dimension of essentialism that still shapes it, what is said of negative theology is also said about deconstruction. That is a significant shift in Derrida's reception of theology.

This is possible because the traumas and tension of negative theology are those of language itself: 'Isn't it also what questions and casts suspicion on the very essence or possibility of language?' (ON, p. 48). Apophasis exceed language, but it remains a language. And so it bears witness to what makes meaning possible and impossible at the same time.

Apophasis, like God, is always becoming nothing: 'negative theology means (to say) very little, almost nothing, perhaps something other than something. Whence its inexhaustible exhaustion' (ON, p. 50). Using language with a striking Christian resonance, this is referred to as the '*Kenōsis* of discourse' (ibid.). Ironically, it is when negative theology takes on its most empty, contentless and non-dogmatic destiny that it resonates with the specifically Christian theme of the self-emptying of God in Christ.

Negative theology speaks by both belonging and not belonging to meaningful language. Its voices are plural, a broken dialogue of radical critique and dogmatic assurance (ON, pp. 66–67). These voices are not wholly distinct from one another. As we have just seen, traces of the Christian narrative are interwoven with an emptiness supposedly foreign to theology. Negative theology testifies, bears witness to what happens when the limits of language are tested and transgressed (ON, p. 54). 'God' functions not merely as the dogmatic end point, the guarantee of the truth founded upon immediate intuition of the divine. After all, negative theology is also an exposé of the inadequacy of such ideas of fullness of intuited meaning, as they are found in contemporary form in phenomenology. In this light, God takes on a very different meaning: '"God" is the name of this bottomless collapse, of this endless desertification of language' (ON, pp. 55–56).

This is not cognitive language, but the language of testimony: 'the trace of this wounded writing that bears the stigmata of its own proper inadequation, signed, assumed, denied' (ON, p. 61). Again we find a reference to the woundedness of Christ at the heart of this most vulnerable and uncertain discourse. Throughout 'Sauf le nom', Derrida tries to keep dogma and deconstruction apart, but their voices cannot wholly be separated, and something of each contaminates the other.

Near the close of the essay, Derrida returns to the notion of God as exemplar. Is God an example of absolute otherness, or the other way round? Can we ever decide this question? Does it matter? For Derrida, it is possible to say that 'Any other is totally other [*Tout autre est tout autre*]' (ON, p. 76), a formula that we will see explored to its limits in *The Gift of Death*. This otherness escapes the bounds of God's unique name, and is found in other people, in what we label 'animals', in all those who call out of us an infinite responsibility. This otherness is both contained within and yet eludes the idiom of Christian revelation. It makes it possible for that very particular tradition to be translated and come into dialogue with others.

The essay notes the tendency within apophatic writings to leave or abandon God in order to let God be (himself). Angelus Silesius uses the German word *Gelassenheit* to signify this movement. The name of God effaces itself, opens itself to being substituted. The process by which it dies is the process by which it lives on. The dereliction of God is also what releases a kind of bliss: not an escape into eternal beatification, but a return to the play of the world and the innocence of becoming. Something of the complexity of this thought is indicated by one of the voices' comments upon Silesius's poetry: 'The abandonment *of* this *Gelassenheit*, the abandonment *to* this *Gelassenheit* does not exclude pleasure or enjoyment; on the contrary, it gives rise to them. It opens the play *of* God (of God with God, of God with self and creation): it opens passion to the enjoyment *of* God' (ON, p. 79).

Again, the ambiguity of this 'of' is underlined. Do we enjoy God or does God enjoy us? Is it God 'himself' who arouses our passion or God as an effect of the play of difference? For Derrida, such questions remain unanswered: 'The desire of God, God as the other name of desire, deals in the desert with radical atheism' (ON, p. 80). Is the other a fount of meaning and promise, or is there only the alien and arid *khora*?

This oscillation between construction and deconstruction is endless. For Derrida, it is also the oscillation between desiring a universal community and language, and the desire to keep the secret safe (ON, p. 83). As we have seen, the 'secret' is what preserves otherness and singularity from being assimilated into the mass or the unblinking gaze of the public. In the essay 'Passions', published alongside 'Sauf le nom' in its English translation, Derrida affirms that the secret has an 'apophatic aspect', but this cannot be reduced to that of a negative theology (ON, p. 24). It is always a matter of testifying to what cannot be brought without loss into the light of knowledge: 'We testify [*témoignons*] to a secret that is without content, without a content separable from its performative experience, from its performative tracing' (ibid.). This secret, then, is not merely nothing. It is something that makes a difference as it is experienced, even if that experience is never fixed, never has the character of a certainty. It is always 'in the trace' of the other, an experience of responsibility, promise and desire that exceeds any programme or rule. At the same time, this secret preserves a solitude or singularity that can never be translated into words, or made public property. For Derrida, this solitude would not be the denial of community, but its essential condition. Put at its most paradoxical: a refusal to respond is the condition that makes responsibility to the other possible, because it alone preserves the difference between self and other (ON, p. 31). Ultimately, this lack of responsiveness can be linked to death, and we see again the way Derrida connects responsibility, selfhood and mortality.

Translation: a machine for making God

Negative theology is a wounded language, a self-emptying logos, a writing that bears the stigmata of its own dereliction and failure. Are these merely Christian glosses on an underlying non-theological structure of differences, or is there something essentially Christian that marks the story Derrida is telling?

The question itself may be misplaced. As we have seen, Derrida's thinking calls into question any idea of simple origins. Once such origins are complicated, the absolute division between the ideal and the real, or the transcendental and the empirical, also flounders. He is not seeking an alternative starting point or foundation, but troubling the motivation behind such a search.

Much turns on the distinction, to which we referred earlier, between revelation and revealability, and the question as to whether one can be translated into the other without remainder. To remind ourselves: revelation concerns the specific, historical event and content of something being communicated to us. Revealability is about the conditions that make any such specific revelation possible in the first place. In a sense, it is another way of stating the difference between, on the one hand, the singular, the particular and the empirical, and, on the other hand, the universal and the ideal.

In *Politics of Friendship*, Derrida poses the issue in this way:

> a thought (ontological or meta-ontological) of conditions
> of possibility and structures of revealability, or of the
> opening to truth, may well appear legitimately and meth-
> odologically anterior to gaining access to all singular events
> of revelation . . . 'In fact', 'in truth', it would be only the
> event of revelation that would open – like a breaking in,
> making it possible after the event – the field of the possible
> in which it appeared to spring forth, and for that matter
> actually did so. The event of revelation would reveal not
> only this or that – God, for example – but revealability
> itself. By the same token, this would forbid us saying 'God,
> for example'. (PF, p. 18)

Derrida's point is closely related to Karl Barth's doctrine of revelation. For Barth, the idea that God's revelation could be prepared for, that it had found any natural point of contact waiting for it within the world or humanity, would be a contradiction of the infinite qualitative difference between God and creature. God would simply be known according to our pre-existing forms of knowledge, and therefore his image would be corrupted, turned into an idol. For Barth, it was axiomatic that only God could reveal God to us in an unprecedented act. That act of revelation creates in us the capacity to receive it, a capacity that was not in existence prior to God's initiative. God, therefore, defines himself, and cannot be reduced to the status of being an example of anything else.

Barth's opponents counter that this undermines the integrity of humanity's response to God. Unless we are able in some way to recognize revelation when it comes to us, we are unable to receive and respond to that event. Barth's strong emphasis on the vertical breaking in of revelation as an absolute surprise stands in tension with the Christian doctrine that the world is and continues to be God's good creation. However corrupt our will and intellect may be, they still retain some vestige of perception and judgement that is at least able to prepare for the possibility of revelation when it comes.

Derrida seems to affirm different aspects of each of these two strategies. On the one hand, he upholds the unpredictability of the future and of the event. Nothing can truly happen without an openness to what is to come that exceeds any set of conditions, any law or programme. On the other hand, if we are truly open to what is to come then we cannot confine it within the limits of one institutionally defined set of dogmas about the content of revelation. There is something in the event of revelation that escapes such constriction, opening it to other interpretations and voices.

Revelation is both translatable and untranslatable at the same time. Recognizing this paradox as something to be lived rather than solved is what disrupts the Aristotelian idea that we can only form friendships of like with like. Perhaps there is a friendship that truly opens us to the other. If so, it can only be experienced because otherness is already at the heart of oneself. This otherness 'would break all ipseity apart in advance' (PF, p. 24), ipseity being the strong sense of identity with self that seems to be the foundation for knowledge of others and the world.

For Derrida, such self-identity is the death of relationship, but he does not appeal to a wholly external cause in order to break it open. He is suggesting that, in order for the event of revelation to surprise and convert us to the other, there must always have been the possibility of otherness lodged within our most intimate sense of self. There is no original self-identity for us who live in language and therefore within time and difference. As Derrida points out elsewhere, 'The identity of a language can only affirm itself as identity to itself by opening itself to the hospitality of a difference from itself or of a difference with itself' (A, p. 10).

Negative theology bears witness to this universal structure, which is at the same time a structure that preserves our singularity and the singularity of every other, of every event. It is a structure that cancels itself, a condition of possibility that is also a condition of the impossible.

The question of this impossible but necessary translation takes centre stage in Derrida's reading of another story of origins, that of the Tower of Babel and the confusion of languages. On the surface, this is a narrative in which the sovereign God punishes his creatures for their pride in trying to reach up to the heavens and knock him off his throne. By dispersing humanity and multiplying their tongues, God secures his uniqueness. In 'Des Tours de Babel', written in 1980, Derrida reads the text differently: as a story about God's own proper name being divided and disseminated: 'And the war that he declares has first raged within his name: divided, bifid, ambivalent, polysemic: God deconstructing' (AR, p. 108). The God of the text still bears within his name a pagan plurality ('Let us descend . . .') and the effect of scattering humanity is also to make the translation of God's name and nature unavoidable.

Derrida notes the ironies of the story. The idealistic and universal dream of the tower builders is also an act of aggrandizement and empire building that would colonize all reality. The aggressive act of a jealous God also makes possible the labour of translation and respect for differences. Derrida is able to depict God divided in his nature, pleading for the translation of his name even as he forbids it: 'God weeps over his name' (AR, p. 118). This experience of radical otherness is not something that happens to God, an accident or contingent consequence of creation. It is God deconstructing (himself?). God's own ipseity is broken open from the first.

The sacred text is exemplary for all meaning. It demands translation, otherwise it would remain inaccessible. However, it must also preserve its own unique untranslatability, without which it becomes something merely formal and empty (AR, p. 132). Meaning demands this essential lack of meaning, just as responsibility demands a lack of responsiveness. Without it, nothing is said, nothing new is ever communicated.

Derrida has already drawn attention to the ways in which negative theology can become a formal, mechanical operation, something done by rote or imitation, lacking any real fullness of intuition at its heart. And yet what seems like a failure of negative theology is also its promise. This emptiness and formalization is not foreign to what apophatics is 'about'. It offers an opening to the other before the other is determined by merely human prejudices. Revealability and revelation need each other, to avoid lapsing into dead abstraction and overbearing dogmatism.

The question appears again in the 1996 essay 'Faith and Knowledge', which is subtitled 'The Two Sources of "Religion" at the Limits of Reason Alone'. Taken as a whole, the title recalls three other classic philosophical reflections on religion: Hegel's *Faith and Knowledge*; Kant's *Religion Within The Limits of Mere Reason*; and Bergson's *The Two Sources of Religion and Morality*. In different ways, each of these works tries to distinguish between the essential and inessential aspects of religion, in the quest for a philosophically defensible and rational faith, which is not weighed down by merely parochial and cultural beliefs and forms of expression.

Derrida's own text deals with issues of calculability and technology, which are at once so alien to religion and yet so much bound up with it. It is divided into fifty-two segments, as if it followed an arbitrary mechanical code. Its own form is therefore a reflection upon both the inevitability of machine-like repetition in all our language of ethics and religion, even as they deal with what is incalculable and wholly other.

In his analysis of the so-called return of religion, Derrida notes how this abstract term is used to cover a hugely diverse set of phenomena. He argues for the impossibility of defining it in any closed or rigid way. Nevertheless, he risks his own generalization by asserting that 'Religion is **the response**' (AR, p. 64). In other words, religion has to do with our address and responsibility to the other. Seen in this way, there is nothing that is unrelated to religion, no purely secular space of morality, law or politics.

Every oath, everything that binds us to the other, produces (as if mechanically) the presence of the deity. At the same time, God remains a witness, an example of the absolute other, undetermined by any particular religious discourse: 'God: the witness as "nameable-unnameable," present-absent witness of every oath or of every possible pledge' (AR, p. 65).

No simple historical story of secularization can comprehend this, whether it is conceived as a progress towards light or a fall into darkness. In the contemporary age, the duality becomes explicit in the constitution of religions themselves. Derrida draws on the distinction of religious types made by his philosophical predecessors, but with a twist. In his version, there are two experiences that come together in what is called religion.

The first is that of faith or belief, of the testimony that cannot be reduced to knowledge. This is something Derrida takes to be a part of every act of language: when I open my mouth to speak, I am asking for you to believe me and trust my words. It need not be part of any explicitly religious discourse.

The second experience is that of the holy, the safe and unscathed. Religion always seeks to secure its own immunity from what is profane, subject to error and decay. The holy remains separate from the world, untouched and uncontaminated in its purity.

Derrida argues that these two 'veins' of religion need to be understood as distinct, although in practice they always occur together. One result of this is the 'autoimmune' reaction of religions to the modern world, in which the means used by religion to propagate and preserve itself are the very things that undermine its uniqueness, much as some viruses cause the immune system to attack the body they are meant to protect. Modern fundamentalisms use technology, for instance, to present themselves and wage war upon secularism and false religions. However, their message is inevitably contaminated by the medium they use, making it into something that can be packaged, repeated, consumed and re-imagined far away from its original context. The pure and sacred space, experience or word is transmitted by means that are defined by mechanical repetition. There is no clear line between the undefiled sanctuary and the profane world of mass communication.

Technology may have transformed this communication, but the issue has always been there for any religion that tries to hold on both to its singular uniqueness and its drive to spread its message to other contexts.

Derrida again refers to the division between revelation and revealability in this context. Is revealability a structure that exists independent of all particular religious expressions and claims? Or does the event of revelation create a new situation out of nothing, making itself possible in its own act of communication? Derrida does not want to lose either end of this *aporia* (the blocked way that one must pass through in order to reach a destination). Faith in the event, faith in the other, goes hand in hand with repetition and translation: 'No faith, therefore, nor future, without everything technical, automatic, machine-like supposed by itera-bility' (AR, p. 83).

Again, we are brought back to the origin, only to be repelled. At the origin of faith there is repetition. Faith cannot articulate itself, cannot even exist without this law of iteration displacing and disrupting the origin since before the beginning. Now, how-ever, Derrida's attention has become much more strongly turned to the other pole of the beginning: towards the future, towards what is to come. As we follow his language shifting from the ques-tion of Being to the promise of language, so this openness to the advent of what is new emerges more insistently in his work. As we will see, it is a trend that is associated in 'Faith and Knowledge' with the messianic, although this is a strange messianism. For one thing, it expects no actual Messiah, it envisages no end point, no guaranteed outcome for our hopes. And it always lives in tension with the thinking of the *khora*, which also returns to haunt this discussion of religion and its other.

Previously, we have noted the strange presence of Christian imagery in Derrida's discussions of negative theology. However, such imagery always tended towards its own self-emptying, as it strayed away from all dogmatic anchorage. We need also to pay attention to the equally unsettling presence of Jewish themes and images in Derrida's texts, which work to disrupt the Christian–Hegelian notion that the final revelation is embodied in the God–man, that in Christ salvation is achieved once and for all, that history now has an assured goal that will result in unambiguous restoration of peace and the expulsion of any evil that remains foreign to peace. This will lead us into a better understanding of why Derrida employs messianic language, even as he keeps his distance from religion, and continues to deal in the desert with radical atheism.

Chapter 5

Messianism and the Other to Come

Columns and cuts: the God of circumcision

The risk, then, is the Jewish reading.

(Gl, p. 84a)[1]

In *Glas*, Derrida stages a deconstruction of Hegel's philosophy of religion. It is well known that Hegel characterized Judaism as a religion of alienation. The God of the Jews was distant, a lawgiver, an unseen commanding voice. In the Temple, the Holy of Holies was empty. No representation of God was possible. While this was a necessary advance on religions that objectified God in a variety of earthly forms and images, it was still a stage that had to be overcome. God and human beings needed to be reconciled, not just kept apart. Judaism's unhappy alienation pointed forwards to its fulfilment and overcoming in the Christian doctrine of the incarnation, the joining of God and man. As Derrida puts it, 'The irruption of the infinite, then of reason, rages like a passion in the Jewish destiny. But the irruption remains abstract and desert; it does not incarnate itself, does not concretely, actually unite itself to the forms of understanding, of imagination, of sensibility' (Gl, p. 47a).

Hegel's portrayal of Judaism is a caricature, standing in continuity with a Christian history of supercessionism. Nevertheless, Derrida uses it against him. Judaism becomes the name of an otherness that resists being incorporated into the system of Hegelian philosophy or Christian theology. Hegel's Trinity is mirrored by his idealization of the (holy) family, in which consciousness is relieved of its isolation. Throughout *Glas*, the bonds of the natural family, of the Trinity and of the union of God and man come unstuck.

It is significant that *Glas* is written as two separate columns, one on Hegel and the other on the poet and thief Jean Genet. Genet's criminality and homosexuality set him apart from the Hegelian ideal. At the same time, that ideal is itself undermined by its inability to integrate all of reality. At various times in *Glas*, therefore, it is the Jew, the woman, the sister, the homosexual, the thief and the bastard child (of Hegel's own imperfect family) who disrupts the system. At one point, Derrida states that 'If God is (probably) a man in speculative dialectics, the godness of God – the irony that divides him and makes him come off his hinges – the infinite disquiet of his essence is (if possible) woman(ly)' (Gl, p. 188a).

The self-division of God, the 'disquiet' of God's essence, recalls the Kabbalistic motif that Derrida explored in his essays on Jabès. The association of the figure of woman and of the Jew with what is marginal and other to the system carries its own risks, of course. It can turn them into ciphers for what is alien and excluded, while leaving the oppressive structures of patriarchy and anti-Semitism untouched. It does little to articulate the real embodied experiences of women and Jews in their diversity.[2]

Given the risk of the Jewish and/or 'womanly' reading, it is important to understand the strategic ruse that is being pursued. Derrida is seeking to disturb classic texts and themes of Western metaphysics from within: 'Isn't there always an element excluded from the system that assures the system's space of possibility?' (Gl, p.162a). By exploring the ways in which Jews, for instance, have been defined by the dominant tradition, he can identify the instability of that tradition. The point is not to confirm the system's interpretation, but to call into question the whole governing logic of centres and margins, insiders and outsiders. If this is done, a space is opened in which the particular others can speak and be heard in their singularity.

The form of these texts is as important as their content. In this light, the division of *Glas* into two columns echoes the scrolls of the Torah, separated in order to be legible during the synagogue service. Describing the service, the scrolls lifted high, visible yet inaccessible, Derrida comments:'Maybe the children who watched the pomp of this celebration, even more those who could lend it a hand, dream about for a long time after, in order to organize all the pieces and scenes of their lives' (Gl, p. 241b). Asking himself what he is doing by recalling this scene, he answers that he is working on the 'origin of literature. Between the two' (ibid.).

The themes that we have been following – the dispersal of languages, God's self-differing, the legibility and illegibility of the revealed law – come together near the end of *Dissemination*, as Derrida discusses the novels of Phillipe Sollers and the way in which they show that any presence or sense of self is always preceded by a text, a web of differences older than consciousness. The symbolism of the glass, transparent column is used by Sollers as an image of the column of a text, always reflecting and dividing the self. Derrida associates this column with a familiar scriptural image, to which we have already referred:

> It is a Tower of Babel in which multiple languages and
> forms of writing bump into each other or mingle with
> each other, constantly being transformed and engendered
> through their most unreconcilable otherness to each other,
> an otherness which is strongly affirmed, too, for plurality
> here is bottomless and is not lived as negativity, with any
> nostalgia for a lost unity. (D, p. 341)

Derrida draws a parallel with 'the ungraspable column of air in the Zohar' (D, p. 342), one of the major Kabbalistic texts, and thus with 'the *zimzum*, the crisis of God, the "drama of God" through which God goes out of himself and determines himself' (D, p. 344). Sollers also uses the imagery of fire, both the fire that consumes and that which is creative, the original fire that is never gathered in some 'focal hearth'. Derrida again links this with a mystical Jewish motif in which the written Torah is only an incomplete revelation of God's will, which is spun out endlessly into the realms of commentary: 'The fires of the Torah, the black fire and the white fire: the white fire, a text written in letters that are still invisible, becomes readable in the black fire of the oral Torah' (D, p. 343).

Beyond the immediate context of an interpretation of Sollers, these references have a larger significance for Derrida's work. The ambiguity of God's name and what it reveals is exposed starkly in the text of Jewish mysticism: 'Indeed, reduced to its textuality, to its numerous plurivocality, absolutely disseminated, the Kabbalah, for example, evinces a kind of atheism, which, read in a certain way – or just simply *read* – it has doubtless always carried within it' (D, p. 344). No eschaton, no fully gathered end point of resolution and meaning can ever be achieved, without the worst possible violence: 'to the extent that meaning presents itself, gathers itself together, says itself, and is able to stand there, it erases difference and casts it aside' (D, p. 351). The dream of metaphysics is disrupted by the column, which has no being, and which interrupts the circular, harmonious rhythm of suffocating closure that Derrida detects in Hegel's dialectics, Freud's Oedipus complex and the Christian doctrine of the Trinity (D, p. 352).

The column, which escapes being and the totalizing ambitions of ontotheology, undoubtedly has phallic overtones. However, if this is so, it is not the power of the erect penis that is envisaged, but a wounded vulnerability. Derrida notes the imagery of cuts, and scissions that is also at play in Sollers' work, associating it with castration, and a fullness of meaning that is never present (D, pp. 300–302). The pen, like the knife, has always incised the paper: writing has always begun, and 'Presence is never present' (D, p. 303).

In a text on the poetry of Paul Celan, this cut is related to that of circumcision, via a meditation on the paradoxical nature of dates. Circumcision happens only once. It is an unrepeatable wound. The question is: can it therefore be dated? Does it belong to a time that can be measured?

Derrida elucidates this with reference to poetry. The poem must both preserve and efface its date, that is, its particular origin. If it is to work as poetry, it must have its own singularity, an absolutely unique voice. However, if the poem is to be read by others, accessible at dates far distant from its own, it must also make an effort to universalize itself: 'One must, while preserving its memory, speak the date, that is to say, efface it, make it readable and audible beyond its singularity' (Sh, p. 311). The date is compared to a cut in the body of the poem, which 'begins in the wounding of its date' (Sh, p. 317). In a phrase whose significance will become clearer further on, we read that 'The date is a specter' (ibid.). It comes back to us as a spectre, because it can never return as fully present and alive, yet return it must. Using imagery drawn from Celan's poetry, Derrida affirms that this is the fragile memory of a past that can never be present: 'what must henceforth commemorate itself is the annihilation itself of the date, a kind of nothing – or ash' (Sh, p. 318).

The date is in turn linked with the Shibboleth. In Judges 12, after the defeat of Ephraim by Gilead, the surviving Ephraimites try to escape by crossing the Jordan. The Gileadites set up checkpoints, and devise a linguistic test to determine who of those crossing the river belongs to Ephraim. Each person is asked to say the word 'Shibboleth'. Because of their dialect, the Ephraimites are only able to pronounce it 'Sibboleth'. Betrayed by the difference of language, they are put to death.

For Derrida, the significance of the story lies in the fact that a difference that is meaningless in itself is actually crucial for making meaning possible. It marks the difference that divides the origin: 'there is no one meaning, no single originary meaning, from the moment there is a date and a *Shibboleth*' (Sh, p. 323). The shibboleth is a mark of difference and singularity. It resists translation, because it is not a concept or piece of knowledge, but a difference that has to be enacted: 'A *Shibboleth* is untranslatable, not simply because of some semantic secret, but by virtue of that in it which forms the cut of a non-signifying difference in the body of the (written or oral) mark' (Sh, p. 324). Derrida is well aware that this mark of difference can also become the excuse for the worst forms of racism and exclusion (as evidenced by the story in which it appears).

Singularity is always at risk precisely because it must always be emptied out into repetition if it is to be understood and remembered:

A date marks itself and becomes readable only in freeing itself from the singularity which it nonetheless recalls . . . So that, commemorating what may always be forgotten in the absence of a witness, the date is exposed in its very essence or destination to annihilation, threatened in its very readability; it risks the annulment of what it saves. (Sh, p. 329)

We are drawn again to 'the essence without essence of ash' that appears often in Celan's poetry. Ash is the trace, fragile, almost nothing, of what has been consumed, and Derrida is mindful of the resonance this has with the consuming fires of the Holocaust. It is the very fragility of life that makes such evil possible.

It is here that Derrida find a surprising role for religion, in blessing or commemorating this ash, all that remains of the other: 'perhaps because it is here, quite simply, that religion begins, in the blessing of dates, of names and of ashes' (Sh, p. 330). Religion is primarily not supernatural reassurance, absolute truth or idealized community, but the witness to the other that asks for faith, not knowledge.

In this text at least, 'religion' does not seem to be that of Christianity, but a certain form of Judaism. Derrida argues that 'Formally, at least, the affirmation of Judaism has the same structure as that of the date' (Sh, p. 337). This is so because 'The Jew is the other who has no essence . . . The Jew, the name Jew, is a *Shibboleth*' (Sh, p. 338). Despised by supercessionist Christianity and assimilated by Hegelian dialectics, the Jew's outsider status returns to haunt the totalizing ambitions of the system. The Jew proclaims a religion at once universal and yet tied to an untranslatable singular history.

In a sense, therefore, all poets are Jewish, outsiders to the system, witnesses to a singular yet universal truth. What is proper to Judaism is circumcised, and thus opened, displaced: 'Anyone or no one may be Jewish. No one is (not) circumcised; it is no one's circumcision' (Sh, p. 341). The cut is also the opening of a door to the stranger, a wound that allows the communication of heart to heart: 'No one's circumcision, the word's circumcision by the incision of Nothing in the circumcised heart of the other, of this one, of you' (Sh, p. 345).

Again we must note the danger inherent in this language of romanticizing the wandering Jew, while simultaneously robbing real Jews of their flesh and blood reality, their own demand for a settled land. Beyond acknowledging the 'terrifying political ambiguity' of the state of Israel (Sh, p. 338), Derrida does not attempt to resolve this dilemma (and we must remember that this essay is primarily a commentary on the poetry of Celan). He insists on the need for a dislocation of essences and identities, even though this risks the assimilation and worse of singularity. Without the openness to the other, identity simply becomes an excuse for opposition, suppression, violence and extermination: the interminable clash of closed identities. Circumcision leaves its mark. It defines us, but not through the possession of some thing, meaning or object. It defines us through dispossession. The specific mark of the Jew thus becomes readable as both the deconstruction of all closed identities and the affirmation of others in all their particularity. That is the risk of the Jewish reading.

The impossible future

In *Archive Fever*, Derrida discusses the writings of Yosef Yerushalmi, and particularly the latter's critique of Freud from a Jewish perspective. Derrida writes that, for Yerushalmi, there is a hope 'proper' to Jewishness that is not defeated by Freud's oedipal pessimism. Beyond any specific religious belief, this would be a 'the opening of a relation to the future, the experience of the future' (AF, p. 72). The turn to an unremembered past, to the cut of circumcision, to the date of the poem that could only become readable even as it is effaced – this loss of a pure and absolute origin is also the possibility of a future.

Judaism, of course, is often viewed (if not caricatured) as a religion of Law. Doctrine is less important than the living of the Law, in all its grandeur, but in all its arbitrariness as well. Is this just a turning to the past, the exclusion of hope in the future based on a dead letter, as Christian supercessionism might suppose?

Although it is not an essay on Judaism per se, it is worth recalling Derrida's seminal piece on legality, 'Force of Law. The "Mystical Foundation of Authority"'. Derrida's argument is that the foundation of a law or legal system must by its very nature fall outside the law it constitutes. This origin is neither legal nor illegal: it asserts itself. There is therefore a necessary violence that founds the law:

> Since the origin of authority, the foundation or ground,
> the position of the law can't by definition rest on anything
> but themselves, they are themselves a violence without

ground. Which is not to say that they are in themselves unjust, in the sense of 'illegal'. They are neither legal nor illegal in their founding moment. They exceed the opposition between founded and unfounded, or between any foundationalism or anti-foundationalism. (FL, p. 14)

Derrida's intention is not to relativize or debunk the idea of law. Law is needed in order to restrain violence. It is public, calculable, regular. However, the fact that it depends upon a forgotten moment outside its system shows that it is also unstable, subject to critique. This is not a counsel of despair, but of hope. Law points beyond itself to justice, by which Derrida has in mind an incalculable affirmation of and hospitality for the other. Derrida goes as far as to say 'Justice in itself, if such a thing exists outside or beyond law, is not deconstructible. No more than deconstruction itself, if such a thing exists. Deconstruction is justice' (FL, pp. 14–15). Remember that deconstruction is not the method or possession of any particular school, much less of Derrida himself. It is another name for the movement of differences, what it makes possible, and what it makes impossible. It is respect for the singularity of the other, who cannot be reduced to part of a system, whose nature cannot be defined in advance according to a fixed rule. In its purity, it can never be achieved or come to rest, because any resting point is partial, and excludes some possibilities or perspectives. However, this does not devalue it or make it unreal: 'Justice is an experience of the impossible' (FL, p. 16). An *experience*: not an intuition, not a comprehension, but an experience nonetheless.

Without this experience of the impossible, Derrida argues, all we have are fixed laws, essences and natures. Nothing new can happen. We and others are defined wholly by the system that consumes us. The Law that we need for our peace and well-being can become the embodiment of the worst violence. That is why the experience of justice needs to be kept alive:

Law (*droit*) is not justice. Law is the element of calculation, and it is just that there be law, but justice is incalculable, it requires us to calculate with the incalculable; and aporetic experiences are the experiences, as improbable as they are necessary, of justice, that is to say of moments in which the decision between just and unjust is never insured by a rule. (Ibid.)

Without the element of the incalculable, there could be no real responsibility. Faced with a choice, we would just consult the appropriate rule that told us what to do. We would become people who just followed orders: 'A decision that didn't go through the ordeal of the undecidable would not be a free decision, it would only be the programmable application or unfolding of a calculable process' (FL, p. 24). An essay on the unremembered violence that founds the law has become something else: an argument for the impossible experience that enables us to be free, responsible to the other and open to a 'relation to the future'. Why the future? Because without justice, there would only be sameness, the end of history. There would just be one thing after another. Justice, which disrupts all origins and all presence, makes a future possible: 'Justice as the experience of absolute alterity is unpresentable, but it is the chance of the event and the condition of history' (FL, p. 27).

There is a hope at work (and at play) here. However, Derrida refuses to assimilate it to any determinate messianic promise. Rather, it is what makes those messianisms possible. It is the indeterminate opening to the future to what is to come (the French for the future, *l'avenir*, contains within it *venir*, the verb 'to come') that Derrida believes underlies or impels particular forms and projects of hope and expectation. Deconstructive justice gives life to hope, but it refuses to be caught in any programme that would concert that hope into the guarantee of a presence, a fulfilment, an end point when all doubt and alienation would be overcome. The undecidable is compared to a ghost, never present and alive, but effectively haunting every decision. It is, we might say, the ghost in the machine of messianism.

Derrida's dealings with Jewishness and with the law provide the context for his development of the idea of a messianism without messianism, particularly in *Specters of Marx*. Near the beginning of that work, Derrida writes that 'No justice ... seems possible or thinkable without the principle of some *responsibility*, beyond all living present, within that which disjoins the living present, before the ghosts of those who are not yet born or who are already dead'

(SM, p. xix). The ghost or the spectre looms large in this re-reading of the relevance of Marx to contemporary politics and ethics. The ghost is not simply an abstract alterity, but the other who calls to us, places demands on us, without ever becoming immediately visible or knowable. Unless thinking and politics allows itself to be addressed by this spectre, it is in danger of reducing life and others to the status of objects to be manipulated. Starting with Hamlet's declaration that 'the time is out of joint', Derrida insists that only if history is related to the incalculable can we avoid reducing others to a homogenized mass.

Following on from his discussion of justice in 'Force of Law', Derrida writes of the 'infinite asymmetry of the relation to the other, that is to say, the place for justice' (SM, p. 22) and of 'justice as incalculability of the gift' (SM, p. 23). The gift will occupy us in the next chapter. For now, suffice to say that the 'pure' gift always escapes the economy of reward, recompense, punishment and revenge. The gift, like justice, is impossible; but the experience of it is necessary if we are to be disjointed, able to relate to others and to the future as the coming of an unforeseen event. For Derrida, this is a 'dislocation in Being and in time itself', one that distances him from Heidegger's continuing wish for the gathering of Being in and through poetic language: 'The necessary disjointure, the de-totalizing condition of justice, is indeed here that of the present – and by the same token the very condition of the present and of the presence of the present' (SM, p. 28). The paradoxical origin of the present, this 'irreducible excess' (SM, p. 27) to any systematic thinking, gives the other and the future their chance.

As he develops this thought, Derrida turns to language drawn from the Judeo-Christian tradition, but he does so in a very particular way. Deconstruction 'would always begin to take shape as the thinking of the gift and of undeconstructible justice, the undeconstructible condition of any deconstruction'. However, this condition would itself remain 'in deconstruction' (SM, p. 28). In other words, we should not deceive ourselves that all this talk of what resists deconstruction is going to deliver to us a justice, a gift, an other who is fully and finally present, defined and whole. There is no supernatural justice or grace waiting behind the scenes, of which particular instances are only partial and imperfect manifestations that await their completion at the end of time. The time is always and forever out of joint. *Différance* is not a veil that can be drawn aside. It is the indispensable condition for thinking, experiencing and acting.

It is with this in mind that Derrida evokes a 'desert-like messianism (without content and without identifiable messiah)' (SM, p. 28). This messianism is always related to a desert that is 'abyssal' and 'chaotic'. There we find 'the excessiveness, the disproportion in the gaping hole of the open mouth' (ibid.). There is a savage genesis at play here. The deeps that ferment before the word of creation is spoken are not just an unfortunate chaos or nullity that must be overcome, but the inescapable face of creation itself, even in their monstrosity.

The hope that engages deconstruction is therefore not a dream of returning to the lost garden of paradise, nor of reaching a final destination. It puts being (thought of as presence) into question. Derrida signals this by playing upon the French phrase for perhaps: *peut-être*. The significance is of course that it contains *être*, meaning 'to be' or 'being'. The 'perhaps' opens the future, and so destabilizes the ground of being itself: 'wherever deconstruction is at stake, it would be a matter of linking an *affirmation* (in particular a political one), *if there is any*, to the experience of the impossible, which can only be a radical experience of the *perhaps*' (SM, p. 35)

This is the reason why Derrida's messianism cannot be identified with a specific and determined imagination of what the 'end' of things might be. It functions to keep history in motion, the future open and hope alive. It aims at 'a messianic extremity, an *eskhaton*' exceeding any historical telos (SM, p. 37). Later, Derrida refers to it as 'structural messianism, a messianism without religion, even a messianism without messianism' (SM, p. 59) and as 'a structure of experience rather than a religion' (SM, p. 168).

The implication is that religion, in its institutionalized and codified forms, offers an authorized access to the ground and telos of hope. It determines how the other appears and what our relation to the other must be. Appealing to revelation, authoritative tradition, self-evident reason or direct intuitive experience, it claims to have found the Archimedean point around which all of reality can be interpreted and gathered. Derrida is not so much rejecting this religion as drawing its limits, and arguing that it always relies on a general structure of life, language and experience. Without the generalized, structural messianism that impels deconstruction, the particular varieties of religious hope would not be possible. At the same time, this general structure is what radically de-structures our hold on reality, knocks the time out of joint.

The point applies in a different way to secular discourses of hope and emancipation, such as Marxism. Against those who want to secure a purely objective and scientific Marxism, Derrida argues that only if this messianic dimension of its project is recognized can it be liberated from dreams of totalizing power, from the temptation to think that history unfolds according to iron-hard rules and that these rules are correctly understood only by the revolutionary vanguard. Such perceptions of Marxist theory, however fair or unfair to Marx's writings, have shaped the worst forms of totalitarian oppression and extermination of those who do not abide by the logic of the system.

In a sense, Derrida is returning to the question of revelation and revealability. To the determinate religions, he is pointing out that their particular expressions of hope and faith rely upon a general possibility of thinking the future and openness to the other that cannot ever be finished or captured. To the Marxists and other advocates of secular emancipation, he is claiming that their own discourses are inextricably linked to forms of hope that have been carried (if not exhausted) by religion. Choosing the particular language of messianism while refusing to give it determined content, is Derrida's way of doing justice to both sides of this divide. The ideal, the transcendental and the universal cannot exist without the real, the empirical and the particular, and vice versa. There is no purely ideal realm, any more than there is a purely empirical one. The origin is ruined; paradoxically, hope is only possible if it thinks that ruin.

This critique applies equally to the totalizing discourses that justify rapacious capitalism, or are complacent about the achievements of liberal democracy in the face of continuing economic and military exploitation. Part of Derrida's argument is aimed squarely at what he calls the 'neo-evangelistic' proclamation of the end of history by Francis Fukuyama, for whom liberal capitalism brings to a close any sense that history has anywhere else to go, any more events to endure (SM, pp. 59–61). For Derrida, this is the latest and possibly most naïve form of Hegel's Christian triumphalism: as if the self and the other were now fully harmonized, recognizing one another at last in Western democracy. Here too, the presumption to know the other, to master the event, is an act of violent exclusion that closes down the future, defaces the other.

The complex weaving of universal openness to the future with the necessarily limited figure of the messianic is dealt with at length by Derrida near the close of *Specters of Marx*. The whole book is a plea for us not to think we can have done with ghosts. They return to haunt us, because life itself is always a slipping away from presence. Unless we recognize this, if we think we have all the hard facts of history in our grasp, we will neither be alive to hope, faithful in our testimony to others, nor vigilant of the cruel phantoms that invade and control our discourses. The messianic keeps ghosts with us, on the edge of life. It therefore has something of the spectral about it too.

Derrida asks 'Can one conceive an atheological heritage of the messianic? Is there one, on the contrary, that is more consistent?' (SM, p. 168). There is always more than one heritage or way of interpreting what has been passed down. He chooses the 'untimely' interpretation that does not make history a closed book:

Ascesis strips the messianic hope of all biblical forms, and even all determinable figures of the wait or expectation; it thus denudes itself in view of responding to that which must be absolute hospitality, the 'yes' to the *arrivant(e)*, the 'come' to the future that cannot be anticipated – which must not be the 'anything whatsoever' that harbors behind it those too familiar ghosts, the very ones we must practise recognizing. Open, waiting for the event *as* justice, this hospitality is absolute only if it keeps watch over its own universality. The messianic, including its revolutionary forms (and the messianic is always revolutionary, it has to be), would be urgency, imminence but, irreducible paradox, a waiting without horizon of expectation. One may always take the quasi-atheistic dryness of the messianic to be the condition of the religions of the Book, a desert that was not even theirs . . . (SM, p. 168)

The messianic desert and the emptiness of the *khora* are brought very close to one another. Derrida acknowledges that critics will see in this 'quasi-transcendental "messianism"' something insubstantial and even despairing. Derrida counters that 'without this latter despair and if one could count on what is coming, hope would be but the calculation of a program' (SM, p. 169). A hope that was guaranteed, that knew what to expect, would not be hope at all. It would be prudence.

The uncalculable future is always associated with the disruption of origins. If the origin of the world and life were single, simple and pure, then it could unfold in unbroken continuity with itself. But this would not actually be life. There could be no desire, no relationship. There would only be more of the same.

'Faith and Knowledge' links the messianic and the *khora* as two names for the 'duplicity of these origins. For here origin is duplicity itself, the one and the other' (AR, p. 55). Beyond the contrast between the general structure of revealability and the particular event of revelation, there is a third place, 'the most anarchic and anarchivable place possible, not the island nor the Promised Land, but a certain desert, that which makes possible, opens, hollows out or infinitizes the other. Ecstasy or existence of the most extreme abstraction' (ibid.). This non-origin can be read in different ways.

One, the messianic, Derrida summarizes as 'the opening to the future, or to the coming of the other as the advent of justice, without horizon of expectation or prophetic prefiguration' (AR, p. 56). In contrast, the *khora* would be radically other to all theological or anthropological figures, heterogeneous to the holy and sacred, to the present, to being. It leads nowhere and gives nothing. It is an 'utterly faceless other' (AR, p. 59).

For Derrida, it is an open question whether the 'desert' of the *khora* can be thought prior to all the particular 'deserts' of religion (where the desert is the place of revelation, of God's self-emptying, of transcendence); or whether, on the contrary, it is only in and through these latter places of encounter that the foreignness of the *khora* can be glimpsed. This dilemma cannot be resolved conceptually or closed down dogmatically, but is lived as an ordeal that must be endured and respected. For Derrida, this would be 'at once the chance of every responsible decision and of another "reflecting faith," of a new "tolerance"' (ibid.). This would not be the tolerance of indifference, or reducing everyone to a carbon copy of the same: 'it would respect the distance of infinite alterity as singularity' (AR, p. 60). This would still be religion – of a sort.

As we have seen, in *Politics of Friendship*, Derrida explores the thought of the future through the notion of the 'perhaps', in which the fixed order of being is troubled and so opened to receive the other. The book calls into question the classical way in which friendship has been delimited by sameness, sharing or belonging to a common essence, kinship or fraternity (the patriarchal overtones of that word being very much to the point). He evokes another kind of relationship, one with the *arrivant*, the other who comes to us unprepared. This coming is essentially connected with the experience of the future: 'the *arrivant* could also be the *perhaps* itself, the unheard-of, totally new experience of the *perhaps*. Unheard-of, totally new, that very experience which no metaphysician might yet have dared to think' (PF, p. 29). It is this 'unheard-of' that resists being included in any calculation of what the future might hold. By its nature, it is an impossible experience, an impossible thought:

> a possible that would only be possible (non-impossible), a
> possible surely and certainly possible, accessible in advance,
> would be a poor possible, a futureless possible, a possible
> already *set aside*, so to speak, life-assured. This would be a
> programme or a causality, a development, a process without
> an event . . . What would a future be if the decision were
> able to be programmed, and if the risk [*l'aléa*], the uncer
> tainty, the unstable certainty, the inassurance of the
> "perhaps" were not suspended on it at the opening of what
> comes, flush with the event, within it and with an open
> heart? (Ibid.)

A real relatedness to the future requires the interruption of our monologues, the suspension of what binds us into a common, taken-for-granted identity. It needs 'the other, the revolution, or chaos' (ibid.).

The critical condition of the 'perhaps' returns again and again in *Politics of Friendship*. It is not the 'perhaps' of indecision and indifference, but a name for what opens the future and makes responsibility and questioning possible. Derrida is keen to distinguish it from anything like sitting on the fence or muddled thinking:

> Our unbelievable *perhaps* does not signify haziness and mobility, the confusion preceding knowledge or renouncing all truth. If it is undecidable and without truth in its own moment (but it is, as a matter of fact, difficult to assign a proper moment to it), this is in order that it might be a condition of decision, interruption, revolution, responsibility and truth. The friends of the *perhaps* are the friends of truth. But the friends of truth are not, by definition, in the truth; they are not installed there as in the padlocked security of a dogma, and the stable reliability of an opinion. If there is some truth in the *perhaps*, it can only be that of which the friends are the friends. Only friends. The friends of truth function without *the* truth, even if friends cannot function without truth. (PF, p. 43)

This makes clearer why Derrida resists equating the messianic with any particular religious dogma. To relate to truth one must acknowledge the moment in which truth is suspended. To relate to what 'God' names, one must take leave of God, let God be, save the name of God by letting it go, letting the name resound with dissonance and difference. Truth requires the risk of friendship, of a faith that, in the moment it gives itself, is without assurance, guarantee or authority.

A further point is that religious truth is not just a matter of propositions that supposedly correspond to reality. It is also the medium through which a community articulates its own identity in relationship to the divine. Derrida is calling attention to the way in which the boundaries of such communities of 'friends' can easily become hardened by forgetting the nature of faith and believing that the truth is within the community's grip. Communion becomes a settled, substantial, given reality, whose definition follows established and authoritative lines. In contrast, in commenting on Nietzsche, Derrida writes of 'a communion of infinite wrenching' (PF, p. 54), a mutual rejoicing that preserves the solitude and singularity of each, a community that does not absorb its members as parts of a greater whole. The distance that Nietzsche recommends in relationships is not an alternative to friendship, but its life.

Inventing spectres

Derrida has been criticized for his reading of Marxism, for dissolving its materialism and analysis of real world classes and economic forces. Could the same be said of the general impetus of his work? In relation to Judaism, to religious institutions, to communities, he seems to strip away all that makes them concrete, embodied, historical phenomena, leaving a trace that is always elusive, and, yes, ghostly. The Jew becomes a cipher for uprooted wandering; the woman for elusive truth; the messianic for an aimless hope; the friend for a distant relation. Is Derrida merely reintroducing an old patriarchal symbolic system, in which what is privileged is disembodied, abstracted, free of all specific context and ties? Is his trace in search of an incarnation that would ground it?

Such a critique would need to reckon with the logic and applications of Derrida's argument. For one thing, the trace or difference requires embodiment, requires space and time to work. It is not set aside in an ideal realm. Its effect is in fact to confuse the ideal and the real. No pure, spiritual presence is given mastery over appearances in Derrida's philosophy.

Second, the negativity in Derrida's thought, while it does not aim at a positive presence or foundation, does open a relationship to the other, to the other in their particularity. Otherness is not domesticated within a system, reduced to being a reflection of myself and my needs. It is secret.

Third, we need to understand Derrida's own critique. He is not seeking to abolish the need for specific communities or religions, any more than he sought to abolish truth and reference. The traces left by Judaism and Christianity in his work are irreducible. However, Derrida does aim to unsettle a certain politics of truth that would deny or suppress the impossible and undecidable aspects of faith, decision, the promise and the gift. These things can only be thought and acted upon in specific material ways and contexts, because there is no meaning apart from this. Their role is to expose the paradoxes inherent in our belief and action, and to elicit our protest when such impossibilities are smoothed over or trampled down in the name of unity, freedom, brotherhood and Truth. They do not paralyze us in abstraction. Without the incalculable and unforeseeable, we would have no decision to make:

> Undecidability . . . is not a sentence that a decision can leave behind. The crucial experience of the *perhaps* imposed by the undecidable – that is to say, the condition of decision – is not a moment to be exceeded, forgotten or suppressed. It continues to constitute the decision as such; it can never again be separated from it; it produces it *qua* decision *in and through* the undecidable. (PF, p. 219)

It is worth noting that one of the targets of *Politics of Friendship* is the patriarchal ideal of friendship as fraternity, a communion of brothers. Without the rupture of the event, of the other, such closed systems could never be challenged or changed. Part of this involves the recognition that such systems are not given facts of nature: 'There has never been anything natural in the brother figure . . . De-naturalization was at work in the very formation of fraternity' (PF, p. 159). This active critique does not rely upon an ideal of self-contained (male) reason, separating itself from what is natural (and maternal) in order to come into its own. No: as with the cut of circumcision, openness to the other leads us to a fundamental vulnerability at the heart of our experience of truth. The humanistic, androcentric ego is forever displaced: 'The passive decision, condition of the event, is always in me, structurally, another event, a rending decision as the decision of the other. Of the absolute other in me, the other as the absolute that decides on me in me' (PF, p. 68).

The absolute other: what religion might well name God. Something happens to us that is akin to a religious experience, but it is not an experience of a presence. It is a response to a call, it is a grace that precedes every action, dethroning our dreams of sovereignty:

> We have begun to respond. We are already caught up, we are caught out, in a certain responsibility, and the most

ineluctable responsibility – as if it were possible to think a responsibility without freedom . . . It is assigned to us by the other, from the place of the other, well before any hope of reappropriation allows us the assumption of this responsibility . . . The altogether other and *every other (one) is every (bit) other*, comes here to upset the order of phenomenology. And good *sense*. That which comes before autonomy must also *exceed* it – that is, succeed it, survive and indefinitely overwhelm it. (PF, p. 232)

If this echoes a Christian language of grace, however, there is a sting in the tail: 'every other (one) is every (bit) other' is perhaps the least worst way of translating the inherent ambiguity of the simple French: *tout autre est tout autre*. It is a phrase we will return to in the next chapter. For now, we need to note its own undecidability. Does the phrase simply affirm the otherness of God, or does it disperse God's presence into the otherness of people and the world? In the moment of response, is it the absolute other, the divine, who addresses me? Or is every other person or being a trace of that absolute otherness? Can we decide? Does it matter?

The echo of Levinas is particularly strong here. For Levinas, God is not known directly, but in the trace left in the face of the other. An undecidable ambiguity remains: is God wholly identified with the transcendence and ethical demand that confronts me and takes hold of me through the encounter with an other person? Levinas wishes to break with the philosophy that privileges an impersonal 'being' or objectivity, subordinating ethics and otherness to the grip of conceptual sameness. Like Derrida after him, he strikes an eschatological note. An 'eschatology of messianic peace' is opposed to the violent, totalizing ambitions of ontology.[3] This eschatology does not promise another world after death, or a revelation of absolute knowledge, but institutes a different relation to the other here and now. It invokes an idea of infinity that ruptures our self-contained world, a 'transcendence with regard to totality'.[4] This infinity is a revelation, but without any dogmatic content:

The idea of Infinity *is revealed* in the strong sense of the term. There is no natural religion. But this exceptional knowledge is no longer objective. Infinity is not the 'object' of a cognition (which would be to reduce it to the measure of the gaze that contemplates), but is the desirable, that which arouses Desire, that is, that which is approachable by a thought that at each instant *thinks more than it thinks*. The infinite is not thereby an immense object, exceeding the horizons of the look. It is Desire that measures the infinity of the infinite, for it is a measure through the very impossibility of measure.[5]

In an essay on the Jewish thinker Franz Rosenzweig, Levinas puts it like this: 'Revelation is precisely an entering–into–relation completely different from the one that corresponds to a synthesis or that can be lodged within a category established between the elements . . . Revelation *establishes* nothing'. Rather there is 'a crossing over toward the Other'.[6]

There is no promise of uniting with God here, for 'Transcendence is to be distinguished from a union with the transcendent by participation'.[7] Desire keeps the self open, wounded, exposed to the other, and God is known in and through this wound, through the vulnerability of the other's face: 'The dimension of the divine opens forth from the human face'.[8] The approach of the Other opens up a distance between us that is necessary for ethics to work: 'The Other is not the incarnation of God, but precisely by his face in which he is disincarnate, is the manifestation of the height in which God is revealed'.[9] Here, incarnation would mean a direct and immediate presence of God. However, in the introduction to the later text *Otherwise than Being*, Levinas uses the language of incarnation in another sense: 'exposure is being incarnate' and 'It is as responsible that one is incarnated'.[10] This incarnation is not the direct embodiment of God's nature, but a passivity, vulnerability and exposure to the other.

This brief discussion of Levinas shows that there is an unavoidable duplicity, if not paradox in his language about the other, transcendence and God. He opposes the reductionism of secular humanism, because it repeats the error of the philosophical tradition, excluding a genuine relationship to what it cannot conceptualize and objectify. This immanent form of thinking has to be broken apart. However, what is revealed in this interruption cannot be codified in a dogma. If it is incarnate, it is only so as the wounding of our self-contained reason and being. 'A voice comes from the other shore',[11] from beyond my world; but this is not a voice from a separate, heavenly, supernatural realm. God is known only in and as the trace of the other. Belief in this God is compatible with a sort of atheism, 'the death of a certain god inhabiting the world behind the scenes'.[12]

The links with Derrida's approach to religion and theology are clear. The undecidable is not a symptom of confusion or indecision, but the inescapable condition of our encounter with the other in responsibility and faith. The other – and therefore the transcendent – comes to us precisely as the one whose status cannot be determined in advance or exhausted by any conceptual scheme.

In the essay 'Psyche: Invention of the Other', Derrida explores this through the paradoxical concept of invention. To invent something is to bring about something new. It is something that is unexpected: 'Never does an invention appear, never does an invention take place, without an inaugural event' (Psy, p. 5). This event opens out to an 'advent' to a future possibility that the invention brings into being.

This is where the paradox begins, because, in order to be recognized and received as new, the invention must be addressed to others, communicated and connected with them in ways they understand, made available to them. The pure moment of origin, of creation, is, like the date, inscribed: 'Invention begins by being susceptible to repetition, exploitation, reinscription' (Psy, p. 6).

Derrida traces the ways in which, in the metaphysical tradition, 'invention' has come to mean something like 'discovery': the uncovering (albeit for the first time) of a truth or possibility that was already there. Even in the work of philosophers who tried to give pride of place to the productive role played by the imagination in human existence, a sense remains that this originality is limited. Referring to Schelling's claim that human activity supplies 'what is missing in the totality of God' (Psy, p. 42), Derrida argues that inventiveness still remains caught in a logic of sameness. It is only by reflecting and carrying forward God's original being that human beings can invent anything. Nothing is *really* new.

In ontotheology, invention is always possible, because it is a way of uncovering some as yet unknown aspect of a being that is already there: 'paradoxically, invention invents nothing, when in invention the other does not come, and when nothing comes to the other or from the other. For the other is not the possible. So it would be necessary to say that the only possible invention would be the invention of the impossible' (Psy, p. 44). The other is not the possible, because that would mean that we were interpreting the other solely according to known rules or concepts. The other would just manifest something that was familiar, and so would cease to be other.

The alternative is to deconstruct this logic, to envision another possibility of inventing the other, 'to offer a place for the other, to let the other come' (Psy, p. 45). Strictly speaking, this would not be an 'invention' of the other, an expression of my power. I can only prepare a place, a welcome for the other. I cannot compel the other to come or show itself in any particular way. 'We' are no longer the centre of the world, we cannot find ourselves anywhere, but wait for the other. We are

> invented only by the other and from the coming of the other that says 'come' and to which a response with another 'come' appears to be the only invention that is desirable and worthy of interest . . . For the other is always the origin of the world and *we are to be invented*. And the being of the we, and being itself. Beyond being. (Psy, p. 45)

Here, again, at the origin of the world, there is no self-same foundation, no power belonging to a contained subject. There is the impossible approach of the other, calling us beyond being. Derrida writes of

> allowing the adventure of the event of the entirely other to come. Of an entirely other that can no longer be confused with the God or the Man of ontotheology or with any of the figures of this configuration (the subject, consciousness, the unconscious, the self, man or woman, and so on). (Psy, p. 46)

Derrida is not advocating a utopian abandonment of the world for otherness, since it is only within the 'economic circle of invention' that this irreducible thought of the other is set in motion. There is no flight to a god behind the scenes of the world. However, nor is there any substitution of a human idea or capacity for God, since this would only amount to playing the same game.

The subtitle of this section of the essay includes the words 'The Invention of God' Is God an invention: made up, projected by us? Does all invention in the end simply belong to God, a pale reflection of the absolute origin? Or is there another possibility: that 'God' is the name of the other who is beyond being, who can never be known as such, but who invents us by an unexpected call? One point is worth noting: Derrida ends the essay with a small dialogue that reflects these ambiguities. The final voice states that 'the call of the other is a call to come, and that happens only in multiple voices' (Psy, p. 47).

If there were to be a theological rendition of this call, then it would have to be a disjointed and disfigured one. It would be a response to the otherness of the divine, without ever finally deciding the 'objective' status of that divinity as a matter of knowledge. It would be primarily ethical, not in the sense of abandoning thinking for the pragmatic, but precisely because the ethical involves thinking most rigorously about the limits of thought. It would be placed within an inheritance, a tradition, institutions, but it would always be destabilizing them though its openness to what is 'to come', to the unforced approach of the other. And it would have to speak in multiple voices, owning up to the plurality that has always constituted it. It would be a queer, postcolonial, heterodox, nonhuman theology that emerged, though not necessarily one that would be unfaithful to what it inherited, and certainly not a reductionist one. The point is that, if this theology were possible, it would also be impossible. Only by living and thinking its own impossibility could it be faithful.

This duality is signalled by Derrida's late tribute to the thinking of Levinas entitled *Adieu*. Derrida's commentary on Levinas is largely positive, grateful even, showing how much his own ethical and religious thinking owes to his friend. For Levinas, Derrida argues 'It is necessary to *begin by responding*' (AEL, p. 24). The other has always gone before us, and interrupted our self-relatedness. The other is not an object of knowledge, but of desire. It is a desire that requires self and other to be separate, because unity would be its death.

However, Derrida also want to think this as radically as possible. If the other is only known by their withdrawal, there could never be the perfect peace Levinas dreamed of. Moreover, our desire for the other or for God would always remain divided in itself. The *adieu* is at once an approach, going towards God (*á-dieu*), and also a leave-taking, departing from God. This divided faith would be God's element (AEL, p. 103). If this is so, why does Levinas assume that God will not abandon us? Derrida raises the question of whether 'the *á-dieu*, like salutation or prayer, must be addressed to a God who not only might not exist (who might no longer or not yet exist) but who might abandon me and not turn toward me through any covenant or election' (AEL, p. 104). Such a possibility seems absurd to Jewish or Christian faith: surely God *is* the one who loves faithfully, without breaking the word that is given? To abandon this premise seems to suggest we have moved away from anything that could recognizably be referred to as God.

In a sense, Derrida is making the point that faith must always risk being misplaced. The other, who lacks any determinate qualities, could just become a spectre, an emptiness. Faith is always dealing in the desert with a radical atheism and with ghosts. And yet it is driven by a desire for the other, and a hospitality that welcomes the risk brought by this other beyond being, and far from all guarantees and assurances (AEL, pp. 111–12). The spectral is not opposed to the spiritual. It is its life.

The *adieu* is the sign of this haunted spirituality, but also of a messianic spirituality that is addressed by the other. It begins by being out of joint. The problem lies in whether this generalized structure of openness really is a 'faith' or fidelity at all. The suspicion Derrida raises against all particular determinate religious traditions and institutions is understandable. However, the other cannot remain an abstraction, disembodied in the sense of being removed from the world of time and difference. Derrida's own thinking points to a truth that is always 'written' or 'placed', a truth that is traced or cut in the flesh of the world. The poem must be read beyond its singular origin, but if it is to say anything at all, it must also speak in figures that are definite, irreducible, which sound in a way that cannot simply be translated into a universal language.

The danger is that if faith always finds its element in indeterminate structures such as messianism without a messiah, then, rather than respecting singularity, it is abolished. The Jew loses flesh and blood reality to become a cipher for alienation. Without a measure of some kind, each poem, each expression of faith is just as good as any other, because they are all equally removed from the emptiness of the *khora* or the blind and directionless movement of *différance*.

Derrida does not intend this 'anything goes' caricature of 'postmodernism'. However, in order to avoid it, is it necessary to return to the questions of particular forms of revelation, even of incarnation, if faith and promise are not simply to be empty words. The register in which Derrida chooses to articulate the structures of language and time resounds with specific ethical and religious themes, with a desire for the absolute other that is never merely neutral or descriptive. If he is right in noticing how the real and the ideal are always contaminated one with the other, then there can be no final suppression of what these themes give to thinking.

We turn, therefore, to the idea of the impossible gift. Perhaps here, the possibilities and risks of how the other *gives itself* might be discerned.

Chapter 6

Touching: The Impossible Gift

What is to come? What will be revealed when the other arrives?

Derrida's turn to the future is a turn to the other to come, to the event and advent of the other. If, for some, his early work seemed to promise only the nihilistic destruction of all objective truth and stable meaning, others have always been disturbed by the frequency with which Derrida turns to religious motifs. Does this entail an alternative abandonment of reason: one that submits thinking to mysticism and consumes the material world in the spectral maw of pious abstraction?

The thinking of the gift engages both of these concerns. For Derrida, a pure gift – one untainted by the economy of exchange, reward, gratitude or self-congratulation – is impossible. It is beyond anything that can be experienced as such, as a simple presence. As soon as a gift becomes a present (and Derrida is well aware of the duplicity of this word's meaning in English), its character as a gift is always compromised. As present, the gift is recognized. It is inserted into a symbolic order, in which its meaning is always structured by ideas of debt and recompense. Even if the donor gives a gift without the knowledge of the recipient, the donor's awareness of giving the gift allows her to reap some reward from it, even if this is only a sense of satisfaction in her own generosity. As soon as the gift appears, there is no gift:

> If there is a gift, the *given* of the gift (*that which* one gives, *that which* is given, the gift as given thing or as act of donation) must not come back to the giving (let us not already say to the subject, to the donor). It must not circulate, it must not be exchanged, it must not in any case be exhausted, as a gift, by the process of exchange, by the movement of circulation of the circle in the form of return to the point of departure. If the figure of the circle is

essential to economics, the gift must remain aneconomic. Not that it remains foreign to the circle, but it must *keep* a relation of foreignness to the circle, a relation without relation of familiar foreignness. It is perhaps in this sense that the gift is the impossible.

Not impossible, but *the* impossible. The very figure of the impossible. (GT, p. 7)

This impossibility is an unresolvable tension in the thinking of the gift. It therefore evokes all those spectres of absurdity and paradox through which deconstruction supposedly attacks the notion of objective truth and meaning. However, it also has another face: the gift seems to be turned towards an ineffable purity that escapes anything our finite and contingent world can contain. The question returns: is Derrida a nihilist, spinning paradoxes in the void? Or is he a closet mystic, leading us to a perfect gift beyond Being?

Of course, neither is the case, at least in any straightforward way. For Derrida, the necessity of thinking the gift's impossibility goes hand in hand with the necessity of dealing with the mundane world of giving and receiving. The gift is not a mystical presence we can encounter, but a rupture within thought and being, which impels us to critical vigilance over every form of economic giving in our experience. The impossible is not a disabling paradox, but an urgency of thinking and acting.

This becomes clearer if we examine more closely what Derrida has to say about the future as the 'to-come', for the future in this sense shares an essential dynamic with the gift. It is ungraspable, unpredictable and cannot be comprehended under any category or notion of presence. As such, the future is the condition for us to have any present, for anything to happen to us or be given to us.

The gift to come

In his 1983 essay 'Of an Apocalyptic Tone Recently Adopted in Philosophy', Derrida addresses the use of quasi-religious imagery in his texts with reference to the future. His title echoes a piece of writing by Kant, who wished to draw a strong line between rational philosophy and the enthusiasm of mystics and visionaries. For Derrida, however, that line is not so easy to draw.

The genre of apocalytpic is represented in the New Testament by the book of Revelation (also known as the Apocalypse of John) and other scattered passages in the gospels and epistles. There is a much wider body of literature in this category in extra-canonical sources. These texts have often been seen as dramatic attempts to predict the future, casting it in terms of a final battle between the forces of light and darkness. However, apocalypse also means something like a drawing aside of a veil, and this literature can also be seen as a vision into a truer, heavenly order of things that is used to critique and subvert current conditions on earth. It offers a gift of truth that brings confidence to persecuted communities that their imperial oppressors, for all their apparent might, are men of straw destined to fall.

Apocalyptic is not simply about prediction, but about empowerment, emancipation and truth won through a critical light. It is not as far from the supposedly rational Enlightenment as Kant and his heirs might wish. As Derrida puts it, 'every apocalyptic eschatology is promised in the name of light' (OA, p. 50).

This does not mean that Derrida is ready to accept without question every truth claim made by apocalyptic writers who claim that they have seen the workings of the heavenly court. However, he does recognize in this movement a desire that punctures dogmatic pretensions, even a desire that can be turned against the claims of apocalytpic itself:

> we cannot and we must not . . . forgo what imposes itself as
> the enigmatic desire for vigilance, for the lucid vigil, for
> elucidation, for critique and truth, but for a truth that at
> the same time keeps within itself some apocalyptic desire,
> this time as desire for clarity and revelation, in order to
> demystify, or, if you prefer, to deconstruct the apocalyptic
> discourse itself. (OA, p. 51)

In this sense, the most 'irrational' of genres harbours the self-critical vigilance that impels all enlightened thinking. It opens the present to its other. Derrida can therefore ask the most daring question: 'wouldn't the apocalyptic be a transcendental condition of all discourses, of all experience even, of every mark or every trace?' (OA, p. 57). He writes of 'the apocalyptic structure of language, of writing . . . *the divisible* envoi *for which there is no self-presentation nor assured destination*' (ibid.).

This dynamic can be identified with neither religious dogmatism nor self-contained reason. It is neither mysticism nor an all-out attack on truth. It deconstructs the divide between the religious and the secular in the name of reason *and* desire, truth *and* faith. Derrida's terse question expresses the tension that this involves: 'Shall we thus continue in the best apocalyptic tradition to denounce false apocalypses?' (OA, p. 59).

Towards the end of the essay, Derrida turns to the invitation that occurs in the book of Revelation: 'Come'. This summons and invitation takes us outside all settled dogmas and fixed positions of rationalism or religion. It beckons us into a future that is not programmed, towards an encounter that has not been scripted in advance. It is both within the apocalyptic discourse, at the same time as it pushes against and through any claim to know the course of what is to come (and so claim a certain power over those who do not know).

For Derrida, 'the event of this "Come" precedes and calls the event' (OA, p. 64). It is a paradoxical call that makes any event possible. It cannot be confined by metaphysical theology or any systematic thinking: '"Come" no more lets itself be arraigned by an onto-theo-eschatology than by a logic of the event' (OA, p. 65).

Derrida is conscious of the risk involved in such a summons. It can be claimed by those who advocate violence and totalitarianism. However, if we are faithful to the call, it confounds any such control, precisely because its source cannot be identified. There is no single, simple origin that issues the invitation, and this is crucial to averting the risk that it will be commandeered in the name of an arrogant domination: '"Come" is *only* derivable, absolutely derivable, but only from the other, from nothing that may be an origin or a verifiable, decidable, presentable, appropriable identity, from nothing not already derivable and arrivable without *rive* [bank, shore]' (OA, p. 66). In this 'apocalypse without apocalypse' (ibid.), the closed totalities of secularism and scientific positivism are riven, derived from a transcendent other, even as their religious counterparts are deprived of their power to name and domesticate that other.

The themes of the coming of the other and the dethronement of gathered power converge in a later text, *Rogues*. Discussing ideas of sovereignty and democracy, Derrida invokes the incalculable nature of the future and the call to respect the singular other. At one point, there is a discussion of Tocqueville's writing on American democracy. Tocqueville suggests that the democratic ideal is already perfectly embodied in the United States (R, pp. 13–16). The social body is wholly unified, and the will of the people is sovereign in the state much as God is sovereign in the universe. For Derrida, this ideal of a finished democracy, a kind of realized eschatology, is full of danger. In its complacency, it assumes that all differences have been or can be overcome. The recent adventures of the United States in the global 'war on terror', spreading 'democracy' through military force as the final solution to barbarism, is never far from Derrida's reflections.

Tocqueville's comparison of the people to God leads Derrida to explore the nature of God in the philosophy of Aristotle. The God of Aristotle is the unmoved prime mover, pure thought thinking itself, wholly self-absorbed. God is the One, the unbroken circle of pure self-presence. He is also the image of the sovereign, dominant in undisturbed exercise of force. Derrida is suggesting that Tocqueville's democratic God is not far from this tyrannical, other-denying power.

The risk that democracy takes this form cannot be eliminated, but it can be checked by a vigilant openness to the other and to the future. In the preface to *Rogues*, we are urged to 'think at once the unforeseeability of an event that is necessarily without horizon, the singular coming of the other, and, as a result, a *weak force*' (R, p. xiv). This weak force has no power, but is unconditional nonetheless. The affirmation of it 'resembles yet again an act of messianic faith – irreligious and without messianism' (ibid.).

Keeping his distance from concrete messianic religion, Derrida now associates this irreligious messianism much more closely with the *khora*, which is not any kind of God or agent. As we have seen, in 'Faith and Knowledge', the messianic and the *khora* are the two names of that 'third place' beyond the duality of revelation and revealability. Both evoke the duplicity of origins. *Rogues* underlines this connection. Without compromising the alien, inhuman and ungodly aspect of the *khora*, it nevertheless becomes a space in which an invitation and a promise can be heard.

Khora is a receptacle, not a giver or a gift. However, in its passivity, it allows the world to take place. Remember how the problem of passivity was at the heart of Derrida's early questioning of the purity of Husserl's attempt to reconstruct and reactivate the origin of the world and of ideal truth. Husserl could not account for this original passivity at the heart of the transcendental self. It suggested an intuition that was not full and present, but wounded at its source.

This unaccountable, savage genesis is productive and creative precisely because of its otherness. Similarly, despite its uncanny and alien nature, *khora* allows a call to rise up and take hold:

> the call for a thinking of the event *to come*, of the democracy *to come*, of the reason *to come*. This call bears every hope, to be sure, although it remains, in itself, without hope. Not hopeless, in despair, but foreign to the teleology, the hopefulness, and the *salut* of salvation. Not foreign to the *salut* as the greeting or salutation of the other, not foreign to the *adieu* ('come' or 'go' in peace), not foreign to justice, but nonetheless heterogeneous and rebellious, irreducible to law, to power, and to the economy of redemption. (R, p. xv)

In the main text, Derrida affirms this as a form of faith, not only in the past, but in what is to come, for 'fidelity, contrary to what we often tend to believe, is first of all a fidelity to . . . to come. Fidelity to come, to the to-come, to the future. Is this possible?' (R, p. 4). The question is a genuine one, for this is a faith in the impossible – that which breaks with the order of what can be measured and calculated.

Later in the book, Derrida dwells upon the nature of this 'impossible' future. He argues that the impossible is not simply privative (a something lacking), not hidden or distant, not a regulative ideal in Kant's sense. It is urgent,

> it announces itself; it precedes me, swoops down upon and seizes me here and now in a nonvirtualizable way, in

actuality and not potentiality . . . Such urgency cannot
be *idealized* any more than the other as other can. This
im-possible is thus not a (regulative) *idea* or *ideal*. It is what
is most undeniably *real*. And sensible. Like the other. Like
the irreducible and nonappropriable différance of the other.
(R, p. 84)

This is a crucial point. At the close of the previous chapter, we
raised the question whether Derrida's messianism is so free of
content, so abstract, that it effaces the otherness and singularity it
is meant to respect. Derrida faces a similar objection from critics
of *Specters of Marx*, who complain about his 'utopian' use of messianic motifs, devoid of determinate content. The suggestion is
that it represents a flight from Marx's real-world materialism into
an ungrounded idealism.

Derrida's response is important:

Messianicity (which I regard as a universal structure of
experience, and which cannot be reduced to religious
messianism of any stripe) is anything but Utopian: it refers,
in every here-now, to the coming of an eminently real,
concrete event, that is, to the most irreducibly heterogeneous otherness . . . Even if messianicity as I describe it here
can seem abstract (precisely because here we have to do
with a universal structure of relation to the event, to the
concrete otherness of him who/that is coming, a way of
thinking the event 'before' or independently of all ontology), we have to do here with the most concrete urgency,
and the most revolutionary as well. *Anything but Utopian*,
messianicity mandates that we interrupt the ordinary course
of things, time and history *here-now*; it is inseparable from an
affirmation of otherness and justice. (MS, pp. 248–49)

The necessary abstraction of the messianic, and, even more, of the
khora, serves a thinking of otherness in all its finite and material
particularity. This strategic abstraction is subversive of ontology,
the assumption that otherness can be comprehended within the
horizon of being, where being is interpreted as presence, foundation, centre, origin and goal. Derrida's concern is that those who

reproach him with a lack of 'realism' have not really thought through what they mean by such a term. 'Realism' (like 'common sense') may in practice commit its proponents to the most abstract philosophical presuppositions about what counts as truth, evidence and knowledge. Reducing the 'real' to a graspable materiality, it can negate otherness and the future. This is the totalitarian danger that haunts 'scientific' Marxism. Once the iron laws of historical inevitability are exposed, there is no room for doubt, dissent or compassion. The same is true of the advocates of capitalism as the end and fulfilment of history.

Derrida's use of religious motifs is one way of interrupting the self-contained worlds of Althusserian Marxism, but also of structuralism in general, of all that cannot think the savage genesis and the undomesticated other. At the same time, these motifs are deliberately uprooted from specific traditions and texts. It is as if Derrida were practising, in his own writing, the transgression of meaning, the mutual contamination of the real and the ideal, of the empirical, the transcendental and the transcendent.

For us, therefore, the question takes a different turn to that offered by Derrida's Marxist critics: if 'God' names the 'bottomless collapse', the 'desertification of language', what links this emptiness to the most particular affirmation of the other? Must what God names be entirely faceless, absent, reserved, and so disembodied? What is the 'real' that escapes the reductions of 'realism'?

This brings us back to the idea of the gift, which has featured prominently in a number of Derrida's texts. How does the gift, which can never be 'present', nevertheless show itself, incarnate itself in a way that sets thinking and ethics in motion?

What gives?

The gift has been a rich theme in anthropological literature, which has explored the nature and significance of gift-giving for social exchanges and structures in general. Derrida's own work discusses key texts by Marcel Mauss and Claude Lévi-Strauss, for example. However, the gift has also taken on other resonances, because of its disputed connection with the whole idea of givenness in the thinking of Husserl, Heidegger and Levinas. The resulting controversy (particularly centred on the work of Jean-Luc Marion) is due to the fact that the gift seems to stand at a boundary between pure philosophical description, and the possibility of revealed religion.

For Husserl, phenomenology sets aside all assumptions about the nature of reality and attends to what is 'given' to consciousness. It does not look for evidence or foundations apart from what gives itself as appearance to be known by the mind. It then seeks in these appearances their ideal essence, and further grounds that ideality in the original constituting intention of the transcendental ego. This ego (which we recall is not to be identified with the empirical self) is, in a sense, the source of the world as an objective, ordered whole. Knowledge is objective when there is a fullness of intuition, when the ego's aim perfectly coheres with what is present to it.

For Derrida, this 'givenness' is problematic. As we have seen, from early on he argues that phenomenology is caught in a double bind; it can never entirely account for its own ground, its own possibility. At the very moment of origin, the ego must be entirely active, and yet it is also passive, itself constituted by time and difference, by another origin it cannot grasp. Like a system or play of mirrors, it can never wholly reflect itself. It can never bring to light what makes reflection possible.

Derrida argues that there is therefore in phenomenology a

> dogmatic or speculative commitment which, to be sure, would not keep the phenomenological critique from being realized, would not be a residue of unperceived naïveté, but would *constitute* phenomenology from within . . . This would be done precisely in what soon comes to be recognized as the source and guarantee of all value, the 'principle of principles': i.e., the original self-giving evidence, the *present* or *presence* of sense to a full and primordial intuition. (SP, pp. 4–5)

If anything, then, the deconstruction of presence seems to be a contradiction of the given, if the latter means what is purely 'present' to consciousness.

However, this is not the whole story. Heidegger, for example, wishes to pay attention to the way Being eludes capture by ideas of presence. As his thought develops, he evokes ideas of a paradoxical givenness, in which Being only gives itself in its withdrawal. Heidegger uses the German term *es gibt*, a term most usually translated as 'there is', but that literally means 'it gives'. Being cannot be objectified or turned into a thing, a theme or a concept. It is not separate entity, but is always the Being of beings. However, thinking the difference between Being and beings is essential for Heidegger, if we are not to reduce all reality to objects that we unthinkingly manipulate. One way of maintaining this distinction without assuming to possess or think Being directly is through the *es gibt*. Being is given, without becoming a present thing or experience, and without there being any identifiable giver who would become the ground of Being. That way lies ontotheology, which Heidegger believed had reduced Being to the status of an exalted entity alongside other entities in the world. This giving without a giver is the experience and thinking of Being's difference, its presence as withdrawal.[1]

In other texts, Heidegger uses the term *Ereignis*, or event. This event is what gives being and time to us, it is the condition for the possibility of our experience of being and time.[2] It is an event without subject or object, in which Being is disclosed in its essential hiddenness. Despite the change in vocabulary, there is no suggestion that the event is any 'thing' or 'being' outside of the gift and withdrawal of being and time. Neither being nor the event can be identified with the God of ontotheology.

In contrast, Levinas sees Heidegger's obsession with Being as subordinating ethics and the call of the other to an impersonal force of sameness and totality. Although this might not be entirely fair to Heidegger, Levinas is convinced that no matter how sophisticated ontology might become, it needs to be displaced by the approach of the other and the ethical responsibility that this imposes upon me. The French phrase *il y a* is the equivalent to *es gibt,* but like the English phrase 'there is', it carries no explicit overtones of giving. In Levinas's work, the *il y a* is the anonymous backdrop of brute givenness, a suffocating shroud that needs to be pierced or thrown off for the ethical relation with the other to appear. The other needs no overarching horizon of meaning or conscious intentionality within which to appear, because the other disrupts all horizons of expectations and all conceptual schemes.[3]

Both Heidegger and Levinas draw upon, but ultimately contest the phenomenological method of Husserl. As we have noted, Derrida also challenges Husserl's notion of givenness, because it suggests a full conscious intuition of objective truth on the basis of the pure presence of the self to itself. However, Marion has argued that it is possible to articulate a very different idea of the gift from within phenomenology. It is useful to outline his thinking, albeit briefly, in order to clarify Derrida's own position.[4]

For Marion, givenness is not merely an impersonal or anonymous horizon of being. Marion explores the possibility of appearances that break thinking out of its preoccupation with being and objectivity. He calls these 'saturated phenomena'. Unlike appearances that are not fully 'given' to consciousness, saturated phenomena are given in excess. They overflow the ability of intuition to grasp and comprehend them.

Marion seeks to stay within the bounds of phenomenology. The given nature of what appears is not attributed to any particular source or structure. It is radical. What is given in a saturated phenomenon exceeds the capacity of the thinking subject, but it cannot be directly derived from any Giver, such as God. Marion is nevertheless suggesting that, at the boundaries of thought, even when all assumptions are laid aside and only appearances are in view, the gift breaks the self-contained nature of thought.

In principle, it seems that any appearance may have this saturated aspect, since all are 'given'. However, Marion does point to more specific instances: the experience of a work of art, of love, joy. One important example is that of being confronted by an icon. Marion distinguishes this from the idol, a dead thing that merely arrests and returns our own gaze. The idol is nothing but the reflection of ourselves, objectified and lifeless. In contrast, the icon exceeds our gaze. It looks at us, holding us in a gaze that cannot be objectified or measured.

Marion is trying to tread very carefully on the boundary between phenomenology and theology. However, the fact that he is also a theologian, and has written works that do identify the source of the gift with a God beyond or without being, has led some to accuse him of smuggling dogmatic theology into the supposedly unprejudiced science of phenomenology. The fact that the 'icon' is given a privileged place in explaining the idea of saturated phenomena suggests as much, as does Marion's ambiguous claims that such appearances are revelatory in a sense that seems to overlap with that of revelation in a specific and dogmatic sense.[5]

Derrida expresses his own reservations about Marion's account of givenness: 'Having *declared* that it excludes any determinable content, why does Marion determine "the pure form of the call" (and therefore of the gift) as call "in the name of the Father"?' (GT, p. 52n). As we have seen, for Derrida, the 'Come' must not be derived from any determined origin, or identified exclusively with the revealed content of any historical faith tradition. The fact that, in his more overtly theological work *God Without Being*, Marion identifies the bishop presiding at the Eucharist as the only true theologian, might only confirm Derrida's queasiness.[6]

Marion's work is extremely detailed and subtle. He agrees with Derrida in wanting to overcome ontotheology, and develop a language about God that does not define God in terms of being or presence. Part of his challenge to Derrida is to be more attentive to the ways in which negative theology undermines the metaphysics of being. God is unknowable, unattached to any name, but is not thereby reduced to an abstraction or emptiness: 'God remains incomprehensible, not imperceptible – without adequate concept, not without giving intuition'.[7] God is 'experienced' though the overwhelming of our intuition, not its barrenness.

Derrida's response is to call into question the link Marion makes between the givenness of appearances and the idea of the pure gift. He argues that 'givenness' always assumes some prior horizon of consciousness and intention. Without this, we must leave the bounds of phenomenology and admit that we are *interpreting* the given as a gift. The gift itself can never appear. It breaks with the horizon of what is 'given', which in Husserl's sense is also what is present. The gift is not and can never be the present in this way.[8]

It is important to see that Derrida does not mean that the impossibility of the gift means that there is no such thing:

> I said, to be very schematic and brief, that it is impossible for the gift to appear as such. So the gift does not exist as such, if by existence we understand being present and intuitively identified as such. So the gift does not exist and

appear as such; it is impossible for the gift to exist and appear as such. But I never concluded that there is no gift. I went on to say that if there is a gift, through this impossibility, it must be the experience of this impossibility, and it should appear as impossible. The event called gift is totally heterogeneous to theoretical identification, to phenomenological identification.[9]

The paradox lies in the impossibility and absence of the gift, which nevertheless enters into our experience. Indeed, it is what sets our experience going. Derrida stresses that the gift cannot be captured and defined within the circle of the economy, of giving and receiving. However, this does not reduce the gift to the status of a blank and empty nothingness:

> The overrunning of the circle by the gift, if there is any, does not lead to a simple, ineffable exteriority that would be transcendent and without relation. It is this exteriority that sets the circle going, it is this exteriority that puts the economy in motion. It is this exteriority that engages in the circle and makes it turn. (GT. p 30)

In a startling adoption of Aristotle's language about God, Derrida even dubs the gift a 'first mover' (GT, p. 31).

However, we need to be clear that the gift is not, like Aristotle's Prime Mover, pure thought thinking itself in absolute self-identity. It is inseparable from the idea of *différance* and the breaking open of origins. As Derrida puts it, 'there is only a problematic of the gift on the basis of a consistent problematic of the trace and the text . . . we are unable to do otherwise than *take our departure in texts insofar as they depart* (they separate from themselves and their origin, from us) *at the departure* [*dès les départ*]' (GT, p. 100). The (pure) origin is secondary, lost in a movement of difference from before any beginning. The experience of the gift is also one of a radical forgetting of a past beyond any recall. This would not be an accidental forgetting that could be remedied given the appropriate prompts and reminders; it is not even the forgetting associated with the psychoanalytical notion of repression. Nevertheless, it is not nothing, not a 'simple non-experience' (GT, p. 17).

The gift does not appear as such, but it leaves its mark in experience. Derrida uses motifs such as the trace, cinders, ashes. The gift is disseminated, fragile, never an object of knowledge. And yet it also demands the most unconditional respect for and witness to the other. Referring to Baudelaire's story of the giving of a counterfeit coin to a beggar, Derrida notes that money, credit and credence go hand in hand. This most economical reality is inhabited by a demand for what exceeds knowledge and measure. In the story, 'Everything is an act of faith' (GT, p. 97).

The gift retains a dual relationship with thought and language, one that Derrida explores through the reading of texts and stories about giving: 'The gift, if there is any, requires and at the same time excludes the possibility of narrative' (GT, p. 103).

It is worth noting that the theological move to narrative in the work of figures such as Hans Frei, George Lindbeck and Stanley Hauerwas offers a way of thinking dogma beyond the rigid dominance of propositional models of truth and language. Christian dogmas are not direct descriptions of an objective content, but ways of shaping the life and worship of communities of faith. Truth lies in the living response of the church to God, not in content that could be examined and argued over through a neutral discourse of reason.

Derrida might well be sympathetic to such a nuanced view of faith. Nevertheless, his argument suggests that the category of narrative is no more neutral than that of reason. Narratives are located, institutionalized and owned. The gift demands narration, a form of language inseparable from time, faith and the other. However, it cannot be confined within a narrative that obeys a determined teleology and authorship. The gift is just what unsettles the origin and end of the story.

The gift thus relativizes all settled structures and starting points, but it does not do so in the name of a hostility to all order and truth: 'as no natural stability is ever given, as there is only *stabilization in process*, that is, essentially precarious, one must presuppose "older" structures, let us not say originary structures, but more complicated and more unstable ones' (GT, p. 95). This is not therefore a reduction to chaos or pure disorder. By keeping open the relationship to the other and to time, it also keeps alive the possibility of what Derrida calls grace. Grace is what surprises us in the gift. Beyond calculation or narration, it is the meeting of our conscious decisions and the chance of an unforeseen future: 'There must be chance, encounter, the involuntary, even unconsciousness or disorder, and there must be intentional freedom, and these two conditions must – miraculously, graciously – agree with each other' (GT, p. 123).

The gift calls for a different thinking of responsibility, a thinking that is explored at length in a work that contains some of Derrida's most striking writing on God and faith.

The heresy of responsibility

The Gift of Death takes its starting point from the work of the philosopher Jan Patocka, who had been involved in resistance to the Communist regime in Czechoslovakia before its collapse. Patocka's work on the historical development of concepts of responsibility in the West leads Derrida to reflect on the way in which responsibility is tied to the idea of the secret. One tradition of thought suggests that I can only be responsible for my actions if I can give a full, clear and open account of why I did this and not that. However, Derrida argues that if we take this to its logical conclusion, it really means the abdication of responsibility. If I can explain all my reasons for acting as I did, then I am basing my actions on publicly available rules. This means that I have not really taken a decision, I have simply acted on a rule. And that means I cannot really be acting responsibly.

Derrida puts things the other way round. True responsibility means my motives and reasons can never be brought fully into the light of day or the clarity of reason. It cannot just be the application or outworking of knowledge. So there is something about responsibility and the responsible person that is hidden from the light of day: not accidentally as though one day it could be revealed if we had the right way of looking at it, but necessarily. That is what Derrida means by the secret: not a contingent bit of knowledge that I happen to know and keep from you, but an essential hiddenness that makes truth and ethics possible. And he links this with the idea that my responsibility is called out from me, provoked by the other. It is not something that I simply possess and can know and account for. I am held in relationship to the other, whose own identity and essence never become a matter of knowledge for me. Again, despite Derrida's reservations, the connections with Levinas are strong.

So responsibility does not centre upon clarity and reason, however important these remain. What comes first is the secret in me and the gaze of the other. Ethics is a matter of witness, risk – and faith: 'responsibility and faith go together, however paradoxical that might seem to some, and both should, in the same movement, exceed mastery and knowledge' (GD, p. 6).

This sounds promising for a theological project that wants to take inspiration from Derrida; not only his critique of the philosophical tradition, but his constructive use of ideas that sound close to the heart of theology. As one might expect, however, matters are not so simple. For one thing, responsibility, like decision, must go beyond what is calculable or governed by pre-existing rules. Derrida points out 'what ties responsibility to *heresy*' (GD, p. 26). Heresy is defined by its root meaning 'choice', but it is hardly accidental that it carries overtones of breaking with, subverting and resisting the concept of orthodoxy.

How is the faith of responsibility related to Christian faith? To explore this further, Derrida examines Kierkegaard's disturbing work *Fear and Trembling*, written under the pseudonym Johannes de Silentio. *Fear and Trembling* is a reflection upon the story of Abraham's willingness to sacrifice his son Isaac. For de Silentio, it is a story glossed over by complacent bourgeois Christians, who praise Abraham for his faith, without stopping to think that on any accepted ethical criteria, Abraham is a criminal and would-be child murderer.

Ratcheting up the horror of the tale, de Silentio uses it to accentuate the absurdity, the offensive scandal that true faith entails. Abraham is willing to give up Isaac and all that Isaac represents, in faith that though dead, Isaac will be returned to him. This faith is willing to suspend the universal norms of ethics. It cannot make itself understood in any human language. It is a decision based on the absurd, a response to God's call as absolute, no matter what.

We can detect the troubling logic at work here, one not so far removed from the actions of the suicide bomber or crusading army. But Kierkegaard's text is not designed to offer easy answers, only to make the scandalized reader face the paradox of faith.

Derrida finds much to affirm in Kierkegaard's emphasis on the secrecy and risk of faith, which cannot be calculated according to any rational measure. However, he is wary of the way Kierkegaard is implicitly giving a Christian gloss to the story, which turns the offence of faith into a question of whether the individual will believe in the sacrificed Christ as the Son of God, the God-Man, the absolute paradox. Derrida is wary because by identifying the other in such a particular and unique way, the offence of faith finds an outlet in violent exclusion, in institutions with a vested interest in perpetuating themselves and securing their identity against all infidels.

So Derrida reads the tale against the grain of Kierkegaard: yes, we must place our response to the wholly other above all the generalized laws of ethics and society. But the wholly other is not necessarily a God, separate from us, detached from the earth, whose incarnation in the Son only serves to underline his paradoxical distance from us. No: every other is wholly other. The acceptance of responsibility, in all its radical excess,

> propels me into the space or risk of absolute sacrifice. There are also others, an infinite number of them, the unnumerable generality of others, to whom I should be bound by the same responsibility ... *Every other (one) is every (bit) other [tout autre est tout autre]*, every one else is completely or wholly other. (GD, p. 68)

Derrida's French formula, which we have met before, and which cannot be translated into English with any elegance, preserves an essential ambiguity: 'It implies that God, as the wholly other, is to be found everywhere there is something of the wholly other' (GD, p. 78). Every other (and we should not rush to assume that this is confined only to human beings) places a unique and binding call upon us. And whatever response we make, we will always be sacrificing the call and needs of some others, of most others. To attend to one person is not to attend to so many others. To feed my cat is not to feed all the other cats in the world. And yet we must respond, we must choose, we must act.

That is the paradox of faith we are caught in, one that always reminds us to test the limits of our allegiances and our hospitality, and to recognize in every other a trace of transcendence. It is part of what lies behind the idea of a 'gift' of death. To give death (the French title of the book is *Donner la mort*) might mean to kill, or, with the addition of a reflexive pronoun, to commit suicide. However, it could also mean giving oneself for the other, offering one's own life in place of the other, and so making a gift of one's own death. I give what I can only give: my time, the time that is singular to me because I am mortal. In a sense, therefore, I can only ever give my death in giving my life for the other.

Derrida is suggesting that this gift of death is not reserved for the most extreme cases of self-sacrifice. It is an everyday event. One gives oneself to and for the other, opening oneself out to a responsibility that might ask everything of us. In the same moment, one cannot attend to all the (other) others who also lay obligations on us. As one gives one's life for some, so one also sacrifices those one cannot serve or save. In different, irreconcilable but necessary ways, death is given. This is not a situation we can avoid. It is the condition that haunts and makes possible our every decision.

If this is so, then it is only as mortals, only as those who can give and receive death, that we are ethical: 'only a mortal can be responsible' (GD, p. 41), because only a mortal knows their own finitude, their unique irreplaceability. Death gives me this responsibility, because it singles me out, exposes me to the absolute risk that giving to the other entails.

We have already seen how Derrida's early work on Husserl insists that life is intrinsically mortal, temporal, finite. An immortal God, therefore, would seem to be the opposite of life. Here, we discover that an immortal God would also be the height of irresponsibility: an invulnerable, unaffected, indifferent God, for whom nothing is ever at stake.

It is striking then that Derrida still does not abandon talk of God. It is a language that can still evoke the experience of the wholly other, confirming our impossible experience and gift of responsibility. Language about God is the impossible language of the gift, but the corollary of this is that 'God' escapes identification, is disseminated into the traces of the world:

We should stop thinking about God as someone over there, way up there, transcendent, and, what is more – into the bargain [pardessus le marché], precisely – capable, more than any satellite orbiting in space, of seeing into the most secret of the most interior places. It is perhaps necessary, if we are to follow the traditional Judeo-Christian-Islamic injunction, to think of God and of the name of God without such idolatrous stereotyping or representation. Then we might say: God is the name of the possibility I have of keeping a secret, that is visible from the interior but not from the exterior ... God is in me, he is the absolute 'me' or 'self', he is that structure of invisible interiority that is called, in Kierkegaard's sense, subjectivity. (GD, pp. 108–109)

Derrida's (perhaps rather tongue-in-cheek) claim is that his heretical ethics is in fact a way of taking the Abrahamic tradition at its word, resisting all the idols that turn God into a super-being far away and cut off from the world, and instead making the issue of faith about how we respond to those around us. And we can only do this if we refuse to let ourselves be translated into abstract, universal norms, laws and rules. If we preserve a radical, hidden, secret subjectivity.

But does this make God simply a projection of myself, an ideal I make up and use to add a little symbolic lustre to my ethical striving? On the one had, we have to acknowledge that there is a real risk here that Derrida in fact empties God of all otherness, and makes God into a capacity of the self. That would surely mean falling back into the self-enclosed humanism from which Derrida is also struggling to be free. The 'satellite' God that Derrida rejects is hardly an image that would be endorsed by any credible theologian today, nor does it reflect the complex ways in which God is thought of in Christian tradition, for instance. Is Derrida setting up a straw-God, easy to knock down, with the result that we have nothing other than immanent forces left to worship?

However, The Gift of Death also makes it clear that the interior secret of the self, what Kierkegaard calls subjectivity, is not a closed in ego-centred citadel. It is precisely the place where the other's approach is felt, the absolute other 'whose name here is God' (GD, p. 66). If God is 'in' me, it is not as a possession or part of my ego.

The gift, whose trace calls me to respond, is only known in an impossible experience of forgetting. God, too, is known as withdrawing, as forgotten, as dispersed. That withdrawal is the condition for me to respond to every other in all their singular mystery, irreplaceable uniqueness and unconditional demand. Derrida is therefore claiming a certain fidelity to the tradition, a fidelity that by *its own logic* deals undecidably with heresy and atheism. After all, 'traditionality is not orthodoxy'.

Forgetting: the incarnation

There is another aspect to this retreating God, which Derrida touches upon in an intriguing way. It comes as part of his discussion of Patocka, and it is far from clear that he would endorse it without qualification. Nevertheless, it is suggestive of another experience of the unpresentable gift of grace:

> On what condition does goodness exist beyond all calculation? On the condition that goodness forget itself, that the movement be a movement of the gift that renounces itself, hence a movement of infinite love. Only infinite love can renounce itself, and, in order to *become finite*, become incarnated in order to love the other, to love the other as a finite other. (GD, pp. 50–51)

The gift, we have seen, cannot appear as such. In that sense, a belief in the unique incarnation of God would be suspect. It would claim too much: that God could be immediately present, fully embodied in an individual whose 'body' is then communicated to an ecclesiastical community, its hierarchy and sacraments. God as incarnate would be the most direct presentation of truth, truth in person, a truth conveyed exclusively by a particular faith tradition. The problem in this for Derrida would be the identification of traces (gospel narratives, iconography, Eucharistic elements) with the substance and fullness of a fully present truth, embodied wholly in Christ. Interpreted in that way, the Incarnation would indeed lend itself to Hegelian philosophy, as the figure and reality of absolute truth. And this truth would continue to depend on ideas of presence that would suppress time, difference, finitude and responsibility.

However, this is of course not the only way of reading the incarnation. For the incarnation could also signal the trace of an otherness that defies ecclesial definition and ownership, and confirms materiality and history as the inescapable context for experiencing the impossible gift. This would be an incarnation of the good, of the gift, that takes us beyond all calculation. It would be the condition of a nondogmatic faith.

The duplicity of incarnation can be traced in a number of Derrida's texts. In 'The Pit and the Pyramid', Derrida discusses Hegel's approach to signs. Hegel integrates history and change into philosophy, seeking to reconcile the finite and infinite through a real historical story of alienation and reconciliation. Despite this, Derrida argues that Hegel still privileges ideas of spirit, ideality and presence. Time and difference are the necessary, but ultimately secondary means for spirit to realize its full unity with itself. Language, and the sign in particular, are defined according to the philosophical hierarchy. Meaning is equated with a soul, deposited in a material body or sign: 'The sign, as the unity of the signifying body and the signified ideality, becomes a kind of incarnation' (M, p. 82). This incarnation is essential to meaning, but only as a stepping stone towards a fuller ideal certainty. The sign and the body, in their externality, have to be overcome, 'incorporated' into spirit. At the same time, however, the very fact that Hegel needs such externality in order for spirit to realize itself opens the door for a deconstructive reading, in which incarnation comes before ideality.

A second instance comes in the discussion of Hegel and Christianity in *Glas*. For Hegel, it is of the nature of spirit that it is divided from itself, in order to come to fuller self-conscious awareness of its truth. The highest 'example' of this is God, and yet, for Hegel, God is not an 'example' at all, since God is another name for absolute, universal spirit. Derrida describes this fundamental self-alienation of God:

cannot God – of himself – fall into the finite, incarnate himself, become his own proper example, play with himself as the infinite becoming finite (death) in order to reappropriate his infinity, to repeat the spirit, that is, to have a son–man who is his own proper seed, his own proper product, his own proper result, his best yield? (Gl, p. 30a)

The gift of the incarnation and of death is not really a gift in Hegel's eyes. It remains a movement confined by a sense of property. It is investment with a guaranteed return, with no real risk involved. Everything is kept within the (holy) family. Incarnation in this sense is no scandal, but the essence of ontotheology. It is a transgression that actually confirms the logic of the metaphysics to which is belongs.

At the same time, the very idea of God divided from himself, of God playing with himself, suggests something more subversive and perverse: an exposure of God as *différance*, which breaks out of the logic of sameness, just as the text of *Glas* is divided to the reader's line of sight, impossible to assimilate into a single reading.

A final example of Derrida's attitude to incarnation can be found in *On Touching*, a text devoted to a reading of the work of Jean Luc-Nancy, but that also interprets many classic philosophical treatments of touch and flesh. Derrida explores the paradoxical nature of touch, which seems to promise an immediate contact with reality beyond us, but which is actually always mediated by surfaces that both reveal and veil what is real.

In a section on the work of the Christian thinker Jean-Louis Chrétien, Derrida explores the Christian interpretation of touch. For Chrétien, our ordinary experience of bodily touch points us to a more fundamental reality, in which the divine spirit touches itself in a pure and immediate way. Sensible touching is 'the incarnate trope and the carnal figure of a purely spiritual touch' (OT, p. 247). At the same time, Derrida acknowledges that Chrétien does not wish to make spiritual truth something abstract and ahistorical. Physical embodiment is 'converted', given its true orientation to spirit by a historical revelation, specifically through the embodied truth of the Incarnation and Eucharist.

Chrétien interprets the Incarnation in terms of the Father reaching out with his 'hand': the Son or Logos. And only God's touch is immediate: 'Immediacy is the absolute truth of divine touching, "the hand of God," his Incarnation in Logos or the Son's flesh' (OT, p. 254). All finite touching is mediated and it is only an illusion to think otherwise. The divine touch invites us to respond in a mutual, reciprocal relationship. As for Hegel, so here, there is a proper 'passage' from the finite to the infinite, the human to the divine, by way of passion, incarnation, transubstantiation (OT, p. 261).

Derrida's reading of Chrétien is respectful, and his book as a whole avoids taking a systematic stance on questions of touch, even as it troubles ideas of immediacy and what is proper or essential to it. However, towards the end of the section we have been looking at, we are returned to an idea of 'spacing', a difference or trace that would disrupt immediacy and that would not be confined within a finite, worldly realm. Derrida also raises the question of substitution, 'the figuration of the unfigurable' (OT, p. 261) in which one figure stands in for something that cannot be presented. Chrétien admits this as possible, but only through the logic of incarnation, 'the gift of a God who makes himself into Man' in which it is God who chooses his own figure, his own 'proper example' to recall what was said in *Glas* (ibid.). In this economy, the essence of God and Man remain untroubled. God remains beyond all substitution and 'though there may be some spacing in it, Incarnation will never be the phenomenon of an irreducible finitude' (OT, p. 262).

Derrida does not directly contradict this logic, but raises the possibility of another way of thinking about substitution, one that draws on the language of prosthetics and transplantation to suggest that the boundary between the original and the substitute becomes harder and harder to determine. If the heart, even the Sacred Heart, can be transplanted, what happens to the idea that all finite touching gets its sense only from God, whose touch is immediate, pure and unbounded? Derrida again invokes the *khora* as the nontheological spacing that makes such ideals possible, as if to suggest that Chrétien's theology of touch ultimately denies and suppresses the difference that it must presume.

Is there another thought of God, and of incarnation, that does not lead the finite back to a pure ground that is wholly spiritual and immediate, which has, in effect, abolished the flesh? Is the Incarnation destined to be an unfortunate necessity or detour for a theology that values disembodied spirit above all?

The Gift of Death at least hints at another way, radicalizes the notion of God's self-emptying as a love that is made flesh, forgetful of its origins, no longer yearning for a return to unity and the immediacy of spirit. The incarnate gift of love could no longer be secured from the risk of death. It would be disseminated, open to substitution, a singular figure for the singularity of every other.

There is at least an echo here of Paul's characterization of the sacrifice of Christ as a free gift, an undeserved act of grace that excludes all boasting (Roman 3.21–31). Paul of course, also refers to the self-emptying of God in Christ as a servant who becomes a slave even to death for our sake (Philippians 2.5–11). The weakness of God is madness to philosophical reason and established religion (1 Corinthians 1.18–25).

It is worth noting that Derrida also links the gift and forgiveness, for both share a similar impossibility:

> There is only forgiveness, if there is such a thing, of the
> un-forgivable. Thus forgiveness, if it is possible, if there is
> such a thing, is not possible, it does not exist as possible, it
> exists only by exempting itself from the law of the possible,
> by impossibilizing itself, so to speak, and in the infinite
> endurance of the im-possible as impossible.[10]

If forgiveness were only to forgive what was forgivable, it would simply be the straightforward application of a rule. But if it is really to forgive, then it must transgress all rules and calculation, and enact an impossible event. Derrida notes that this is what forgiveness shares in common with the gift: 'Forgiveness as the impossible truth of the impossible gift'.[11]

This radically incarnate God has been hinted at before, in the God who separates himself from himself, appears only as the passing of difference or the trace of the other. In *Rogues*, having discussed the implicit theological foundations of ideas of sovereignty, Derrida opens another way of reading the divine, one that is open to the coming of the other and the promise of the future:

> In speaking of an ontotheology of sovereignty, I am
> referring here, under the name of God, this One and

Only God, to the determination of a sovereign, and thus indivisible, omnipotence. For wherever the name of God would allow us to think something else, for example a vulnerable nonsovereignty, one that suffers and is divisible, one that is mortal even, capable of contradicting itself or of repenting (a thought that is neither impossible nor without example), it would be a completely different story, perhaps even the story of a god who deconstructs himself in his ipseity. (R, p. 157)

Such a god would not be protected by the solidity of metaphysical foundations for 'nothing is less secure than a god without sovereignty' (R, p. 114). But perhaps, for Derrida, this is the only possibility of salvation, not in the sense of being redeemed, kept safe and sound, freed from finitude, but in the sense of being opened to the *salut* or salutation of the other.

This would be the vulnerable incarnation of the gift, not in a perfected body, but in the fragility of remains, what Derrida also calls cinders or ash:

I understand that the cinder is nothing that can be in the world, nothing that remains as an entity [*étant*]. It is the being [*l'être*] rather, that there is – this is a name of the being that there is but which, giving itself (es gibt ashes) is nothing, remains beyond everything that is (konis epekeina tes ousias) remains unpronounceable in order to make saying possible although it is nothing. (C, p. 73)

Derrida writes of a 'vulnerable tenderness, with the patience of a cinder' (C, p. 35), whose effect is that of 'bestowing grace and dissemination at the same time' (C, p. 39). In this 'dispersion without return' we find that 'the cinder is not, is not what is' (C, p. 27). This is a despairing hope, a faith and grace that remains to us after the Holocaust and the genocides the world has endured.

Paradox and uncertainty surround the vanishing appearance of this grace. Its incarnation is also its betrayal as soon as that incarnation is fixed and defined. In Marion's terms, the icon can always become an idol, and we have to choose how to see it: 'betrayal is a revelation ... manifestation of the impossible truth on which it will have been necessary, at every instant, and despite repetitions, to decide once and for all' (C, p. 26).

Cinders, like many of Derrida's texts, speaks with plural voices. It does not offer a thematic description of the gift, but performs a faithful response to it, which is inevitably agnostic. One voice confesses: 'An order or a promise, the desire of a prayer, I do not know, not yet' (C, p. 27).

This unknowing is echoed elsewhere in Derrida's work, where we read of a faith or confession that 'has nothing to do with truth' (Circ, p. 107), of the 'sacred truth of this nonknowledge' (Circ, p. 142), of 'believing, the only relationship possible to the other as other' (AF, p. 94).

In *The Gift of Death*, Derrida confesses and declares: 'Our faith is not assured, because faith can never be, it must never be a certainty' (GD, p. 80). As I have stressed throughout this chapter, this is not an abandonment of reason, but a way of thinking what reason must always owe to faith. *Rogues* also invokes 'the rational space of a hypercritical faith, one without dogma and without religion, irreducible to any and all religious or implicitly theocratic institutions' (R, p. 153). Rational, irreligious – but faith, nonetheless. A theology that deconstructs itself, always vigilant, always questioning the ways in which the otherness of the other is reduced.

A theology of the question, a theology radically in question haunts Derrida's work, but it is not one that will leave the politics of orthodox truth undisturbed. As he insists in *Memoirs of the Blind*, something comes before the knowledge that seeks to mirror the world: there is a 'blessing before the knowing' (MB, pp. 29–30). Indeed, he goes further and says that 'at the origin of the *graphein* there is debt or gift rather than representational fidelity' (MB, p. 30). Is there a way open here for grace, for creation, for revelation? Perhaps; but it is not a straight way, not one that will support an idea of revealed truth as a set of certified propositions, for Derrida adds: 'the fidelity of faith matters more than the representation, whose movement this fidelity commands, and thus precedes. And faith, in the moment proper to it, is blind' (ibid.).

Chapter 7

Gift or Poison? Theological Responses to Derrida

Gift or poison? Derrida has noted the duplicity built into a number of languages, whereby words meaning gift or remedy also have sinister overtones of what comes to threaten and blight the one who receives what is given. It is an indication that the gift for us is always impure. To receive the gift, to welcome the other, is always to take a risk. There is no guarantee that the other comes to us with friendly intentions.

A similar uncertainty surrounds Derrida's use of religious motifs. Do they offer a constructive alternative to a theology still dominated by a metaphysics or presence, certainty and totality? Or do they corrode the truth of religion from within, emptying it of all particular content and driving its adherents into the desert of nihilism? Is Derrida just dressing up his atheism in religious garb?

Up to this point, references to secondary literature on Derrida has been kept to a minimum, in order to allow the reader to engage with his own works in greater depth, without that reading being dictated by a prior theological agenda. Derrida has often been the target of ill-informed commentary, which has avoided the awkward necessity of reading what he actually wrote. My hope is that those who have followed this essay so far, even if unfamiliar with much of Derrida's work, will have a better grasp of the motivation and breadth of his dealings with theology.

However, the way in which Derrida has been received and interpreted by theologians also plays an important role in this story. As we will see, Derrida's positions have been understood in very different ways by commentators who cannot be accused of knowing his work in a superficial way. Exploring this contested arena will help us to discern what, if any, are the risks and opportunities Derrida's legacy offers to theology.

The primary focus will be on responses that come from a Christian theological backdrop. This is not to suggest that other religious traditions have nothing to say. There have been significant engagements with Derrida's relationship to Judaism (some of which we will touch on later), and a smattering of other texts relating his work to Buddhist and Hindu themes.[1] In the main, however, the academic setting of theology in which Derrida's work has been received has been dominated by Christian voices. Perhaps this reflects the 'globalatinization' of which Derrida himself writes in 'Faith and Knowledge', the strained universalism of a highly Eurocentric and specifically Christian discourse.

For ease of navigation, the chapter is divided into a number of sections. It is not the case that all the thinkers gathered in each section share the same views, but the format suggests ways of interpreting the variety of responses to Derrida in a coherent way. Naturally, we cannot hope to do justice to the complexity and depth of the each writer we cover here. The reader is invited to pursue these hints and openings further into the texts themselves.

Nihilism and the death of God

One of the first substantial attempts to relate Derrida more closely to theology was the 1982 collection *Deconstruction and Theology*, which included a contribution from one of the original 1960s Death-of-God theologians, Thomas Altizer. In the first essay of the book, Carl Raschke boldly affirms that deconstruction 'is in the final analysis *the death of God put into writing*'.[2] Dissolving any notion of God as a stable presence or absolute truth, Derrida's work suggests a radically incarnate understanding of the divine dispersed in writing: 'The divine word, the *sacra verba*, is truly made flesh; it reaches its kenotic consummation, its radical otherness, in a theology which is nought but a writing about theology'.[3]

Altizer's own contribution recognizes the complexity of Derrida's theology, and the influence upon it of Kabbalism and the idea of God's self-alienation.[4] This does not spell the end of theology, however, for the desire for a unifying centre and therefore the idea of God remain 'inescapable'.[5] For Altizer, Derrida's Judaism offers the promise of a new beginning for Christian thinking. God is seen withdrawing from the world as the absent origin. Altizer claims that this absence of God sets history free, history now understood as the total presence of difference itself.[6] God dies and is discovered anew in the movement of time, in consciousness and language. God is exiled from himself and embodied in the world. This self-embodiment of God brings history to an end, because history no longer has any stable ground or reference point beyond itself. The death of God is both a 'Christian nihilism'[7] and an experience of 'absolute grace' as God's identity and ipseity 'has now passed into the centre of the world.[8]

Altizer's focus on the Kabbalah is taken up in some significant readings of Derrida from a Jewish perspective. Eve Tavor Bannet argues that deconstruction is 'an opening to the infinitely Other',[9] which is 'a deconstructed God, the Jewish God become pure *Ein Sof* and pared down to the mystery of his infinite Otherness'.[10] The Kabbalistic motif is pursued further: 'In Derrida, as in *kabbalah*, the world is only possible by virtue of a certain contraction and withdrawal of the deity, and the world is henceforth separated from the deity by an abyss'.[11] What results is akin to atheism. Whatever 'God' names can take no determinate form, for 'To think of God as a subject, as a Creator or Speaker, is to reduce his Otherness'.[12]

Bannet concludes that '*différance* is God and is not God'.[13] It cannot be prayed to, nor can it be encountered. There is no divine plan or providence. For Derrida, therefore, the world is absurd, lacking all real referents, a pure fiction. Texts refer only to themselves.

The problem here is that Bannet constructs an ideal of radical alterity that ends by collapsing all differences into self-reference. It struggles to take account of later ideas of the messianic in Derrida (partly due to its date of publication), and does not do justice to his continuing insistence on the value of truth and reference, however complicated these values become. As Allan Megill puts it, 'If Derrida champions a postmodernist, "poetic" interpretation, he also champions, as Reb Derrida, the "rabbinical" interpretation that still seeks a truth in things'.[14]

Susan Handelman also associates Derrida with the Rabbis. However, her emphasis falls upon the endless nature of commentary that is the lifeblood of Rabbinic or Talmudic Judaism. According to Handelman, Christianity seeks an end to interpretation by presenting Jesus as the incarnate (final) Word. The Rabbis place metaphor above literality, and a relational truth above one based on substances. The Biblical text becomes self-referential and endless, an infinite world of meaning: 'For the Jew, God's presence is inscribed or traced within a text, not a body. Divinity is located in language, not person'.[15] Handelman's thesis is that this style of interpretation is enjoying a new life in contemporary literary theory, with its stress on the death of the author and the endlessness of intertextual meaning.

Derrida is associated with this trend in a dramatic way. Handelman claims that he wants to 'erect a new religion of Writing'[16] and that he is 'the new high priest of the religion of absence'.[17] The result is that he seeks to subvert the possibility of any thinking other than his own, since all truth and meaning are now displaced and caught in the endless web of writing. His thought seeks to free itself from all foundations while claiming 'to be the origin and law of everything'.[18]

Both the praise and the criticism is surely overblown, because Handelman's equation of deconstruction with a religion of pure absence is a misreading. Derrida does not simply invert the value placed upon absence and presence, but seeks to situate them and their relationship differently. Nor does he deny all textual reference to an outside, or close down all otherness, quite the contrary.

The irony of Handelman's anti-literal, anti-incarnational approach is that, by leaving all differences flattened out, it becomes a pure presence, a literal embodiment of the divine as text, as writing that refers to nothing but itself. There is surely a strange and unwitting connection here with the death of God theology of Altizer, one that is reflected in other essays in *Deconstructing Theology*.

For instance, the theme of incarnation is present in Mark C. Taylor's essay, where he argues that 'A death of God (a)theology, which is really a radical Christology, finds its completion in the crucifixion of the individual self and the resurrection of a universal humanity'.[19] God is kenotically emptied out into the flow of the world, and incarnation becomes a kind of embodied *différance*.

It is a thought that is developed at greater length in Taylor's *Erring: A Postmodern A/Theology*. The point is made again that '*deconstruction is the hermeneutic of the death of God*'.[20] For Taylor, it means the end of the substantial self, the end the 'book' as the totality of meaning, and the death of God. However, in this death something of the sacred continues to be experienced. For Taylor, writing becomes the principal matrix through which to understand 'the infinite play of the divine milieu'.[21]

Taylor is advocating a radical change in the understanding of the referent of Christian discourse by correlating deconstruction with the incarnational grammar of that discourse. Incarnation is thus seen as a deconstructive event in which 'the death of God can be understood in terms of a radical Christology that prepares the way for reinterpreting the divine. From an a/theological perspective, Jesus is manifested as word and word is read as writing'.[22] A/theology deconstructs the traditional metaphysical notion of a unified and existent God and sees the divine dispersed into difference.

Taylor's 'undeniably ambiguous' a/theology[23] resists the assimilation of discourse about the divine to the ontological commitments of classical Christian theology. His position is therefore a little more subtle than Raschke's, because there is still a need for a hermeneutic, an act of interpretation of the death of God that does not simply end all talk of the divine. Clearly, this divine will look very different from the metaphysical notion of God as a necessary being. Nevertheless, Taylor still affirms that deconstruction 'harbors a radically new theology, a secular, post-ecclesiastical theology'.[24]

As we have seen, the figure of incarnation and self-emptying plays a key part in an account of the self-deconstruction of the Absolute into the economy of differences that constitute the world. In this Christology, God is poured out without remainder: 'Radical christology is thoroughly incarnational – the divine "is" the incarnate word. Furthermore, this embodiment of the divine is the death of God'.[25] 'God' no longer corresponds to a being or to Being, for 'God is what word means and word is what 'God' means'.[26] God is no longer characterized by identity and ipseity but is virtually equated with difference.

There is no God beyond the interlacings of textuality and therefore no eschaton to aim for, no paradise against which to judge our plight. There is only the passion of language:

The Crucified is the cruciform word that is always already inscribed in the eternally recurring play of the divine milieu. Scripture marks the *via crucis*, in which all creation involves dismemberment and every solution presupposes dissolution. When *die Mitte is überall*, transitoriness and passage need no longer be repressed. Arising and passing can be welcomes as 'productive and destructive force, as *continual creation*.'[27]

Despite the subtlety with which Taylor works out this position, it must be asked whether he, any more than the other writers we have touched on so far, genuinely stays with the undecidability of deconstruction. Their use of the trope of incarnation (especially when allied to Altizer's notion of total presence) suggests a total emptying out of God into writing, God embodied as the trace. This risks losing sight of ways in which God names a future and an otherness that resist embodied immediacy. The undecidability in Derrida's thinking, which still maintains contact with reference and the singular otherness named by God, here becomes 'decided', a sacralization of purely immanent flows.

Admittedly, this is potentially unfair, as each of these writers envisage a new beginning for the divine in language. The divine milieu of writing is one of creativity and destruction, and offers the experience of a 'mazing grace'.[28] Nevertheless, the identification of the divine with writing does raise a significant question: has the otherness 'God' names been comprehended and contained within an idea of writing or history that is all-consuming and foundational?

We will return to Mark C. Taylor's later constructive position in another section. For now, we turn our attention to a radical theologian who stands at the forefront of those who have recognized Derrida's religious importance in the British context: Don Cupitt.

In the mid-1980s, Cupitt remarks that Derrida

is the modern Kierkegaard. As Kierkegaard had to use stratagems to subvert Hegelianism, so Derrida has to use stratagems to subvert the pretensions and the realist illusions of Western reason, and to coax us through to the new way of thinking. A similar deconstruction of all false, nostalgic, otherworldly and metaphysical styles in theology is now needed in order to purify religion.[29]

As we can already see from these words, Cupitt calls religious thought and practice to break with realism, the idea that religious language copies or describes an objective supernatural reality, a final Truth 'out there' beyond the world. His early work in this vein was Kantian, arguing that God should be seen as a regulative moral and spiritual ideal, symbolizing the religious requirement. Anything else was a distraction from the religious life, a claim to knowledge of the divine that could not be justified. Religion becomes a matter of the heart and of subjectivity.

Under the influence of Derrida, however, Cupitt's thought becomes much more centred on language itself. Language, he argues, is composed of differences, and no term in language can hook up to a reality beyond itself. Citing Wittgenstein and Derrida, he claims that 'The surface play of phenomena – words, signs, meanings, appearances – *is* reality. Why seek to downgrade it? The fatal illusion is to believe that we can pierce the veil and find more-real and unchanging verities behind it'.[30] Taylor's radical Christology finds its echo here too: 'That is how the message of the Incarnation of God in Christ is now to be understood: God enters into contingency, "God" dies, and now – everything that lives is holy'.[31]

Cupitt clearly wishes to oppose the Platonic hierarchy that subjects time to eternity, desire to reason, appearance to essence, female to male. He argues from the differential nature of meaning to a thoroughgoing relativism of truth: 'Strictly speaking, words are related only to each other. There is no "finalistic" or pre-established bond at all between language and reality. Reference is merely conventional. There is no Meaning out there and no Truth out there'.[32] Cupitt argues from Derrida's critique of Husserlian presence and Heidegerrian nostalgia for Being that Derrida himself is 'satisfied with the secondariness of the sign'.[33]

All of our words are humanly created and historically evolving, which means there is no fixed point outside language that grounds it or to which it refers. Cupitt makes the point drawing on the well-known Derridean phrase:

'There is nothing outside the text', for however far we go
in chasing after some extra-textual reality which can
function as an objective criterion for checking the text, we
will still be operating within the realm of text. Our relation

to whatever we describe as 'reality' will still be subject to the textual logic which governs all thought. We never grasp objective 'natural presence' in a clear-cut, univocal way, for the very act of grasping is itself language-shaped.[34]

For Cupitt this means embracing a kind of nihilism, in which all fixed truths and values are set in flux, with nothing to ground them. However, the experience of this void has intense religious possibilities, as Derrida's own turn to theological motifs demonstrates: 'both in Nietzsche and in Derrida there is what the financial markets call a "dead cat's bounce". They drop into nihilism so suddenly and startlingly that in both of them there is a rebound, an indirect and negative return of religious ideas after nihilism'.[35] Cupitt argues that a religion after nihilism is possible, one that affirms life, contingency, and becoming, and that is free from otherworldliness and dogma.

A striking account of what a Derridean God might look like is given in 1987 book from which we have already quoted, *The Long Legged Fly*. Cupitt is describing a postmodern interpretation of culture as a shifting system of signs that has no transcendent source or end. A theology of culture would invoke a God who seems to share significant characteristics with *différance*:

> its God, insofar as it has one, must be radically transcendental and decentred. He is no sort of being. He is reached only by a regressive or transcendental analysis which goes back from our world to the world of linguistic meaning, and then to the character of that world of meaning as one in which nothing is selfsame and everything is relative and differential . . . So this world of meaning is nothing but a dance of difference in the Void; and *God* functions to remind us of that. He is so far back that he is not only prior to being, but he is prior even to the distinction between necessity and contingency. For on the one hand he is radically contingent in himself, being mere difference and otherness, a non-thing; while on the other hand there being just such an ultimate difference-in-nothingness is a necessary condition for the emergence of anything whatever.[36]

There is a resonance here with the idea (which we will encounter again in the work of Catherine Keller) of God as matrix of possibilities.[37]

However, we need to note that Cupitt is not embracing this as the only possible theological future. Also in *The Long-Legged Fly*, he outlines a utopian theology of desire (drawing on Deleuze) and theology of the cessation of desire (drawing on Buddhism). The end of objective theism and realism offers an opening to theological creativity and a plurality of perspectives. Cupitt is also critical of Derrida. He disagrees with the latter's resistance to mysticism, arguing that it has nothing to do with the metaphysics of presence, but is itself a radical and deconstructive theology of writing and secondariness.[38] He also notes that his thinking of life and being is more emotivist and biological than Derrida's[39]; indeed, his later writings are more inclined to drop any reference to God in favour of a post-metaphysical idea of Life.

Cupitt engages with Derrida for his own strategic purposes. Although his own thinking is mobile, he tends to fall back upon a humanistic constructivism, in which language creates reality from nothing. It is debatable whether deconstruction can be equated with this form of anti-realism, not least because its destabilizing effect opens language to an irreducible and nonhuman other. Like Taylor, Cupitt tends to resolve the paradoxical tensions of impossibility in a way that does not recognize that ideas of ordinariness or secondariness are themselves 'constructed', but not by anything like a human subject or even language itself. The result is a philosophy that risks simply mirroring the ideological flows of liberal capitalism, in which infinite choice has consumed actual difference.

A different orthodoxy

Given these potential pitfalls of the a/theological or anti-realist approach, it is perhaps not surprising that some of Derrida's interpreters have taken a very different tack. Accepting the reading of him as a nihilist, they have contrasted this strongly with a reading of orthodox Christian doctrine. The intention, however, has been nuanced: not a complete rejection of Derrida's agenda, but an argument that only orthodox Christian theology does real justice to issues of time, difference and embodiment.

A relatively early example is that put forward by Robert Magliola's *Derrida on the Mend*. Much of the book discusses Derrida's work in the light of its relationship to the Buddhist philosophy of Nagarjuna. However, its conclusion is that Derrida's deconstructive thought is in need of correction by a properly 'logocentric' discourse, grounded in revelation. This turns out to 'confirm in unexpected ways the conciliar definitions of the Trinity'.[40]

Magliola's reasoning is that, whereas Derrida views the Trinity as the epitome of self-enclosed identity, in fact it shows that the Christian God is made up of real, differentiated relationships. Revelation offers us 'a Trinity which is sacred difference'.[41] Christ's revelation and the teaching magisterium of the Church '*deconstruct* trinitarian theories which propose a self-enclosed entitative triadic model'.[42] Through the Holy Spirit, God is disseminated. The Trinity is constituted by purely negative or relational differences, 'a God of perpetual alterity' who supersedes Jewish monotheism and the nihilistic difference of Derrida.[43]

Magliola reflects the exuberance and creativity of recent Trinitarian theology. The recovery of a sense that Christian doctrine is not to be defined by the narrow theism of modernity or the God of philosophical metaphysics has unleashed a constructive critique of Enlightenment scepticism. God is relational, differentiated and people created in God's image are not isolated subjects, but are defined in and through otherness.

However, at the same time one can hardly fail to notice Magliola's serene confidence in the absoluteness of the teaching authority of the Church. Notions such as orthodoxy and revelation are not subjected to any real critique. The way in which his text is performed belies its surface meaning, since its logic has little respect for differences, or for any contextualization of ecclesiastical power. Its overt supercessionism in relation to the Jewish faith suggests that the caricatures of Hegel's all-consuming system have not been entirely banished.

John Milbank also offers a robustly orthodox theology, but one that tells its critical story with more depth and rigour, and that does not appeal to timeless foundations. He is a leading light in the 'Radical Orthodoxy' movement, which resists the modern assumption that there can be a neutral secular reason separate from any theological underpinnings. Such an idea of reason, Milbank argues, rests on its own undisclosed theological myths. Principal among these mythological themes is the notion that the world is founded on a violent struggle of forces, in which peace and goodness are always reactive and secondary. Against this, Milbank affirms a Christian narrative in which God's created peace is primary, and violence appears when the analogical participation of the world in God is severed.

A related argument is put forward by David Klemm, who argues that 'Derrida can be read as a kind of crypto-theologian, whose writings offer a sophisticated negative version of the ontological argument for the existence of God'.[44] For Klemm, Derrida's texts move us to an unknowable goal through negation. The origin and end of this movement can be named *différance* or God.[45] However, at the end of the day, Derrida refuses the name of God. His hidden theology is parasitical and secondary, because *différance* cannot truly take God's place: 'deconstruction cannot be theologically meaningful by its own lights; it requires the light of another, which it must deny'.[46]

For Milbank, the issue is more pointed: Derrida's crypto-theology is not just parasitical, it is anti-Christian. Derrida is put forward as a leading representative of a postmodern nihilism, which claims to do away with all foundations, but in fact asserts war and conflict as the ultimate reality. Derrida is therefore classed as a nihilist for whom violence and anarchy are the formative reality.[47] This is due to the dualism Derrida asserts between transcendental *différance* and conventional worldly systems of language and communication. In essence, Derrida privileges negativity and absence. Being is alienated from itself through its fall into language, leaving our own use of signs hopelessly cut adrift from meaning and reality. The 'writing' that Derrida celebrates is disembodied. It is nothing more than the ideal, death, deferral, the nihil.[48] For Milbank, this demands a reversal: only by affirming that our language and acts of creativity participate by analogy in God's can we be saved from an abstract, world-denying and negative idealism.

It is a point made at length by another Radical Orthodox theologian Catherine Pickstock. She contests Derrida's reading of Plato, arguing that, like the Sophists, Derrida fetishizes dead, idealized writing.[49] Plato's affirmation of speech is not a violent gesture that suppresses time and difference, but an invitation to an embodied form of communication, best expressed in worship and liturgy, in which the speaker is drawn to the Good beyond being. In contrast, 'Derrida's emphasis on writing is a denial of the living and dying physical *body*'.[50] Whereas Socrates appeals to the inspirational presence of the Muse, a personal metaphor for creative participation, 'Derrida's written model suggests no people at all, only a word which comes from nowhere, an autonomous word which conceals or violently eradicates its origins and dictates to its "author", rendering him entirely passive before a disembodied and (spiritual?) power'.[51] Derrida's 'play' masks an obeisance to a sinister deity, one whose otherness is the denial of our integrity.

The result is that, for all his talk of difference, Derrida is incapable of making any particular differences significant in themselves. *Différance* is an abstract, catch-all category that levels all real differences, whereas Plato's relation of the world to a Good beyond itself actually allows differences and innovations to appear, be interpreted and evaluated. For Derrida, difference is indistinguishable from indifference, or, worse, from a meaningless violence.[52]

In the light of this, Pickstock shares Milbank's negative assessment of Derrida as a nihilist, whose nihilism is actually the symptom of false worship and idolatry: 'his exaltation of the *nihil* is tantamount to an abasement before the perfect abstract and graspable object . . . his exaltation of absence and postponement turns out to be but the inevitably nihilistic conclusion of a rationalism indifferent to the specificities of human place, time, and desire'.[53] Emptiness and deferral become Derrida's gods, and 'Derrida simply does not consider the Platonic alternative that instead of being at once radical absence *and* original presence, the good might be an inaccessible and inexhaustible plenitude'.[54] Radical Orthodoxy's God is an overflowing fullness, and nothing can truly be known apart from God. There is no secular space or thought that is not actually a counter-religion to Christianity, a nihilistic worship of nothingness and war.

Milbank takes particular issue with Derrida's idea of the impossible gift. As we have seen, for Derrida, the gift is annulled as soon as it appears as such. Even the least awareness of its character as gift compromises its purity and entangles it within an economy of exchange. For Milbank, however, the idea of the 'pure' gift is self-defeating. It is part of a postmodern ethics of absolute sacrifice to the other, in which my alienation from the other, the necessity of death, are taken as axiomatic.

Against this, Milbank opposes the redemptive function of gift-exchange, in which the gift inaugurates a truly mutual relationship. Ethics of total self-sacrifice (like that of Derrida, but Levinas and Marion are also in view here) do not truly value the other, because they refuse an ongoing relationship with a particular, embodied other in favour of self-annihilation. The abstraction of nothingness and death are the real heart of such an ethics.

Milbank proposes instead that 'the ethical is only genuinely imaginable as a mutual and unending gift-exchange',[55] in which there is a genuine openness to the surprise of divine grace and to the reality of resurrection. It is the hope for resurrection that affirms that God's will for us is not death, but a life renewed for relationship. Furthermore, it is not the case that the content of the gift is indifferent. It is only through the specific character of the gift that makes a difference to us that it can really count as a gift. A gift cannot be anything; it must be appropriate.

Against Derrida, Levinas and Marion, Milbank insists that making the gift unilateral, undetermined and from an undecidable origin turns it into a blank, a nothingness that has no effect on our ethical life. This would be the gift of 'an abstract God' for 'where there is no intimation *whatsoever* of the donating source, a gift is simply an impersonal intrusion, whose lack of objectifiable content further renders it arbitrary on our part to interpret it as a gift, rather than as a violent rupture'.[56]

Derrida's God, then, would be an abstraction, the negation of worldly life and loves, little more than a monster demanding sacrifice and offering only violence or indifference. Such a reading certainly offers a challenge to the way in which Derrida oscillates between messianic hope and the barren inhumanity of the *khora*. The latter provides Derrida with a language with which to resist capture by dogmatics, but it also risks dissolving all particularities, and therefore all grace, otherness and hope.

However, Radical Orthodoxy also misses certain essential aspects of Derrida's work. There is a consistent note of affirmation, of saying 'yes, yes' to the other, which is more than abasement to an abstract God. The other is respected only as singular. Moreover, what is named by the trace or 'writing' is not a timeless and abstract ideal, for the boundary between the ideal and real is precisely what calls for deconstruction. The trace is always embodied in fragile, vulnerable cinders, which call for blessing, witness and respect. As we have seen, the gift too must still be thought as engaging our economies, and thus calling us to a greater vigilance about the gifts we offer and the sacrifices we make or demand. None of this endorses a pagan religion of worshipping violence.

Moreover, Radical Orthodoxy's assertion of its Platonized Christian narrative risks its own ahistorical idealism. The serenity of its self-contained orthodoxy, and the violence of its own rejection of all other standpoints as nihilistic calls for a deconstructive reading. The rootedness of this story in an idealized notion of the church and the Eucharist in particular invite reflection on the dangers associated with identifying historical institutions with the outward manifestation of God's will.

Above all, it is important to note that Derrida's texts do not simply state a 'position', whether that be atheism, the death of God, nihilism or even a new theology. They perform and deform languages about God, in order to take us to the limit where the other approaches. The other will always defy capture in a narrative, and this is what Derrida's use of the gift or the messianic keeps alive: not a dead God, but God otherwise.

Dialogues and disputes

A number of theologians have attempted a more constructive dialogue with Derrida. They look for ways in which his work can illuminate theological themes, while seeking to complement or correct his shortcomings. For example, Oliver Davies devotes a section to Derrida in *A Theology of Compassion*, a work that tries to re-think a Christian version of ontology that does not give priority to fixed ideas of totality and identity. For Davies, it is important to take note of thinkers such as Derrida, who have deconstructed the historical privilege given to Being as a form of presence. However, Davies contends that Derrida's departure from metaphysics cannot claim to be absolute, for it could at any point lead to return of the divine voice. Ultimate reality could be not just absence, but a relation to the wholly other as prayed to, and therefore as God.[57] For Davies, Derrida remains stuck in a thinking of absence, but his work does at least open the door to a return of the theological

From a more evangelical perspective, Bruce Ellis Benson finds in Derrida a positive resource for contending against conceptual idols and the arrogance of assuming we have ideas that can comprehend God (an arrogance Benson associates particularly with Platonism). He therefore welcomes Derrida's call to a critical vigilance. However, he takes Derrida to task for separating faith from dogma, for dogma is what gives particular form and content to faith. He charges Derrida with a dogmatism of his own for tarring all dogma with the same brush.[58] Benson also wonders if Derrida is not himself too Platonistic, because the ideals and hopes Derrida articulates are never incarnated.[59] They seem to be detached from all embodiment, a criticism that echoes that of Milbank and Pickstock. Benson insists that, for Christians, it is a given that the Messiah has come, but that this does not necessarily entail the kind of theoretical idolatry that Derrida rightly warns of.

James Smith makes a similar point in what is a largely positive reading of Derrida's relevance to theology and the church. He welcomes the deconstruction of modernity's superstitious belief in the neutrality of reason and the centrality of the individual, arguing that 'Derrida offers insight into the structure of creation'.[60] In other words, we are always in the position of interpretative readers of the world. Far from setting us on the slippery slope to relativism, this is consistent with a theology of grace:

> What is required to interpret the world well is the necessary conditions of interpretation – the right horizons of expectation and the right presuppositions. But as Paul repeatedly emphasizes, these conditions are themselves a gift; in other words, the presuppositions and horizons that make it possible to properly 'read' creation are grace gifts that attend redemption and regeneration.[61]

Smith also accepts that everyone has presuppositions that affect their interpretation. Again, however, this is not an excuse to give up on truth, but a challenge to Christians not to suppress their own starting point in faith:

> if one of the crucial insights of postmodernism is that everyone comes to his or her experience of the world with a set of ultimate presuppositions, then Christians should not be afraid to lay their specifically Christian presuppositions on the table and allow their account to be tested in the marketplace of ideas.[62]

Of course, none of this engages directly with Derrida's critique of the metaphysics that has directed much Christian theology Derrida would question the idea that the 'right' horizons can simply be given to us, or that presuppositions are fixed starting points. If the simplicity of God as the absolute origin is called into question, such 'givens' and 'presuppositions' will themselves be troubled.

Avoiding these difficult questions, Smith offers his criticisms of Derrida instead. As we have already seen, Derrida is accused of dualism (Cartesian in form this time), because he equates any attempt to determine otherness (by giving it a particular shape or interpretation) with violence.[63] Smith counters that this is akin to Gnosticism, which condemned the finite world as intrinsically evil, and longed for a purely spiritual redemption. Christians refuse to demonize creation and the material world. Indeed, they affirm the scandal of particularity: that God was made man at a determinate point in time and history.[64] For Christians, it is possible to name God and know his will.

The idea of Derrida's 'dualistic' rejection of finitude continues to be a theme for theological commentators. In the light of our own discussion, it is hard to justify this interpretation of his work. Derrida is not 'against' finitude or particularity. Such an accusation seems bizarre given even a cursory reading of his texts. What he does do is resist any assimilation of finitude into a discourse that claims to know its limits and centre, and that takes its stand on a presence that escapes the play of time and difference. When we begin to ask how Christians know that God is incarnate in Christ, taking refuge in abstractions of revelation risks evading the very difficult question of what makes such revelation intelligible and secure. Derrida's resistance to determination is a resistance to the power of institutional orthodoxies, not a refusal of the real world.

Graham Ward offers a more in-depth reading, in a bold move that links Derrida with Barth's uncompromising theology of revelation. Centred on the claim that 'language is always and ineradicably theological',[65] Ward argues that Barth offers a theological reading of what Derrida calls *différance*.

For Barth, God is wholly other. Language about God is only analogical because God elects to make it so. Revelation alone can lead us to 'read' correctly: 'we read the language as analogous by revelation through revealedness to the revealer. Our reading by faith, therefore, is a participation in the Trinity'.[66] God is not grasped directly through any concept we manufacture, but is known in the rupture God opens up in our world through Christ.

Derrida also is a thinker of what cannot be reduced to a theme or grasped in a concept. This means that, for all his reservations about theology, there is 'an acknowledgement of an uneradicable metaphysical complicity which Derrida is concerned to expose as frankly theological in its presuppositions, that gives rise to theological motifs and explicit theological references within Derrida's work'.[67] Although Derrida is himself not a Christian, and does not recognize the role played by Christ in Barth's theology, nevertheless Derrida's 'act of transgression, of crossing the boundary and affirming an absolutely other and an infinitely other, is an act of faith'.[68]

Ward thus takes a nuanced view of deconstruction's relationship to theology. The economy of *différance* 'seems to deny the theological categories of revelation and the eschaton, on the one hand, and yet require them, on the other'.[69] Derrida cannot be assimilated into theology, because while philosophy in general is free to keep open the question of what is 'outside' the world, theology has made a decision that this other is God. Ward is clear that 'neither "trace" nor *différance* can be understood theologically as names for God' and makes the point (against Kevin Hart, whose work we shall consider later) that 'negative theology is a language-use. *Différance* is a language condition'.[70] The two discourses cannot be equated.

At the same time, Ward believes that '*Différance* calls the theological into play, lends weight to the ineradicable nature of the theological question in and of language ... *Différance*, examined theologically, becomes the play between the presence and the impossibility of God'.[71] Seen in reverse, this means that a certain agnosticism must be preserved within theology, for God cannot be pinned down and defined. This is acknowledged in Barth's approach, in which 'the truth of theology lies in the necessity yet impossibility of rendering an account'.[72]

For Barth, Christ, 'like *différance*, transcends difference and metaphysical polarities and "makes the movement of signification possible"'.[73] The difference is that the nature of Christ is not a static structure, but a personal reality whose meaning must be narrated. Christ enters the world, and through this event of revelation, God allows certain words and stories to bear his otherness.

It must be noted that this sympathetic account of Derrida is somewhat offset by the more critical approach Ward takes in other texts, in which Derrida's refusal of the decision to name God theologically is held against him. In *Cities of God*, Derrida is accused of only being able to 'transcendentalize aporia'.[74] In other words, Derrida leaves us in eternal suspension. A definite theology is needed to redeem the situation (albeit Ward continues to stress the open nature of theological narratives). Reflecting his own association with Radical Orthodoxy, Ward declares that

> Only theology can do this; for only theology reflects upon
> the relationship between the uncreated creator and
> creation *on the basis* of what Godhead has revealed about
> both itself and its desires and designs with respect to
> creation. The theological makes differences different, makes
> particularities singular and concrete.[75]

A similar point is made in Ward's contribution to *Questioning God*, in which he argues that Derrida's form of questioning gets stuck in abstract indecision, never bearing fruit in any kind of real relationship to the other. Derrida lacks an eschatological vision of relationship fulfilled and creation enjoyed. As a result, his God can only ever be a 'bad' infinite, an endless monotony of deferral, leading nowhere.[76]

It is strange that, as Caputo notes in the same volume, Ward abandons his earlier, more nuanced reading, in favour of a doctrinaire rejection.[77] Derrida always insists that undecidability does not mean the absence of decision. Rather, the fact that decisions cannot be programmed in advance is what makes them possible in the first place. The messianic demands an urgent response in the here and now. Ward's own association of Derrida with Barth suggests a creative interplay of deconstruction and theology, linked by both affirmation of the other and a proper vigilant agnosticism.

A more open-handed welcome for Derrida's thought is offered by Kevin Hart, whose project is explicitly aimed at the promotion of a 'non-metaphysical theology'.[78] Hart concurs with Derrida's deconstruction of the metaphysics of presence, but argues that this deconstruction is already at work within theology. For instance, 'scripture performs the deconstruction of the metaphysical element within theology',[79] and we must note that the French word used for writing – *écriture* – can also be translated as 'scripture'. The implication is that the Scriptures cannot be reduced to a set of philosophical propositions. Their dynamic narratives and plurality of voices and genres disrupt such appropriation.

The most striking instance of deconstruction at work in theology is that of mysticism, apophatics or the *via negativa*. For Hart, negative theology calls ontotheology into question, indeed it deconstructs positive theology.[80] As he puts it, 'My position is not that deconstruction is a form of negative theology but that negative theology is a form of deconstruction'.[81]

Negative theology disputes any attempt to create a conceptual web in which to capture the divine. This is not the same thing as atheism: 'one may hold that there *is* a God but that there is no *concept* of God to which one can appeal that can ground one's discourse about God and the world'.[82] God is known by faith, not by knowledge, and it is this basic dynamic that deconstruction reflects.

Derrida therefore 'argues against God conceived, experienced or used as a mode of presence, though not against God as such'.[83] For Hart, this means that there must be a positive tradition of revelation on which negative theology can do its deconstructive work. Although Derrida himself does not take this step, his writings clarify the vocation of theology:

> Each theology claims priority: without negative theology,
> God talk would decay into idolatry, yet without positive
> theology there would be no God talk in the first place. It is

a permanent task of religious thought to keep the negative and the positive in play, to demonstrate that the impossible is not in contradiction with the possible. What Derrida helps bring into focus is that the possible and the impossible are not to be resolved dialectically or logically: they arrange and rearrange themselves in the negative form of an aporia.[84]

What does this mean for the way God is understood or experienced? Hart argues that the Christian experience of God is one of absolute interruption, not presence.[85] Only by faith is God known. The Christian tradition preserves God's otherness, not least through the doctrine of the Trinity, which refuses to fix God as an isolated 'being'. Hart writes of the 'God whose very act of being is otherness' and whose revelation is not a transfer of information, but a disclosure that we also are 'being-in-relation'.[86]

As we have already seen, Hart has been criticized by Graham Ward for equating deconstruction and negative theology too directly. It might also be said that his appeal to 'faith' remains unexamined. It is not simply that the Christian has a faith that Derrida lacks, but that the latter calls for a different understanding of faith, one that affirms the other without finally deciding where the call to fidelity comes from.

Hugh Rayment-Pickard also takes issue with Hart. He argues that Hart assimilates Derrida to negative theology because he assumes that deconstruction is something like the critique of reason developed by Kant. In other words, it aims to draw the limits of what can possibly be known and said about God. As Rayment-Pickard points out, Derrida distances deconstruction from this kind of critique. Notions such as *différance*, the trace and the gift are not only conditions for the possibility of truth and meaning, but for their impossibility as well. Deconstruction crosses the boundary between timeless structures of knowledge and particular facts and events. Time and difference infect everything, calling for a much more radical questioning of God than that proposed by negative theology: 'the point of these refutations and deconstructions is to clear the path not for a new kind of negative theology – still less a positive theology – but a theology of impossibility'.[87]

Rayment-Pickard pushes negative theology beyond itself when he writes that 'The application of any predicate, even existence, would "restrict" the divine. A true conception of God must transcend all predicates, even to the extent of becoming "impossible".[88] He makes the crucial point, missed by many other Christian theologians in dialogue with Derrida, that 'For Derrida, the self-contradiction of God is not a problem, indeed it may be the essence of divinity'.[89] Such a strange theology promises that God has a life after the death of all residual presence. Indeed, it provokes a renewal of theological questioning: 'God's impossibility acts therefore not to deaden religious feeling or to close down theological discussion but to draw it out'.[90]

How does this impossible God connect with the theology that has gone before? Rayment-Pickard points to deconstruction's drive to combat idols and affirm the irreducibility of paradox as elements that have a resonance within Christian faith. However, the key question remains: how to figure or imagine an impossible God?

Rayment-Pickard draws attention to Derrida's use of the chi, or X, to signify the impossible crossing of negative and positive, concealment and revelation. Could this be a sign also of the crossing point of the life and death of God, of God read as the difference between life and death? After the horizon of theology has been erased, God is known in the difference that survives presence and absence.[91] Rayment-Pickard is careful to point out that this should not be taken to mean that difference can now be equated with some determinate theological idea: 'the chi is not meant as an icon of any kind . . . but as a transcendence of the icon: a self-erasing intersection'.[92] God could be known only as the broken figure. And this thought offers an intriguing connection between impossibility as the crossing point of the life and death of God, and a paradoxical Christology, focussed upon the cross. Again, Rayment-Pickard is cautious: 'the chi might be Christological (or perhaps it would be better to say christogrammatological) on the condition of Christology thinking itself heterologically through its alternatives'.[93]

This thought is left tantalizingly undeveloped, but it suggests an engagement with Derrida's work from a Christian perspective that does not assume Christianity is a given that can be unaffected by the thought of God in and through difference.

What might a theology look like that, without succumbing to the death of God, exposed itself to deconstruction in this way? Would it be anything more than the hollowed out shell of a dead tradition? Or would it be the starting point for a new way of thinking about God?

Another thinking of God

Perhaps the most significant interpreter of Derrida's religious thought is John Caputo, whose many publications on hermeneutics and the touching points between philosophy and theology continually play on the possibilities of deconstruction. His book *The Prayers and Tears of Jacques Derrida* has been highly influential in drawing attention to the persistence and importance of religion in Derrida's writings.

Caputo describes his own position in these terms: 'Religion on my telling is a pact or "covenant" with the impossible. To have a religious sense of life is to long with a restless heart for a reality beyond reality, to tremble with the possibility of the impossible'.[94] There are clear overtones of Derrida's own thinking of the impossible here, and this is no accident. For Caputo, the witness to impossibility is the religious lifeblood of deconstruction.

In the introduction to *God, the Gift and Postmodernism*, Caputo and his co-editor Michael Scanlon set out their stall (in a very Caputo-esque manner!):

> *deconstruction is structured like a religion.* Like a *prayer* and tear for the coming of the wholly other (*tout autre*), for something impossible, like a messianic prayer in a messianic religion, *viens*, like a vast and sweeping *amen, viens, oui, oui.* Like a *faith* in the coming of something we cannot quite make out, a blind faith where knowledge fails and faith is what we have to go on ... Deconstruction thus turns out to be not the final nail in the coffin of the old God, but rather the affirmation of the religious.[95]

The distance kept by Derrida from determinate religious institutions is not seen as a weakness by Caputo. Rather, it is a way of affirming the unknowing at the heart of faith, and the inescapability of interpretation, passion and risk. Deconstruction is a repetition of religion's inner dynamic:

> Deconstruction regularly, rhythmically repeats this religiousness, *sans* the concrete, historical religions; it repeats nondogmatically the religious structure of experience, the category of the religious. It repeats the passion for the messianic promise and messianic expectation, *sans* the concrete messianisms of the positive religions that wage endless war and spill the blood of the other, and that, anointing themselves God's chosen people, are consummately dangerous to everyone else who is not so chosen.[96]

Derrida's thought invites the coming of the other, the address of the other, and this is an irreducibly religious motif. Deconstruction is 'the thought, if it is a thought, of an absolute heterogeneity that unsettles all assurances of the same within which we comfortably ensconce ourselves'.[97] It is not against God or faith, but it draws the limits of what metaphysics can achieve in theology. In so doing, it opens the way for another way of understanding faith apart from dogmatic certainty or mystical intuition: 'a deconstructive theology would find it necessary to deny hyperessentialism in order to make room for faith. *Il faut croire*'.[98]

One aspect of a deconstructive theology would thus be the limitation of knowledge. The Augustinian question that often reappears in Caputo's texts – 'What do I love when I love my God?' – is a genuinely open one. No single name, narrative or tradition can claim ownership of God. Even more importantly, the issue of what God 'is' becomes displaced, for God is no longer defined within a horizon of being and presence: '*différance* makes – or should make; this is part of the ethics of deconstruction – the theist worry about what we affirm when we affirm our God, even as it makes the atheist worry about what is denied when God is being denied'.[99]

Deconstruction does not decide to call the other 'God' in any direct way. Caputo explores this suspension via the logic of exemplarity, a logic Derrida disturbs by making it uncertain just where the chain of examples ends in the proper original. For Caputo, this vertiginous relativity has a therapeutic effect on religious faith: 'Is God an example of justice, or justice of God? Does it matter?'[100] Faith is not denied by this uncertainty. In fact, it is the oscillation and difference at the heart of what 'God' names that give faith its chance: 'The deconstruction of faith, which has *nothing* to do with its simple destruction – *au contraire!* – saves faith from closing round itself by opening this wounded discourse to the wound of translatability or substitutability'.[101]

The uncertainty of God's name seems to draw deconstruction close to negative theology, to a generalized apophatics that runs free of ecclesial order. However, Caputo insists that this is only a small part of the story. Deconstruction is 'more prophetic than apophatic'.[102] Its openness is to the future, and the God of deconstructive theology is a God who is to come: 'Cast in a deconstructive slant, God is not the possible, but the impossible, not the eternal but the futural'.[103] This gives to deconstructive its subversive ethical edge:

> Deconstruction takes the form of a certain re-ligious
> responsibility to what is coming, to what does not exist.
> Deconstruction turns on a certain pledging of itself to the
> future, on a certain *religio* that religiously observes its
> covenant with the *revenant* and *arrivant,* to what is coming
> back from the past, and to what is arriving from the past as
> the future. Deconstruction is, in that sense, a messianic
> religion within the limits of reason alone, that is, it is
> inhabited and structured in a messianic-religious way.[104]

The rationality of this faith means it remains critical of fundamentalism and distant from determinate faiths: 'it reminds us that we do not know what God is, or whether we believe in God, or whether what we believe in is God or not, or what we love when we love our God'.[105]

Caputo is willing to push the radical nature of this theology far enough to argue that 'The name of God is not the name of some "theological" being or object. "God" is given only in praying and weeping . . . in religious experience, in a certain passion for the impossible'.[106] God is simply the other evoked by prayer, even a 'placeholder' for the secret that preserves others in their singularity and prevents us closing down the unforeseeable future. In this context, Caputo holds on to the importance of thinking the *khora* as a necessary protection against determining and controlling the referent of religious language. The God to whom we pray could be the emptiness of an inhuman desert. Without this possibility, faith would harden into dogmatism.

In his later work, *The Weakness of God*, Caputo maintains what he calls an 'unholy communication' between *différance* and God. He goes further in specifying that God is not a being or object, but an event, whose name shelters a weak force of love and justice.[107] This dynamic event of God resonates with Derrida's questioning of the simplicity of origins:

> Suppose, indeed, that the event that is astir within the name of God is stationed, not on the side of the *arche* and the *principium* or of timeless being and unchanging presence, or of the true, the good, and the beautiful, but on the side of the an-archic and subversive, as the driving force of a divine subversion? ... Suppose the name of 'God' harbors an event of solicitation, that it solicits us by being situated, not inside churches on the high altars, but with the beggars with outstretched hands on the church steps?[108]

Recalling Derrida's 'god without sovereignty', Caputo states that

> I do not think of God as an omnipotent onto-theo-cosmo-logical power source for the universe, but as the unconditional demand for beneficence that shocks the world with a promise that is not kept, as the heart of a heartless world, as the call from below being that summons us to rise beyond being, beyond ourselves. I think of the world as addressed by a call, not produced by a cause, as an addressee, not an effect, and of God as a call, not a cause, as a beneficence, not a sovereign power.[109]

Is this God merely a human creation, a name for wishful thinking? Caputo maintains that this is not the case. He proposes neither anti-realism (God as the projection of human wishes) nor the realism that turns God into an object of knowledge, but a 'hyper-realism' in which what 'God' names calls us beyond ourselves and beyond what is given towards the other, the future and a justice to come.[110]

Compared to Radical Orthodoxy, the God offered by Caputo is ontologically thin. This would not worry him, since faith is not a matter of getting hold of a final Truth or Reality. His deconstructive theology ethicizes God without reducing God to ethics, avoiding what he sees as the one-sidedness of the death-of-God movement without ending up in the arms of institutional religion. A question remains of how this God is to be figured, imagined and related to a world of time and embodiment. It is clear that Caputo thinks there are better and worse ways of responding to the event and call of God. Doesn't this push us once more to consider the truth that lies in determinate religious traditions (or even traditions yet to be invented?). The absence of any final Truth is not, as Caputo would accept, the end of truth.

This invites us to reconsider the work of Mark C. Taylor, whose *Erring* does seem to sound an apocalyptic note of the end of God, self and truth. Caputo distances himself from Taylor, because he believes the latter's approach is too reductionist, too quick to deny the otherness of God.[111] However, Taylor would not accept that his position is simply a negative one. It is a result of reading Kierkegaard's idea of the infinite qualitative difference between God and humanity together with Derrida's *différance* with a view to a more radical thinking of otherness: 'A/theology is not the opposite of theology and must not be identified with atheism. Neither exactly positive nor negative, a/theology draws on the resources of deconstruction to develop a nonnegative negative theology that seeks to think what Western ontotheology leaves unthought'.[112]

For Taylor, this reflects the affirmative nature of deconstruction, without reducing it to a repetition of theological metaphysics. In place of God, Taylor prefers to talk about the sacred. The sacred is neither present nor absent, neither being nor non-being. It is the 'approach of the unapproachable'.[113] It reveals by not revealing, a secret without content. It is the lack that, like the gift, opens responsibility and passion. For Taylor it calls for a response of agape, of unconditional giving and gratuitous loving. Without being any kind of determinable entity, the sacred offers a kind of grace. It lets be by letting go.[114] Withdrawing as it draws near, it keeps love, passion and desire alive: 'Unlike God, whose eternal presence some believe delivers satisfaction, the sacred, which is never present without being absent, brings dissatisfaction that knows no rest'.[115]

In his most recent work, *After God*, Taylor develops this post-theistic religious sensibility further. For Taylor, the idea of God has been used to plug a hole in the universe, to shield us from the uncanny void:

God is not the ground of being that forms the foundation of all beings but the figure constructed to hide the originary abyss from which everything emerges and to which all returns. While this abyss is no thing, it is not nothing – neither being nor nonbeing, it is the anticipatory wake of the unfigurable that disfigures every figure as if from within. Far from simply destructive, disfiguring is the condition of the possibility of creative emergence.[116]

This creative emergence gives rise to complex systems that have no absolute centre or ground beyond themselves, but that are composed of dynamic relationships. It leads Taylor to a thinking of the Infinite that, like the sacred in his earlier work, displaces God. The 'creative process of the Infinite' is 'the creative interplay in which identity and difference are codependent and coevolve'.[117] The Infinite is at play in natural, social, cultural, technological systems, as the condition of their life and growth, but it is not a supernatural entity:'the Infinite is neither above nor below, neither behind not beyond, the finite, but is the divine milieu in which everything is relative because all is related'.[118]

Taylor offers an intriguing post-metaphysical approach to thinking the otherness of the divine in a way that connects with his understanding of complex emerging systems at every level of life. Although he has been accused of identifying deconstruction too readily with the death of God in *Erring*, his later development shows a creative and constructive employment of Derridean ideas in new contexts. A kind of 'process' thinking of the sacred is out-lined, in which relativity is the matrix for creative and critical thought and ethics.

The theological potential here is confirmed by the work of Catherine Keller, whose ecofeminist process theology also draws significantly upon Derrida. Keller resists the traditional metaphysical idea that God creates the world out of nothing, believing it reflects an idea of patriarchal power over and contempt for evolving matter. The God who exists in self-contained identity prior to creation is displaced by a God known as the creative process of difference. For Keller, this is an alternative to both anti-realism and the metaphysics of presence, one that is shaped by Derrida's deconstruction of God's simplicity and of origins:

> Would a third way, neither nihilism nor *ex nihilism*, lie in the affirmation of a difference – a difference bursting into supernovas, squalling infants, turbulent texts – that is not preceded by its logos? Then the difference released in the deconstruction of origin as the pure *nihil* signals an impure alternative. The affinity of tehom to Derrida's *différance* lies there where the latter leaves its 'trace' in writing. Might we then read its elusive 'always already' in the salt water deposited in the second verse of the Bible? We might then track this precreation trace back out through the prolific play of difference flooding 'the creation', unfolding in its light and dark, its swarming multiples, its 'creeping things unnameable'. Spurred on by the more recent grammatology of Derrida's beginnings, we need no longer derive these swarming, bifurcating multiples from the undifferentiated Origin of a simple Creator. Difference marks an originating and *originated* beginning.[119]

Where Keller breaks company with Derrida is in reading this difference as a depth from which life emerges, not merely as the play of traces on the surface of life. The idea of the deep allows her to explore alternative imagery for the divine. The *khora* becomes, not a barren desert (a very patriarchal image of lonely aridity) but a fecund matrix, a womb of possibilities and new life.[120]

Keller thus embraces a panentheism in which 'Becoming is not outside of God nor God outside of becoming',[121] for God is the plural 'matrix of possibilities'.[122] In concert with other process and feminist theologians, Keller sees divine transcendence in relational, immanent terms, as the emergence of newness and the call beyond fixed ways of thinking and frozen hierarchies.

From a feminist point of view, however, the question arises as to whether the kind of thinking represented by Taylor and Keller dissolves identity so radically into the flux that it offers no standpoint from which to critique dominant norms. As Elizabeth Schüssler Fiorenza argues, what is important is not simply a celebration of 'difference' as an abstraction, but attention to the difference that can be made by women in acts of struggle against concrete socio-economic oppressions.

It is important to note that feminist thinking has itself witnessed numerous challenges to the notion of fixed or essential identities, while seeking to articulate how this multiplicity can have disruptive and liberating potential. There is scope here for a more constructive engagement with Derrida's work, as evidenced by Ellen Armour's significant feminist theological reading.

Armour is seeking a way to challenge the way in which white feminist theology and theory is so often blind to racial difference, subsuming it in an all-encompassing notion of sexual difference. Reading Derrida together with Irigaray, she seeks to push the thinking of difference beyond essentialism and abstraction towards a recognition of the multiple ways in which difference is marked and performed.

She says of her own work that 'what follows is as much an intervention *in* deconstruction as an intervention *using* deconstruction'.[123] Her reading resists the easy dismissal of Derrida's work as nihilistic. Instead, she acknowledges his contribution to a critique of the 'specular' nature of philosophy, in which all difference is ultimately reduced to sameness.

Armour explores the ways in which 'the figures of woman and God go together in Derrida's work'[124] and the nature of *différance* as 'nonoriginary origin'.[125] Although critical of tendencies to equate woman with what is insubstantial and elusive, she sees Derrida's work as potentially subversive of dominant modes of thinking gender and race, partly because it deals with the bigger question of the underlying systems that produce and interpret difference. As 'God' is a principle anchor of such a system, Derrida's 'theological' critique is especially important: 'Feminist theology has a stake in undercutting the mastery of this God [of the

specular economy] in order to make room for other manifestations of the sacred'.[126] In particular, Derrida offers a deconstruction
of the alliance of God, unity and the word of the father as the
centre or apex of metaphysical systems of truth. For Armour,
'Feminist theology would surely recognize an ally in Derrida's
solicitation of God the father'.[127]

The subversive and creative potential of Derrida's work for
theologians attempting to open theology to new possibilities is
evident. This does not add up to a coherent or systematic view-
point, but perhaps that is the point. Derrida's philosophical and
religious strategies serve to expose the systematicity of theology
to what always eludes the system. It is performative rather than
simply theoretical and it evokes multiple enacted responses. And
yet there does seem to be something of a shared agenda even
among the diversity. Radical Orthodoxy, a/theology, anti-realism,
process and feminist theologies are all seeking ways to overcome
the theism of modernity and the domination of theology by a
metaphysics of sheer presence and unity.

Denials and substitutions

For all their differences, the thinkers we have touched on so far
are largely agreed that Derrida is a significant conversation partner for theology. Even when his ideas are rejected as nihilistic,
they are still rejected as an alternative theological myth set over
and against the Christian narrative.

However, it is not obvious to all that Derrida has any connection with theology at all. A case in point is Martin Hägglund's
uncompromisingly atheistic reading. Hägglund argues that
Derrida is proposing a 'radical' atheism. This is distinguished from
a more conventional atheism that denies the existence of God.
In its radical, Derridean form, atheism claims that the very nature
of life in time makes the existence of God impossible, because
God as traditionally conceived would be the negation of life,
meaning and desire.

Hägglund's starting point is Derrida's deconstruction of pure
presence. All presence and all identity is divided in itself. Nothing
can exist that is not contaminated by space and time, where

contamination 'is not a privation or a lack of purity – it is the originary possibility for anything to be'.[128] Drawing on Derrida's use of the idea of autoimmunity, Hägglund argues that any claim to a truth or identity that escapes the becoming-space of time and the becoming-time of space inevitably undermines itself. Without being exposed to time and alteration, without therefore being exposed to what prevents it ever being perfectly realized, such truth or identity would be nothing at all.

This inevitably affects the possibility of God:

> spacing is the condition for the living as such . . . spacing is the condition for everything that can be thought and desired . . . What traditionally has been figured as the most desirable – the absolute being of God or the immortality of the soul – is here figured as the most undesirable: as the pure indifference of death that would annihilate the impure indifference of life.[129]

For this line of argument, it is axiomatic that a God who would be exposed to the passing of time could no longer be God: 'If the perfection of God were essentially exposed to the coming of time, it would not be perfect since it could be altered at any juncture'.[130]

An important corollary of Hägglund's argument is that there is no ethical content to Derrida's talk about openness to the other. The other, like the gift, is completely undetermined. The other could therefore be a threat, an enemy, someone who comes to destroy us. There should be no presupposition that the other is good. Openness to the other does not provide a basis for any ethical norms. It is descriptive rather than prescriptive.[131] It is the necessary condition for there to be life at all. It does not provide us with normative guidance on how that life is to be lived. That is left to our decision making.

Hägglund draws on a theme we have noted at several points in our reading of Derrida: the association of life and responsibility with mortality. Life, by its very nature, must be lived in time, and this excludes the very possibility of a timeless, immortal being. This is essentially what distinguishes Derrida's *différance* from negative theology. There is no promise of an escape from time to achieve union with the eternal. Rather, 'God is as dependent on temporal finitude as everyone else'.[132]

Hägglund undoubtedly reflects a significant element of Derrida's approach, one that should not be downplayed by those seeking in him a theological helpmeet. The God that approaches and withdraws through deconstruction is a God exposed to mortality, risk and division. However, must we agree that this is the same as saying that there is no God at all? Is this really the radical atheism that Hägglund assumes it to be?

For one thing, Hägglund does not seem to do justice to the particular choice of terminology favoured by Derrida. Messianism, justice, hospitality, friendship and democracy to come, all signify the openness to the other that is indeed risky and threatened. However, they bear within themselves an *affirmation* that is not merely the affirmation of a neutral description, but an ethical and even religious one. If Derrida's language is performative, it brings into being a kind of promise, rather than simply offering an objective account of the conditions of life.

Indeed, why even speak of promise, faith or grace if these words are utterly equivocal and bear no relation to their formation in religious and ethical discourse? Hägglund notes that justice for Derrida is incalculable, but he does not connect this with the statements that justice is undeconstructible or that deconstruction 'is' justice. He rightly observes the impossibility of the gift, but does not take account of the fact that for Derrida, this does not mean that there is no gift. We only 'experience' that gift in forgetting it, as it is incarnated, disseminated, engaged in finitude. Nevertheless, this is still an experience of the impossible. Hägglund does not seem to want to stay with this paradox and undecidability, but to identify with a rather one-sided atheism. More than an empty openness seems to be at work in Derrida's rhetoric.

Hägglund also assumes that unless 'God' refers to a static, timeless, immobile presence, then it has no content or reference at all. There are indeed places in Derrida's texts where God functions in this way. However, God has an afterlife, beyond the metaphysics of presence, and Derrida is certainly open to this possibility even if he does not affirm it as such. The dialogue between Heidegger and Christian theologians that closes *Of Spirit*, the divided voices that reflect the plural meanings of negative theology in *Sauf le*

Nom, the association of God with the secret and responsibility in *The Gift of Death*; all these instances and others that could be added testify to Derrida's wish to resist reducing theology to a univocal meaning to be summarily discarded.

Hägglund is aware of the theological readings we have discussed, but his preconceptions about what God is prevent him from reading them accurately. For instance, John Caputo is accused of assimilating Derrida's thought to a hope for the kingdom of God as pure, timeless bliss.[133] This fails to take account of Caputo's insistence on the undecidability of what God refers to, the nature of faith as performance rather than description, and the indirect and poetic nature of his own writing. Anyone versed in Caputo's hermeneutics and his satirical style could hardly mistake his words for a literal description of heaven! Again, it is the performative aspect of the texts that unravels a univocal interpretation.

It is worth contrasting Hägglund's position with that of the philosopher Hent de Vries. De Vries does not write as a theologian, but nevertheless argues that Derrida's use of religious language cannot be overlooked. Sensitive to the process whereby the real and the ideal, the empirical and the transcendental are always contaminating one another, de Vries claims that the religious nature of Derrida's language cannot be merely accidental. Even as he sets that language to work in different ways, it is still related to the particularity of its history.

For de Vries, 'God' bears a specific legacy, and thus becomes a privileged way of naming otherness and singularity. The effect of Derrida's work is to undermine any stable division between the secular and the religious: 'even the most secular, profane, negative, or nihilistic of utterances, directs or redirects itself unintentionally and unwittingly toward the alterity for which – historically, systematically, conceptually and figuratively speaking – "God" is, perhaps and so far, the most proper name'.[134] For instance, Derrida recognizes the violence that seeks to impose an impossibly static and exclusive identity through the use of religious dogmas, but this is not the only way in which such language can be used: 'this violence at the source of the self also reveals the need to affirm an original and originary messianicity. The latter term hints at an openness toward the future, but an openness that is nonetheless opened up by a singular trait'.[135]

The generalized messianicity that Derrida appeals to is therefore inseparable from historical messianisms, not least because the former does not exists in any separate timeless or transcendental form: 'the concrete positive revelations or messianisms are not so much instantiations of a pregiven and stable "structure of openness", since the latter has no existence "outside", "before", or "without" them'.[136] These are not static concepts, but dimensions of a movement of faith and responsibility that is foreign to any conceptual or dogmatic resolution: 'Messianicity and messianism thus stand in a relation of mutual implication and oscillation of an elliptical movement in which the one pole calls forth the other, even though the one and the other are, in a sense, incommensurable'.[137]

De Vries organizes his analysis around the figure of the *adieu*, which is at once the approach to and departure from God. In the light of this, Derrida can be seen as both denying and affirming theology in a 'hyperbolic' way, outbidding traditional theology to signal a more radical otherness.[138] This position is summed up as *'being at once extremely close to and, as it were, at an infinite remove from this heritage'.*[139]

Duplicity is therefore intrinsic to Derrida's writings, which 'can be taken to reaffirm, if not justify, both the traditional ontotheological notion of God and whatever has come to take its place, or the place of God's name, including its most radical negations and denegations'.[140] This is not simply a feature of those writings, however, but also of the God they evoke. God names a self-contradiction, a 'perverformativity' that deconstructs and deforms itself. As de Vries insists, 'There is no prayer without idolatry'.[141] Whenever the other is addressed, her otherness is inevitably, but necessarily compromised.

Nevertheless, this does not mean that talk of God can be simply eliminated, at least for the foreseeable future, while history bears the marks of theological interpretation. Derrida's own undecidable logic means that one cannot treat ideas such as *différance* or the trace as somehow foundational and immune from the contamination they set in motion, while talk of God is always secondary: 'But if "God" is one of the names – indeed the most exemplary name – of the trace, then the latter is no more originary than the former' (357).[142] Theology *and* deconstruction are called to resist the logic of foundations, which surely rules out the 'radical atheism' proposed by Hägglund.

Conclusion: A Useless, Indispensable Name

Animals and monsters

According to Ellen Armour, 'Encounters between Derrida and theology, in particular, have been dominated by multifaceted and multilayered misconstruals of his work'.[1] The previous chapter helps to show that this is not the whole story. Theologians have engaged at some length and depth with Derrida's work, albeit with very different presuppositions and conclusions.

Nevertheless, even if we accept that Derrida has had an impact on theology, it is hard to determine its exact status. Any body of work of such depth and complexity is bound to inspire an irreducible diversity of readings, but Derrida's ambiguity for theology is more intrinsic. His work explores what makes a diversity of readings possible in the first place. This can only ever be articulated in an indirect, performative gesture, because this cannot be a matter of bracketing out the world and taking a look at its essential hidden workings behind the scenes. Derrida's readings intervene, mechanically replicating and unpredictably innovating a non-logic of contradiction and dissemination.

Take a helpful, if fairly crude categorization of some of the major theological approaches available in modern theology: the experientialism of Schleiermacher, the transcendentalism of Rahner and the theology of revelation articulated by Barth. These are not meant to be exhaustive of all that contemporary theology offers, but they can perform a heuristic function.

For Schleiermacher, our sense of God is rooted in a fundamental sensibility, a feeling of absolute dependence upon the infinite. This is not merely a subjective, passing feeling, but a feeling that

encompasses pre-reflective knowing. It is an experiential orientation of the whole self to the divine. Rahner's approach is related,
but he stresses the transcendental openness of human being to
God. Our nature is constituted by this a priori unthematized
structure of being, which is universal. It makes knowledge and
freedom possible. Barth rejects these two options, maintaining
that God's infinite qualitative difference from us cannot be reduced
by appeals to anything within or constitutive of human experience. Human religion produces only idols. Only the free
self-revelation of a wholly other God can create in us the capacity
to receive God's word.

Can Derrida's thinking be correlated with any of these theological options? Only if we assume that what Derrida offers is a
certain system or set of theological propositions, organized around
a source or founding principle. However, as we have seen throughout this study, Derrida calls into question all such unified or simple
origins. As his works are staged, internally divided, plurivocal,
crossed by voices of promise and prophecy, or emptied out in the
collapse and desertification of language, they offer a different kind
of reading.

So, in one sense, Derrida is very much a theologian of experience, but of the experience of the impossible, of the gift and the
promise. Experience is not any sort of univocal basis for truth,
but is paradoxical, spun between the otherness that evokes it but
withdraws from it. Derrida is also a transcendental theologian,
exploring what makes the world possible for us. However, he is
also the one who shatters transcendentalism, because *différance*, the
trace and the furtive God not only make things possible, they
make them impossible as well. The line between the transcendental and the empirical is never fixed and clear. Truth does not exist
in a pristine ideal state from which it falls into time and language.
It is always truth in transgression.

What of revelation? We have seen how Graham Ward has
creatively placed Derrida and Barth side by side. The latter is a
theologian of the wholly other, whose thought unsettles our self-
enclosed humanism. So there is a connection with Derrida.
However, Derrida does not simply tell the story of what God does,
appealing to a revelation that imposes itself on us without condition. He stays with the unresolved tension between revelation and

revealability. The two call for each other, contaminate one another. And perhaps that means they each relate to a 'third place', to the non-origin of difference and hope that can be named the messianic or the *khora*, but that in each case prevents us simply assuming we can know what it is for God to act and speak and show himself. Or name himself.

God deconstructs; God becomes our thief, the space that insinuates between me and my words, the catastrophe of language, the secret that can never be told, the gift that can never be given. Can any of this be taken literally, or seriously? Yes: if we accept that the 'literal' is always the repeated performance of an impossible experience, and seriousness is other side of play. Derrida's theology does not sediment out into propositions and credal formulae, but is a moving network of provocations. It teases, lures, offends. And in so doing, it draws our attention to an intrinsic element of what it is to speak theologically, to construct theological systems and statements. There must always be an element of deadly and earnest jesting that hollows out such discourses.

Such a hollowing out is therapeutic, because it loosens the grip of theology on its own sources and standards, stops it believing in its own ideology. It is ethical, because it allows space for the other, even the other we would not welcome, even the other who is not human. It is also theological, if we accept that the name of God can only be named in faith, in a performance that is both a life or death decision and utterly ironic.

Derrida is concerned with and for the other. He does not set up camp within atheism, secularism or humanism. A significant way in which this is signalled is his growing concern for animal others. For Derrida, the animal is an instance of the wholly other: a gaze and a claim that interrupts the self-enclosed borders of our human identity. This is so because the way we articulate and defend that identity is inseparable from the ways we separate ourselves from and define what is not human 'The animal looks at us, and we are naked before it. Thinking perhaps begins there' (AT, p. 29). And animals, in particular, have borne the weight of the human project.

Could the animal (and Derrida reminds us that there is no such thing as an animal in general, only an irreducible plurality) be in the trace of God? Could the look with which it exposes and unmans us be the savage genesis of another way of thinking the divine? At the least, such questions begin to unpick the sure and certain boundaries between Christianity and its pagan and poly-theistic others:

> Must not this place of the Other be ahuman? If this is indeed the case, then the ahuman, or at least the figure of some – in a word – divinanimality, even if it were to be felt through the human, would be the quasi-transcendental referent, the excluded, foreclosed, disavowed, tamed, sacrificed foundation of what it founds. (AT, p. 132)

Divinanimality: what a word. Is Derrida deifying cats? Or is he performing and perverting our settled notions of the divine, a perverformance in which the most serious ethical concern for the other is inseparable from the satire on our self-professed certainties. Could God be named in any other way?

The word 'divinanimality' evokes a scene: one that might hint at a mediating but broken image of the call to ethics and faith that echoes in Derrida's texts. Jesus is driven into the desert by the Holy Spirit. In Mark's gospel, the account is as terse and arid as sandworn rock: 'And the Spirit immediately drove him out into the wilderness. He was in the wilderness forty days, tempted by Satan; and he was with the wild beasts; and the angels waited on him' (Mark 1.11).

Jesus finds his calling in the desert, the way opened for him by the Baptist, clothed in camel's hair, and the Spirit that descended as a dove. In the midst of the wastes, Jesus finds he is not alone, not without community. Yes, there is the tempter. But there are also the wild animals and the angels, the nonhuman others with whom he is bound in relationships of solidarity and ministry. In the desert, Jesus begins the work that spells an end to sacrifice: animal, human, divine.

The story is a parable of exposure: the exposure of the false power represented by Satan, but also the exposure of God in the human Jesus, indissolubly linked to the strangeness of other species. God exposed: human, but not defined by a narrow human-ism. God emptied: but emptied for a relationship of compassion that does not depend on a shared language.

Conclusion

The formless desert is a place of creation. It brings us back to the beginning, where things are never simple. Derrida notes how, in the story of Genesis, God lets Adam or Ish name the animals on his own. God watches, but does not know what to expect. It is as if, Derrida suggests, God were allowing himself to be surprised: 'This "in order to see" marks at the same time the infinite right of inspection of an all-powerful God *and* the finitude of a God who doesn't know what is going to happen to him with language. And with names' (AT, p. 17).

A God who can be surprised: could this be the figure for God's exposure, God's passion in the play of the world? It would demand that we think very differently about ideas of providence, election and the language of God's plan. But perhaps the challenge to that closed theology is already to be found within Christian revelation: the exposure of a God who is forsaken, a God who becomes passive to the world. This is not a new idea, as process theologians and others have testified; but they still remain potentially confined by the telos of humanism, the dream of a final harmony and perfection of the human. If theology is called to witness to the passion of God, there must be a weakening of such claims to know the end of the story, the end of man, from a human point of view. Despite the understandable lure of such titles as the humanity of God and the human face of God, we are challenged also to think the ahumanity of God, and to break the link between incarnation and a certain ideology of the human.

Can what comes to pass in and through the name of God and the figure of the incarnation be something other: a monstrous, inviting birth?

The ruses of life

In an interview conducted for a book on John Caputo's thought, Derrida acknowledges the role played by religious and theological thinkers such as Caputo and Mark Taylor in receiving and interpreting his work. He states that he has been aware for some time that 'deconstruction could appear as an enemy and a fascinating ally' or 'a good strategic lever for theologians', since 'the

213

deconstruction of metaphysics or ontotheology didn't simply mean attacking God, the Divine, or the Sacred' (BP, p. 24).

Asked about the undecidability between God and the impossible in Caputo's writings, Derrida responds that 'the difference between the passion for *the* impossible on the one hand, and the passion for "God" on the other, is the *name*. "*The* impossible" is not a name, it is not a proper name, not some*one*' (BP, p. 28). But what is it that God names? As the interview proceeds, we find Derrida engaged in a (deliberately?) contorted improvisation.

We are told that 'God would mean this. The one who could finally make possible what I am sure is impossible' (BP, p. 29). This seems clear: 'God' names the personal being who brings salvation about, a salvation Derrida cannot believe in. However, on the very same page we read that 'God is not some*thing* else or some*one* else, that is the product of a phantasm or a desire. God is precisely what produces this neurosis or this pathology. That's what God is' (ibid.). The interviewer, Mark Dooley, asks 'A neurosis?' and one can sense surprise and incomprehension.

God has gone from being the personal guarantor of salvation to the one who makes possible our neuroses. Has Derrida become a Freudian, for whom religion is a neurotic symptom? Not quite, because this neurosis is not one we can do without. It is something to do with the restlessness of life, the possibility for creation and innovation. Even when life is interpreted in the most naturalistic way, 'God' can still name what impels it, what troubles it, what causes it to fold back on itself, interrupt itself, what allows the other to appear: 'Once you've reduced all this to a movement in life, to an evolution in a very flat positivistic way, you realize that this does not serve to deny the existence of God. It is God' (BP, p. 30). In quick succession, we are told that God is the secret, the possibility of the lie; we are offered an invitation: 'Let us call life, and the ruses in life, "God"' (ibid.); we hear that '"God" is the name of the limit, the *absolute* limit, *absolute* transcendence, *absolute* immanence' (BP, p. 31).

This God, who a few moments before seemed safely defined as a personal being recognizable to theists, now breaks out of those constraints, The border between 'God' and the impossible looks far less secure. God has got out of hand. God is wherever life is doubled, contradictory, where it hits and transgresses limits, where the passage of the absolute becomes dangerous. God, the ruse. Small wonder that Derrida says 'It is a useless, indispensable name' (BP. p. 31). It haunts him, because it is the name through which the absolute other and its transgressions have been articulated.

Then we learn the secret: 'when *I* use it [the word "God"] I do so with tongue in cheek' (ibid.) His tongue has been firmly planted in his cheek, so we should not be surprised that his words have been mumbled and unclear. The speaking tongue was suspended. It let something other than plain meaning be said.

Has Derrida been having us on all along? Is it all a joke? Perhaps. But perhaps it is the kind of jest that makes it possible to speak differently of an impossible experience of the other, a singular gift:

> translation-proof, grace would perhaps come when the time of writing of the other absolves you, from time to time, from the infinite *double-bind* and first of all, such is a gift's condition, absolves itself, unbinds itself from the double-bind, unburdens or clears itself, it, the language of writing, this given trace that always comes from the other, even if it is no one. To clear oneself of the gift, of the given gift, of giving itself, is the grace I now know you have and in any case that I wish for you. This grace is always improbable: it is never proved. But must we not believe it happens? That was perhaps, yesterday, belief itself.
> (OA, p. 26)

Notes

Introduction

1 Kirby Dick and Amy Ziering Kofman, *Derrida: Screenplay and Essays on the Film* (Manchester: Manchester University Press, 2005), pp. 121–22.

2 Particularly notable with regard to Derrida are John Caputo and Michael Scanlon (eds), *God, the Gift and Postmodernism* (Bloomington: Indiana University Press, 1999) and John Caputo, Mark Dooley and Michael Scanlon (eds), *Questioning God* (Bloomington: Indiana University Press, 2001).

3 Caputo, Dooley and Scanlon, *Questioning God*, p. 2.

4 Søren Kierkegaard, *Concluding Unscientific Postscript to the Philosophical Fragments Volume 1* (Princeton: Princeton University Press, 1992), p. 145.

5 An excellent account of the fear provoked by deconstruction in this and other affairs is given in James Smith, *Jacques Derrida: Live Theory* (London: Continuum, 2005), pp. 1–8.

6 Yvonne Sherwood and Kevin Hart (eds), *Derrida and Religion: Other Testaments* (London: Routledge, 2005), p. 29.

7 Ibid., p. 30.

8 See the sketch provided by Geoffrey Bennington (Circ, pp. 325–36); also see Jason Powell, *Jacques Derrida: A Biography* (London: Continuum, 2006).

Chapter 1

1 See Martin Heidegger, *Being and Time* (Oxford: Blackwell, 1962), pp. 41–48.

2 David Wood and Robert Bernasconi (eds), *Derrida and Différance* (Evanston: Northwestern University Press, 1988), p. 3.

3 Ibid., p. 4.

4 Friedrich Nietzsche, *Beyond Good and Evil* (Harmondsworth: Penguin, 1973), pp. 27–28.

5 See, e.g., Edmund Husserl, *Cartesian Meditations* (Dordrecht: Martinus Nijhoff, 1977). Other significant works include *Logical Investigations: Volume 1* (London: Routledge, 2001); *Logical Investigations: Volume 2* (London: Routledge, 2001); *Ideas Pertaining to a Pure Phenomenology and to a Phenomenological Philosophy: General Introduction to a Pure Phenomenology (First Book)* (Dordrecht: Kluwer Academic Publishers, 1983); *Ideas Pertaining to a Pure Phenomenology and to a*

Notes

Phenomenological Philosophy: Studies in the Phenomenology of Constitution (Second Book) (Dordrecht: Kluwer Academic Publishers, 1990); *The Crisis of European Sciences and Transcendental Phenomenology* (Evanston: Northwestern University Press, 1970).

6 What follows is particularly indebted to a number of major studies: Leonard Lawlor, *Derrida and Husserl: The Basic Problem of Phenomenology* (Bloomington: Indiana University Press, 2002); Paola Marrati, *Genesis and Trace: Derrida Reading Husserl and Heidegger* (Stanford: Stanford University Press, 2005); and Hugh Rayment-Pickard, *The Impossible God: Derrida's Theology* (Aldershot: Ashgate, 2003), pp. 21–68.

7 See Dominique Janicaud, *Phenomenology and the 'Theological Turn'* (New York: Fordham University Press, 2000).

Chapter 2

1 Catherine Keller, *The Face of the Deep: A Theology of Becoming* (London: Routledge, 2003).

2 Ferdinand de Saussure, *Course in General Linguistics* (London: Duckworth, 1983).

3 See Claude Lévi-Strauss, *The Raw and the Cooked: Introduction to a Science of Mythology* (London: Pimlico, 1995).

4 Martin Heidegger, *Identity and Difference* (Chicago: Chicago University Press, 2002), p. 58.

5 Ibid., p. 72.

Chapter 3

1 Rodolphe Gasché, *The Tain of the Mirror: Derrida and the Philosophy of Reflection* (Cambridge, MA: Harvard University Press, 1986).

2 Ibid., p. 21.

3 Ibid., p. 102.

4 See Rodolphe Gasché, 'God, for Example', in *Inventions of Difference: On Jacques Derrida* (Cambridge, MA: Harvard University Press, 1994), pp. 150–70.

5 J. L. Austin, *How to Do Things with Words* (Cambridge, MA: Harvard University Press, 1975).

6 Søren Kierkegaard, *Concluding Unscientific Postscript to the Philosophical Fragments Volume 1* (Princeton: Princeton University Press, 1992), pp. 123 and 630.

7 Martin Heidegger, *Being and Time* (Oxford: Blackwell, 1962), pp. 32–35.

8 See Emmanuel Levinas, *Totality and Infinity* (Pittsburgh: Duquesne University Press, 1999). Levinas' later work did take account of Derrida's critique. See *Otherwise than Being or Beyond Essence* (Pittsburgh: Duquesne University Press, 1999).

Notes

Chapter 4

1 See also Jacques Derrida, 'Passions: An Oblique Offering' (ON, pp. 3–31); Jacques Derrida and Maurizio Ferraris, *A Taste for the Secret* (Cambridge: Polity, 2001).

2 See Martin Heidegger, 'What is Metaphysics?' in David Farrell Krell (ed.), *Basic Writings: Martin Heidegger* (London: Routledge, 1993), pp. 89–110.

3 See John Caputo, *The Prayers and Tears of Jacques Derrida: Religion Without Religion* (Bloomington: Indiana University Press, 1997), p. 43.

Chapter 5

1 Please note that references to *Glas* also note which of the two columns on each page is being cited. The columns are designated 'a' and 'b' for the left-hand and right-hand sides, respectively.

2 For feminist receptions of Derrida, see Ellen Feder, Mary Rawlinson and Emily Zakin (eds), *Derrida and Feminism: Recasting the Question of Woman* (London: Routledge, 1997); Nancy Holland (ed.), *Feminist Interpretations of Jacques Derrida* (University Park: Pennsylvania State University Press, 1997); and Ellen Armour, *Deconstruction, Feminist Theology, and the Problem of Difference: Subverting the Race/Gender Divide* (Chicago: Chicago University Press, 1999). For explorations of his relationship to Judaism, see Steven Shakespeare 'Thinking About *Fire*: Derrida and Judaism' in *Literature and Theology*, Vol. 12, No. 3 (September 1998), pp. 242–55; and Bettina Bergo, Joseph Cohen and Raphel Zaqury-Orly (eds), *Judeities: Questions for Jacques Derrida* (New York: Fordham, 2007).

3 Emmanuel Levinas, *Totality and Infinity* (Pittsburgh: Duquesne University Press, 1999), p. 22.

4 Ibid., p. 23.

5 Ibid, p. 62.

6 Emmanuel Levinas, *In the Time of the Nations* (Bloomington: Indiana University Press, 1994), pp. 157–58.

7 Levinas, *Totality*, p. 77.

8 Ibid., p. 78.

9 Ibid., p. 79.

10 Emmanuel Levinas, *Otherwise than Being or Beyond Essence* (Pittsburgh: Duquesne University Press, 1999), p. xiii.

11 Ibid., p. 183.

12 Ibid., p. 185.

Chapter 6

1 See Martin Heidegger, 'Letter on Humanism', in David Farrell Krell (ed.), *Basic Writings: Martin Heidegger* (London: Routledge, 1993), pp. 213–65.

Notes

2 See Robyn Horner, *Rethinking God as Gift: Marion, Derrida and the Limits of Phenomenology* (New York: Fordham University Press, 2001), p. 35

3 Emmanuel Levinas, *Existence and Existents* (The Hague: Martinus Nijhoff, 1978), p. 65.

4 See especially Jean Luc-Marion, *God Without Being: Hors-Texte* (Chicago: Chicago University Press, 1991) and *Being Given: Toward a Phenomenology of Givenness* (Stanford: Stanford University Press, 2002).

5 Horner, *Rethinking God*, p. 153.

6 Marion, *God Without Being*, p. 153.

7 John Caputo and Michael Scanlon (eds), *God, the Gift and Postmodernism* (Bloomington: Indiana University Press, 1999), p. 40

8 Ibid., pp. 58–59.

9 Ibid., p. 59.

10 John Caputo, Mark Dooley and Michael Scanlon (eds), *Questioning God* (Bloomington: Indiana University Press, 2001), p. 48

11 Ibid.

Chapter 7

1 See, e.g., Harold Coward 'A Hindu Response to Derrida's View of Negative Theology' and David Loy, 'The Deconstruction of Buddhism', both in Harold Coward and Toby Foshay (eds), *Derrida and Negative Theology* (Albany: State University of New York Press, 1992), pp. 199–226 and 227–53, respectively. See also Harold Coward, *Derrida and Indian Philosophy* (Albany: State University of New York Press, 1990); and Robert Magliola, *Derrida on the Mend* (West Lafayette: Purdue University Press, 1984).

2 Thomas Altizer *et al.* (eds), *Deconstruction and Theology* (New York: Crossroad, 1982), p. 3.

3 Ibid., p. 14.

4 Ibid., pp. 148–49.

5 Ibid., p. 155.

6 Ibid., p. 156.

7 Ibid., p. 176.

8 Ibid., p. 174.

9 Eve Tavor Bannet, *Structuralism and the Logic of Dissent* (London: Macmillan, 1989), p. 222.

10 Ibid., p. 184.

11 Ibid., p. 189.

12 Ibid., p. 190.

13 Ibid., p. 199.

14 Allan Megill, *Prophets of Extremity: Nietzsche, Heidegger, Foucault, Derrida* (Berkeley: University of California Press, 1987), p. 337

15 Susan Handelman, *The Slayers of Moses: The Emergence of Rabbinic Interpretation in Modern Literary Theory* (Albany: State University of New York Press, 1982), p. 89.

Notes

16 Ibid., p. 164.
17 Ibid., p. 172.
18 Ibid., p. 174.
19 Altizer, *Deconstruction*, p. 73.
20 Mark C. Taylor, *Erring: A Postmodern A / Theology* (Chicago: Chicago University Press, 1984), p. 6.
21 Ibid., p. 11.
22 Ibid., p. 15.
23 Ibid., p. 13.
24 Mark C. Taylor, *Deconstructing Theology* (New York: Crossroad and Scholars' Press, 1982). p. xix
25 Taylor, *Erring*, p. 103.
26 Ibid., p. 104.
27 Ibid., p. 118.
28 Ibid., p. 182.
29 Don Cupitt, *Only Human* (London: SCM, 1985), p. xii.
30 Don Cupitt, *The Long-Legged Fly* (London: SCM, 1987), p. 20.
31 Ibid., p. 75.
32 Don Cupitt, *Radicals and the Future of the Church* (London: SCM, 1989), p. 11.
33 Cupitt, *Long-Legged Fly*, p. 21.
34 Ibid., p. 193.
35 Don Cupitt, *Above Us Only Sky* (Santa Rosa: Polebridge, 2008), p. 17.
36 Cupitt, *Long-Legged Fly*, p. 107.
37 Don Cupitt, *The Religion of Being* (London: SCM, 1998), p. 53.
38 Don Cupitt, *Mysticism after Modernity* (Oxford: Blackwell, 1998).
39 Cupitt, *Religion of Being*, p. 123.
40 Magliola, *Derrida on the Mend*, p. x.
41 Ibid., p. 134.
42 Ibid., p. 135.
43 Ibid., p. 149.
44 David Klemm, 'Derrida's Open Secrets: Not Negative Theology', in Robert Scharlemann (ed.), *Negation and Theology* (Charlottesville: University Press of Virginia, 1992), pp. 8–24 (8).
45 Ibid., p. 12.
46 Ibid., p. 17.
47 John Milbank, *Theology and Social Theory: Beyond Secular Reason* (Oxford: Blackwell, 1990), p. 278 and pp. 308–15.
48 John Milbank, *The Word Made Strange: Theology, Language, Culture* (Oxford: Blackwell, 1997), p. 70.
49 Catherine Pickstock, *After Writing: On the Liturgical Consummation of Philosophy* (Oxford: Blackwell, 1998), p. 8.
50 Ibid., p. 19.
51 Ibid., p. 22.
52 Ibid., pp. 36–37.
53 Ibid., p. 47.
54 Ibid., p. 11.

55 John Milbank, *Being Reconciled: Ontology and Pardon* (Oxford: Blackwell, 2003), p. 154.

56 Ibid., p. 156.

57 Oliver Davies, *A Theology of Compassion* (London: SCM, 2001), pp. 128–29.

58 Bruce Ellis Benson, *Graven Ideologies: Nietzsche, Derrida and Marion on Modern Idolatry* (Downers Grove: InterVarsity, 2002), p. 165.

59 Ibid., p. 167.

60 James Smith, *Who's Afraid of Postmodernism? Taking Derrida, Lyotard and Foucault to Church* (Grand Rapids: Baker Academic, 2006), p. 35.

61 Ibid., p. 49.

62 Ibid., p. 55.

63 Ibid., p. 121.

64 Ibid., p. 122.

65 Graham Ward, *Barth, Derrida and the Language of Theology* (Cambridge: Cambridge University Press, 1995), p. 9.

66 Ibid., p. 15.

67 Ibid., p. 182.

68 Ibid., p. 188.

69 Ibid., p. 216.

70 Ibid., p. 226.

71 Ibid., p. 232.

72 Ibid., p. 244.

73 Ibid., p. 248.

74 Graham Ward, *Cities of God* (London: Routledge, 2000), p. 253.

75 Ibid., p. 254.

76 John Caputo, Mark Dooley and Michael Scanlon (eds), *Questioning God* (Bloomington: Indiana University Press, 2001), p. 285.

77 Ibid., p. 293.

78 Kevin Hart, *The Trespass of the Sign: Deconstruction, Theology and Philosophy* (Cambridge: Cambridge University Press, 1989), p. 41.

79 Ibid., p. 60. For a related approach, see Merold Westphal, *Overcoming Ontotheology: Toward a Postmodern Christian Faith* (New York: Fordham University Press, 2001).

80 Hart, *Trespass*, p. 95.

81 Ibid., p. 186.

82 Ibid., p. 28.

83 Kevin Hart, 'Jacques Derrida: The God Effect', in Philip Blond (ed.), *Postsecular Philosophy: Between Philosophy and Theology* (London: Routledge, 1997), pp. 259–80 (273).

84 Ibid., p. 278.

85 Caputo, Dooley and Scanlon, *Questioning God*, p. 198.

86 Ibid., p. 200.

87 Hugh Rayment-Pickard, *The Impossible God: Derrida's Theology* (Aldershot: Ashgate, 2003), p. 126.

88 Ibid., pp. 143–44.

89 Ibid., p. 145.

Notes

90   Ibid., p. 147.
91   Ibid., p. 162.
92   Ibid.
93   Ibid., p. 163.
94   John Caputo, *On Religion* (London: Routledge, 2001).
95   John Caputo and Michael Scanlon (eds), *God, the Gift and Postmodernism* (Bloomington: Indiana University Press, 1999), p. 4.
96   John Caputo, *The Prayers and Tears of Jacques Derrida: Religion Without Religion* (Bloomington: Indiana University Press, 1997), p. xxi.
97   Ibid., p. 5.
98   Ibid., p. 6.
99   Ibid., p. 13.
100 Ibid., p. 53.
101 Ibid., p. 63.
102 Ibid., p. xxiv.
103 Ibid., p. 113.
104 Ibid., pp. 149–50.
105 Ibid., p. 151.
106 Ibid., pp. 288–89.
107 John Caputo, *The Weakness of God: A Theology of the Event* (Bloomington: Indiana University Press, 2006), pp. 24–26.
108 Ibid., p. 34.
109 Ibid., p. 39.
110 Ibid., p. 123.
111 Caputo, *Prayers,* p. 14.
112 Mark C. Taylor, *About Religion: Economies of Faith in Virtual Culture* (Chicago: University of Chicago Press, 1999), p. 40.
113 Ibid., p. 41.
114 Ibid., p. 45.
115 Ibid., p. 47.
116 Mark C. Taylor, *After God* (Chicago: University of Chicago Press, 2007), p. 345.
117 Ibid., p. 346.
118 Ibid., p. 347.
119 Catherine Keller, *The Face of the Deep: A Theology of Becoming* (London: Routledge, 2003), p. 10; see also pp. 163–65.
120 Ibid., pp. 165–76.
121 Ibid., p. 180.
122 Ibid., p. 181.
123 Ellen Armour, *Deconstruction, Feminist Theology, and the Problem of Difference: Subverting the Race/Gender Divide* (Chicago: Chicago University Press, 1999), p. 42.
124 Ibid., pp. 52–53.
125 Ibid., p. 61.
126 Ibid., p. 62.

127 Ibid., p. 72. Another significant feminist theological writer who draws on Derrida's work to complicate notions of truth and meaning is Grace Jantzen. See her *Becoming Divine: Towards a Feminist Philosophy of Religion* (Manchester: Manchester University Press, 1999).

128 Martin Hägglund, *Radical Atheism: Derrida and the Time of Life* (Stanford: Stanford University Press, 2008), p. 37.

129 Ibid., p. 28.

130 Ibid., p. 30.

131 Ibid., p. 31.

132 Ibid., p. 143.

133 Ibid., p. 120–24.

134 Hent de Vries, *Philosophy and the Turn to Religion* (Baltimore: Johns Hopkins University Press, 1999), p. 26.

135 Ibid., p. 22.

136 Ibid., p. 311.

137 Ibid., p. 333.

138 Ibid., p. 52.

139 Ibid., p. 79.

140 Ibid., p. 89.

141 Ibid., p. 139.

142 Ibid., p. 357.

Conclusion

1 Ellen Armour, *Deconstruction, Feminist Theology and the Problem of Difference: Subverting the Race/Gender Divide* (Chicago: University of Chicago Press, 1999), p. 46.

Select Bibliography

Selected works by Derrida

Speech and Phenomena (Evanston: Northwestern University Press, 1973).

Of Grammatology (Baltimore: Johns Hopkins University Press, 1976).

Writing and Difference (London: Routledge, 1978).

Dissemination (London: Athlone, 1981).

Margins of Philosophy (New York: Harvester, 1984).

Memoires for Paul de Man (New York: Columbia University Press, 1986).

'Shibboleth', in Geoffrey Hartman and Sanford Budick (eds), *Midrash and Literature* (New Haven: Yale University Press, 1986), pp. 307–47.

Glas (Lincoln: University of Nebraska Press, 1986).

Limited Inc (Evanston: Northwestern University Press, 1988).

Edmund Husserl's Origin of Geometry: An Introduction (Lincoln: University of Nebraska Press, 1989).

Of Spirit (Chicago: University of Chicago Press, 1989).

Cinders (Lincoln: University of Nebraska Press, 1991).

'Force of Law: The "Mystical Foundation of Authority"', in Drucilla Cornell, Michel Rosenfeld and David Gray Carlson (eds), *Deconstruction and the Possibility of Justice* (London: Routledge, 1992), pp. 3–67.

'How to Avoid Speaking: Denials', in Harold Coward and Toby Foshay (eds), *Derrida and Negative Theology* (Albany: State University of New York Press, 1992), pp. 73–142.

Acts of Literature (London: Routledge, 1992).

'Of an Apocalyptic Tone Newly Adopted in Philosophy', in Harold Coward and Toby Foshay (eds), *Derrida and Negative Theology* (Albany: State University of New York Press, 1992), pp. 25–71.

Given Time 1: Counterfeit Money (Chicago: University of Chicago Press, 1992).

Aporias (Stanford: Stanford University Press, 1993).

'Circumfession', in Geoffrey Bennington and Jacques Derrida (eds), *Jacques Derrida* (Chicago: University of Chicago Press, 1993).

Specters of Marx (London: Routledge, 1994).

On the Name (Stanford: Stanford University Press, 1995).

The Gift of Death (Chicago: University of Chicago Press, 1995).

Points . . . Interviews 1974–1994 (Stanford: Stanford University Press, 1995).

Politics of Friendship (London: Verso, 1997).

Archive Fever: A Freudian Impression (Chicago: University of Chicago Press, 1997).

Monolingualism of the Other or the Prosthesis of Origin (Stanford: Stanford University Press, 1998).

Adieu to Emmanuel Levinas (Stanford: Stanford University Press, 1999).

'Marx and Sons', in Michael Sprinker (ed.), *Ghostly Demarcations: A Symposium on Jacques Derrida's Specters of Marx* (London: Verso, 1999), pp. 213–69.

Of Hospitality (Stanford: Stanford University Press, 2000).

On Cosmopolitanism and Forgiveness (London: Routledge, 2001).

(with Maurizio Ferraris), *A Taste for the Secret* (Cambridge: Polity, 2001).

Without Alibi (Stanford: Stanford University Press, 2002).

Acts of Religion (London: Routledge, 2002).

'The Becoming Possible of the Impossible: An Interview with Jacques Derrida', in Mark Dooley (ed.), *A Passion for the Impossible: John D. Caputo in Focus* (Albany: State University of New York Press, 2003), pp. 21–33.

The Problem of Genesis in Husserl's Philosophy (Chicago: University of Chicago Press, 2003).

On Touching (Stanford: Stanford University Press, 2005).

Sovereignties in Question: The Poetics of Paul Celan (New York: Fordham, 2005).

Rogues (Stanford: Stanford University Press, 2005).

Psyche: Inventions of the Other Volume 1 (Stanford: Stanford University Press, 2007).

Psyche: Inventions of the Other Volume 2 (Stanford: Stanford University Press, 2008).

The Animal That Therefore I Am (New York: Fordham, 2008).

Other works relevant to Derrida, religion and theology

Altizer, Thomas et al., *Deconstruction and Theology* (New York: Crossroad, 1982).

Armour, Ellen, *Deconstruction, Feminist Theology and the Problem of Difference: Subverting the Race/Gender Divide* (Chicago: University of Chicago Press, 1999).

Bannet, Eve Tavor, *Structuralism and the Logic of Dissent* (London: Macmillan, 1989).

Benson, Bruce Ellis, *Graven Ideologies: Nietzsche, Derrida and Marion on Modern Idolatry* (Downers Grove: InterVarsity, 2002).

Bergo, Bettina, Cohen, Joseph and Zaqury-Orly, Raphel (eds), *Judeities: Questions for Jacques Derrida* (New York: Fordham, 2007).

Blond, Philip (ed.), *Post-secular Philosophy: Between Philosophy and Theology* (London: Routledge, 1997).

Caputo, John, *The Prayers and Tears of Jacques Derrida: Religion without Religion* (Bloomington: Indiana University Press, 1997).

——*On Religion* (London: Routledge, 2001).

——*The Weakness of God: A Theology of the Event* (Bloomington: Indiana University Press, 2006).

Caputo, John and Scanlon, Michael (eds), *God, the Gift and Postmodernism* (Bloomington: Indiana University Press, 1999).

Caputo, John, Dooley, Mark and Scanlon, Michael (eds), *Questioning God* (Bloomington: Indiana University Press, 2001).

Select Bibliography

Coward, Harold, *Derrida and Indian Philosophy* (Albany: State University of New York Press, 1990).

Coward, Harold and Foshay, Toby (eds), *Derrida and Negative Theology* (Albany: State University of New York Press, 1992).

Critchley, Simon, *The Ethics of Deconstruction* (Oxford: Blackwell, 1992).

Cupitt, Don, *Only Human* (London: SCM, 1985).

—*The Long-Legged Fly* (London: SCM, 1987).

—*Radicals and the Future of the Church* (London: SCM, 1989).

—*The Religion of Being* (London: SCM, 1998).

—*Mysticism after Modernity* (Oxford: Blackwell, 1998).

—*Above Us Only Sky* (Santa Rosa: Polebridge, 2008).

Davies, Oliver, *A Theology of Compassion* (London: SCM, 2001).

de Vries, Hent, *Philosophy and the Turn to Religion* (Baltimore: Johns Hopkins University Press, 1999).

—*Religion and Violence: Philosophical Perspectives from Kant to Derrida* (Baltimore: Johns Hopkins University Press, 2002).

Dick, Kirby and Kofman, Amy Ziering, *Derrida: Screenplay and Essays on the Film* (Manchester: Manchester University Press, 2005).

Feder, Ellen, Rawlinson, Mary and Zakin, Emily (eds), *Derrida and Feminism: Recasting the Question of Woman* (London: Routledge, 1997).

Gasché, Rodolple, *The Tain of the Mirror: Derrida and the Philosophy of Reflection* (Cambridge, MA: Harvard University Press, 1986).

—*Inventions of Difference: On Jacques Derrida* (Cambridge, MA: Harvard University Press, 1994).

Hägglund, Martin, *Radical Atheism: Derrida and the Time of Life* (Stanford: Stanford University Press, 2008).

Handelman, Susan, *The Slayers of Moses: The Emergence of Rabbinic Interpretation in Modern Literary Theory* (Albany: State University of New York Press, 1982).

Hart, Kevin, *The Trespass of the Sign: Deconstruction, Theology and Philosophy* (Cambridge: Cambridge University Press, 1989).

—'Jacques Derrida: The God Effect', in Blond, *Post-secular Philosophy*, pp. 259–80.

Holland, Nancy (ed.), *Feminist Interpretations of Jacques Derrida* (University Park: Pennsylvania State University Press, 1997).

Horner, Robyn, *Rethinking God as Gift: Marion, Derrida and the Limits of Phenomenology* (New York: Fordham University Press, 2001).

Janicaud, Dominique, *Phenomenology and the 'Theological Turn'* (New York: Fordham University Press, 2000).

Jantzen, Grace, *Becoming Divine: Towards a Feminist Philosophy of Religion* (Manchester: Manchester University Press, 1999).

Keller, Catherine, *The Face of the Deep: A Theology of Becoming* (London: Routledge, 2003).

Lawlor, Leonard, *Derrida and Husserl: The Basic Problem of Phenomenology* (Bloomington: Indiana University Press, 2002).

Madison, Gary (ed.), *Working through Derrida* (Evanston: Northwestern University Press, 1993).

Select Bibliography

Magliola, Robert, *Derrida on the Mend* (West Lafayette: Purdue University Press, 1984).

Marrati, Paola, *Genesis and Trace: Derrida Reading Husserl and Heidegger* (Stanford: Stanford University Press, 2005).

Megill, Allan, *Prophets of Extremity: Nietzsche, Heidegger, Foucault, Derrida* (Berkeley: University of California Press, 1987).

Milbank, John, *Theology and Social Theory: Beyond Secular Reason* (Oxford: Blackwell, 1990).

—*The Word Made Strange: Theology, Language, Culture* (Oxford: Blackwell, 1997).

—*Being Reconciled: Ontology and Pardon* (Oxford: Blackwell, 2003).

Mitchell, W. J. T. and Davidson, Arnold, *The Late Derrida* (Chicago: University of Chicago Press, 2007).

Pickstock, Catherine, *After Writing: On the Liturgical Consummation of Philosophy* (Oxford: Blackwell, 1998).

Powell, Jason, *Jacques Derrida: A Biography* (London: Continuum, 2006).

Raschke, Carl, *The Next Reformation: Why Evangelicals Must Embrace Postmodernity* (Grand Rapids: Baker Academic, 2004).

Rayment-Pickard, Hugh, *The Impossible God: Derrida's Theology* (Aldershot: Ashgate, 2003).

Reynolds, Jack and Roffe, Jonathan, *Understanding Derrida* (London: Continuum, 2004).

Rollins, Peter, *How (Not) to Speak of God* (London: SPCK, 2006).

Scharlemann, Robert (ed.), *Negation and Theology* (Charlottesville: University Press of Virginia, 1992).

Shakespeare, Steven, 'Thinking About *Fire*: Derrida and Judaism', in *Literature and Theology* Vol. 12 No. 3 (1998), pp. 242–55.

—'A Hiding to Nothing. Cupitt and Derrida on the Mystery Tour', in Gavin Hyman (ed.), *New Directions in Philosophical Theology. Essays in Honour of Don Cupitt* (Aldershot: Ashgate, 2004), pp. 101–16.

—*Radical Orthodoxy. A Critical Introduction* (London: SPCK, 2007).

Sherwood, Yvonne (ed.), *Derrida's Bible: (Reading a Page of Scripture with a Little Help from Derrida)* (London: Macmillan, 2004).

Sherwood, Yvonne and Hart, Kevin (eds), *Derrida and Religion: Other Testaments* (London: Routledge, 2005).

Smith, James, *Jacques Derrida: Live Theory* (London: Continuum, 2005).

—*Who's Afraid of Postmodernism? Taking Derrida, Lyotard and Foucault to Church* (Grand Rapids: Baker Academic, 2006).

Taylor, Mark C., *Deconstructing Theology* (New York: Crossroad and Scholars' Press, 1982).

—*Erring: A Postmodern A / Theology* (Chicago: Chicago University Press, 1984).

—*About Religion: Economies of Faith in Virtual Culture* (Chicago: University of Chicago Press, 1999).

—*After God* (Chicago: University of Chicago Press, 2007).

Ward, Graham, *Barth, Derrida and the Language of Theology* (Cambridge: Cambridge University Press, 1995).

—*Cities of God* (London: Routledge, 2000).

Select Bibliography

Westphal, Merold, *Overcoming Ontotheology: Toward a Postmodern Christian Faith* (New York: Fordham University Press, 2001).

Wood, David and Bernasconi, Robert (eds), *Derrida and Différance* (Evanston: Northwestern University Press, 1988).

Wyschogrod, Edith, *Saints and Postmodernism: Revisioning Moral Philosophy* (Chicago: Chicago University Press, 1990).

Index

Index

Index

Index

Index